Jossey-Bass Teacher

Jossey-Bass Teacher provides educators with practical knowledge and tools to create a positive and lifelong impact on student learning. We offer classroom-tested and research-based teaching resources for a variety of grade levels and subject areas. Whether you are an aspiring, new, or veteran teacher, we want to help you make every teaching day your best.

From ready-to-use classroom activities to the latest teaching framework, our value-packed books provide insightful, practical, and comprehensive materials on the topics that matter most to K–12 teachers. We hope to become your trusted source for the best ideas from the most experienced and respected experts in the field.

The Joyful Reading Resource Kit

Teaching Tools, Hands-On Activities, and Enrichment Resources, Grades K–8

Sally M. Reis

with

Rebecca D. Eckert
Elizabeth A. Fogarty
Catherine A. Little
Angela M. Housand
Sheelah M. Sweeny
Brian C. Housand
Lisa M. Muller
Erin E. Sullivan

JOSSEY-BASS
A Wiley Imprint
www.josseybass.com

Published by Jossey-Bass
A Wiley Imprint
989 Market Street, San Francisco, CA 94103-1741—www.josseybass.com

Library of Congress Cataloging-in-Publication Data

Reis, Sally M.
    The joyful reading resource kit : teaching tools, hands-on activities, and enrichment resources, grades K-8 / Sally M. Reis ; with Brian C. Housand . . . [et al].
        p.   cm.
    Companion to: Joyful reading : differentiation and enrichment for successful literacy learning, 2009.
        ISBN 978-0-470-39188-4 (paper)
        1. Reading (Elementary)   2. Reading (Middle school)   3. Children—Books and reading.   4. Individualized reading instruction.   I. Housand, Brian C.   II. Reis, Sally M. Joyful reading.   III. Title.
    LB1573.R44   2009
    372.41—dc22
                                                                                                            2009007144

Printed in the United States of America
FIRST EDITION
PB Printing   10 9 8 7 6 5 4 3 2 1

Contents

About This Book   ix

About the Authors   xi

Introduction: ***The Schoolwide Enrichment Model for Reading*   1**

General Tools and Resources   5
Using Bookmarks to Scaffold Thinking   7
SEM-R Bookmarks   9
Weekly Teacher Log   39
SEM-R Quality Indicator Checklists   43

Phase One: **Support Materials for Book Hooks   47**

Reading Comprehension Strategies in the SEM-R   49
Making Connections   49
Determining Importance   50
Questioning   50
Visualizing   50
Making Inferences   51
Synthesizing   51
Metacognition   51
Books That Act as Hooks   53
Lists of Recommended Books   57
Award Winners   57

Choice Winners *60*

Classics *60*

Author *62*

Genre *65*

Reading Level *71*

Frequently Asked Questions About Phase One   81

Phase Two: **Support Materials for Independent Reading   83**

Choosing Books for Independent Reading: Making
the Right Match   87

Word-Reading Level *87*

Complexity of Content *87*

Linking Students to Appropriate Books *88*

Supporting Students in Selecting Books   91

Conferencing Strategies   95

Management Tips for Supporting Independent Reading   99

Progress Assessment Rubric   103

Providing a Purpose for Reading   105

Using Student Reading Logs   109

Schoolwide Enrichment Model for Reading Student
Reading Log   111

Sample Student Reading Log   117

Frequently Asked Questions About Phase Two   123

Phase Three: **Support Materials for Student-Selected Activities   127**

Reading Interest-a-Lyzer   129

Renzulli Learning   133

*Helping Teachers Provide Enriched, Differentiated Learning
for All Their Students* *134*

The Renzulli Learning System *135*

Creativity Training Activities   141

General Strategies for Creativity Training *141*

Introductory Lessons in Creative Thinking *145*

Activities for Exploring Creativity   149

Activity 1: If I Wrote the Book (Transforming Figures) *149*

Activity 2: Rhyme Time (Creating Rhymes) *153*

Activity 3: The Doodler (Elaborating) *157*

Activity 4: Spin a Story (Developing Fluency) *161*

Activity 5: Consequences (Speculating and Imagining) 165

Activity 6: Cartoon Captions (Writing Humor) 169

Activity 7: Way-Out Words (Linking Words and Symbols) 173

Activity 8: Make-a-Sentence (Creating Ideas from Words) 176

Activity 9: Changing Things (Brainstorming) 179

Activity 10: Can You Design It? (Planning) 182

Reading on the Internet 187

Authors' and Publishers' Sites 187

Online Books 188

Take a Test Drive! Exciting Web Sites for Students to Try 191

SEM-Xplorations: Enrichment Projects 201

1. Build a Bridge 203

2. Experiment with Sound 210

3. Investigate Local History 218

4. Create an Artifact Box 228

5. Draw a Comic Strip 234

6. Design a City of the Future 244

7. Create an Illustrated Book 248

8. Invent Something New 264

9. Write a Short Story (Grades K–4) 273

10. Write a Short Story (Grades 5–8) 283

Frequently Asked Questions About Phase Three 297

Frequently Asked Questions About the SEM-R 299

SEM-R Glossary 303

About This Book

The Joyful Reading Resource Kit serves as a companion book to *Joyful Reading: Differentiation and Enrichment for Successful Literacy Learning, Grades K–8*. Both books have been designed for one purpose—to help teachers inspire their students to love reading and at the same time build their self-regulation and discipline in order to read independently for sustained periods of time. *Joyful Reading* introduces teachers to the Schoolwide Enrichment Model for Reading (SEM-R), an innovative approach to reading instruction designed to give children the chance to learn to enjoy reading and the time within their school day to read books of their own choice. *The Joyful Reading Resource Kit* provides teachers with tools, book lists, student activities, and other resources to help them implement the SEM-R successfully, either as part of a language arts program or as a separate literacy component. Research conducted on the SEM-R has demonstrated that students who participate in this program have higher reading fluency and comprehension compared with students who receive more traditional reading instruction. The SEM-R is especially effective in enhancing student engagement and motivation to read and has been implemented in schools across the country. Teachers have been elated with the results, reporting how the program enables even the most resistant readers to read more challenging material on a regular basis and, most important, to discover the enriching rewards of reading. Teachers also report that the program is practical and easy to implement. Introduced in three phases, the SEM-R is dynamic and designed for flexibility in order to meet teachers' and students' needs. *Joyful Reading* and *The Joyful Reading Resource Kit* will provide you with everything you need to make the SEM-R work in your classroom.

We acknowledge all of the teachers and administrators who have implemented the SEM-R over the last decade for their dedication and support, as well as their suggestions to improve our work.

About the Authors

Sally M. Reis is a Board of Trustees Distinguished Professor of educational psychology at the University of Connecticut, where she also serves as principal investigator of the National Research Center on the Gifted and Talented. She was a teacher for fifteen years, eleven of which were spent working with gifted students at elementary, junior high, and high school levels. She has authored more than two hundred publications and has traveled extensively across the country to conduct workshops and provide professional development on enrichment programs and gender equity programs for school districts. She is coauthor of *The Schoolwide Enrichment Model, The Secondary Triad Model, Dilemmas in Talent Development in the Middle Years,* and *Work Left Undone: Choices and Compromises of Talented Females.* Sally serves on the editorial board of *Gifted Child Quarterly* and is a past president of the National Association for Gifted Children. She is also a fellow of the American Psychological Association.

Rebecca D. Eckert is a professor in the Neag School of Education at the University of Connecticut, where she works with college students as they prepare to become teachers. In her former role as the gifted resource specialist for the National Association for Gifted Children, Becky co-edited the book *Designing Services and Programs for High-Ability Learners* with Jeanne Purcell. Her previous work at the National Research Center on the Gifted and Talented included participation on the research team that developed and implemented the Schoolwide Enrichment Model for Reading. Her research interests include talented readers, recruitment and preparation of new teachers, arts in the schools, and public policy and gifted education. She is a former middle school teacher with experience in geography, history, and theater arts.

Elizabeth A. Fogarty graduated with a Ph.D. in reading and gifted education from the University of Connecticut and moved to North Carolina, where she now teaches at East Carolina University. She teaches classes in literacy and elementary education, is the author of several articles, and travels often to facilitate staff development for teachers in schools throughout the country. Her research interests include talented readers, differentiation, and teacher effectiveness.

Catherine A. Little is assistant professor in educational psychology in the Neag School of Education at the University of Connecticut. She teaches courses in gifted and talented education and in the education honors program, and she serves as program advisor to UConn Mentor Connection. Catherine received her Ph.D. in educational policy, planning, and leadership with an emphasis in gifted education administration from the College of William and Mary. Her research interests include professional development, talent development in teachers, curriculum differentiation, and perfectionism in gifted students. She presents regularly at state and national conferences and in local school districts, and she has written or co-written several curriculum units as well as book chapters and journal articles related to curriculum implementation and other issues in gifted education.

Angela M. Housand, a research associate with the Neag Center for Gifted Education and Talent Development and assistant professor at the University of North Carolina–Wilmington, has a doctorate in educational psychology with an emphasis in talent development and gifted education and educational psychology. A former teacher and a published author, Angela works as an instructor and as a presenter and leader of workshops on self-regulation, meeting the needs of talented readers, theories of cognitive development, program planning, creativity, and curriculum differentiation.

Sheelah M. Sweeny recently graduated from the University of Connecticut with a doctorate in curriculum and instruction, focusing on literacy instruction and a concentration in educational psychology in the area of gifted and talented education. She is assistant professor of reading at Rhode Island College and is interested in reading instruction for all students, including high-ability readers; instruction in comprehension strategies; and integration of new literacies throughout the curriculum. Her dissertation research focused on instructional reading conferences within the Schoolwide Enrichment Model for Reading.

Brian C. Housand completed his doctorate at the University of Connecticut with an emphasis in gifted education and instructional technology and is assistant professor at East Carolina University. Brian is author of the column "Technology

Untangled," which appears in the National Association for Gifted Children's newsletter *Teaching for High Potential.* His research interests include instructional technology, new literacies, and the selective underachievement of gifted students. Brian is currently exploring what it means to be creative in a digital age.

Lisa M. Muller graduated from American International College with a master's degree in forensic psychology. She has been working as a program specialist at the Neag Center for Gifted Education and Talent Development since 1999.

Erin E. Sullivan is completing her doctoral work in school psychology, counseling psychology, and gifted education at the University of Connecticut. Erin's research interests include social-emotional issues in gifted youth, underachievement, behavioral interventions, and gifted girls and women.

Introduction

The Schoolwide Enrichment Model for Reading

The Schoolwide Enrichment Model for Reading (SEM-R) is an enrichment-based reading program that can be differentiated to meet students' individual needs. The program encourages students to read books of their own choice for a period of time during the school day and has been proven by research to benefit underachieving and talented readers alike. As described in *Joyful Reading: Differentiation and Enrichment for Successful Literacy Learning, Grades K–8,* the SEM-R has three goals: increasing students' enjoyment of reading and their positive attitudes toward it, encouraging students to pursue independent reading at an appropriately challenging level, and improving reading fluency and comprehension. *Joyful Reading* guides teachers in the SEM-R instructional approach, which can be incorporated into any language arts or reading program. This companion book, *The Joyful Reading Resource Kit,* provides teachers with tools, book lists, and student activities that are useful for implementing the program in any classroom.

The SEM-R consists of three dynamic phases of reading instruction that are designed to enable flexibility of implementation in response to teachers' and students' needs. In general, each phase occurs on a daily basis; however, the time allotted to each phase will vary over the course of implementation as students increase their capacity for self-regulation and thus their capacity for independent reading. The approach is based on Joseph Renzulli's Enrichment Triad Model (1977), which includes three levels of enrichment. The three levels in the SEM-R focus on exposure to books, self-selected reading with instructional differentiation, and investigations of self-selected topics. The three levels in SEM-R expose children to wonderful literature, like Type I in the triad, train students in self-directed, regulated reading, like Type II in the triad, and give students opportunities to pursue interest-based, self-selected reading projects, like in Type III of the triad model.

Phase One: Hooking Kids on Reading

In Phase One of the SEM-R, teachers plan read-aloud sessions called *book hooks,* using segments from a wide selection of wonderful literature for students interspersed with higher-order questioning and instruction in thinking skills. Phase One exposes students to a wide variety of books and develops listening comprehension and critical thinking skills. During Phase One, teachers read aloud from high-quality, engaging literature and use follow-up strategies that include higher-order questioning and instruction in thinking skills. Bookmarks with higher-order questions (included in this book) are used to help students use critical thinking skills in these read-aloud sessions. This book provides teachers with suggestions for engaging students' interests and helping them to enjoy listening to excerpts from high-quality biographies, other nonfiction books, mysteries, poetry, historical and science fiction, and other genres.

Phase Two: Supporting Independent Reading

In Phase Two of the SEM-R, students engage in supported independent reading (SIR) for thirty-five to forty-five minutes each day, reading from books of their own choice and engaging in periodic teacher-led reading conferences that are tailored to their individual needs. During SIR time, teachers use the individual student conferences to guide each student in selecting challenging books and to provide differentiated instruction in reading strategies and skills. Phase Two develops students' ability to engage in independent reading. Students choose books based on their interests, with the requirement that the reading level must be above a student's current reading level, to ensure that students have a challenging reading experience. Reading material for these sessions is at least one or two years above each student's current reading level, and teachers are trained to assess students individually in order to ensure appropriate levels of challenge. During Phase Two, students read independently and also participate in individualized reading conferences with adults. During these conferences, classroom teachers or instructional aides assess students' reading fluency and comprehension and provide individualized instruction in the use of vocabulary skills and high-level strategies such as predicting, using inferences, and making connections. Teachers emphasize higher-order themes and critical questions, especially with talented readers.

Phase Three: Facilitating Interest and Choice

In Phase Three of the SEM-R, students are encouraged to move from teacher-directed opportunities to self-chosen enrichment activities, still pursuing their areas of interest and improving reading fluency and comprehension. Teachers provide options for activities that extend students' interests, and students select and eventually even propose their own options. Activities might range from a continuation of self-selected reading to book discussion groups, creativity training, visits to Web sites, or self-directed explorations. Activities might also include computer-based reading and research activities, investigation centers, activities that develop advanced thinking skills, independent projects, or book chats.

———————

This resource book is divided into four sections. The first section contains basic tools and resources for implementing the SEM-R and is followed by sections relating to the three phases of the SEM-R. The fourth section is followed by frequently asked questions about the SEM-R as well as a glossary of terms. We hope that you find these materials and ideas helpful to you!

Reference

Renzulli, J. S. (1977). The Enrichment Triad Mode. A plan for developing defensible programs for the gifted and talented: II. *Gifted Child Quarterly, 21,* 227–233.

General Tools and Resources

This first section of the book includes tools and resources that are useful across different phases of the SEM-R.

Using Bookmarks to Scaffold Thinking

In the beginning of this section, we explain how the SEM-R bookmarks can be used across all phases of the SEM-R. We focus on how the bookmarks can be used by teachers to introduce reading strategies as part of exciting book hooks in Phase One of the SEM-R. Teachers also regularly use the bookmarks during Phase Two as part of the differentiated reading conferences they conduct with students. In Phase Three, bookmarks can be used to guide students who are having small group literature circle discussions as well as for students who are interested in writing and responding to questions about books they are reading. They can also be used to prompt students who are working on reading creativity training activities and who are interested in designing book jackets or other creative options.

SEM-R Bookmarks

The entire series of SEM-R bookmarks are included in this section of the book as well, including a pattern for blank bookmarks so that you can create bookmarks that list your own questions. We have developed bookmarks across all literary aspects of teaching reading, such as setting, plot, theme, narrative style, as well as genres, such as fiction and nonfiction. We have also embedded reading strategy instruction across all of our bookmarks and likened them to state standards, as well. The bookmarks were designed to be used across all different books to help teachers facilitate conferences with books that they have not read.

Weekly Teacher Log

The teacher log is introduced in this section because it is used as a planning guide for all three phases of the SEM-R. The teacher log is used to plan book hooks, to keep track of books that have been used in various genres, and to monitor the introduction of reading strategies across phases.

SEM-R Quality Indicator Checklists

The last part of this section discusses quality indicators. Our research on the SEM-R has demonstrated that teachers who take the time to plan how to implement the SEM-R have better outcomes in the classroom. During the years in which we have conducted this research, we have been able to identify the indicators of high-quality activities associated with each phase. These guidelines for high-quality work in all three phases are included in this section to provide teachers with goals and standards for the most successful implementation of the SEM-R.

Using Bookmarks to Scaffold Thinking

A series of reproducible bookmarks has been developed that can be used in both Phase One and Phase Two of the SEM-R. The sample questions included on the bookmarks apply to a variety of genres and are intended to help students think analytically about both fiction and nonfiction literature. The bookmarks can be used in several ways. In Phase One, teachers use bookmark questions during read-alouds to help stimulate student thinking and provide practice in applying complex comprehension strategies. Some teachers laminate the bookmarks and keep one set with them, often in a folder or on a ring, so that they can easily use the bookmarks to guide their Phase Two conferences with students. Teachers usually make one master copy of the bookmarks, keeping that set intact for their own use, and then distribute additional copies of bookmarks to students. Many teachers place copies of the bookmarks in the books in their SEM-R classroom library.

Following are some simple suggestions on how to use the SEM-R bookmarks to assist students who need additional support in thinking about literature.

1. During the read-aloud, teachers can model their own process of applying comprehension strategies by answering some of their own questions. In addition, they can think aloud in order to make overt the cognitive steps that they go through to answer the question. For example, the teacher might ask, "How would the problem change if the story took place elsewhere?" To model how to answer, the teacher could say, "I'll show you how I might answer that question. First, I would think of a different place or setting—maybe here in Willimantic. Then I would think about what is different between Willimantic and the setting in the book. [She would then talk about some of these differences.] Now, I would think about how these differences might change the problem."

2. When students answer questions during the read-aloud, teachers can ask about the steps of the thinking process that led to their response. That is,

teachers can help students to think aloud about how they answered the question.

3. Teachers can provide practice by asking and answering the same types of questions with the class on consecutive days or for multiple books.

4. When answering bookmark questions (whether orally or in writing), one important concept to emphasize with students is that providing a plot summary does not necessarily mean that you have completely answered a question. Students should be encouraged to provide opinions and hypotheses that can be supported by evidence that they have collected from the book. One way to emphasize this concept is to encourage students to focus on one bookmark question during supported independent reading and to use the bookmark to mark a page on which evidence to answer the question can be found. In this way, the student will be able to easily locate the evidence during an individual conference.

5. During individual conferences with students, teachers can support the development of complex and critical thinking skills by asking some of the same questions that were discussed during that day's read-aloud (or previous days' read-alouds). Again, the teacher can prompt students to talk through how they came up with their responses.

6. If a student is not able to answer a question during an individual conference, again, the teacher can model answering the question by thinking aloud in order to demonstrate the cognitive steps that the student would use to respond to the question.

7. Three blank bookmark templates have also been provided for you and your students. Teachers have found that encouraging students to craft their own questions about literature can build a deeper understanding of literary analysis and develop higher-order thinking.

SEM-R Bookmarks

Just the Facts 1

A **character** is an imaginary person represented in a novel, poem, short story, or any other work of fiction.

A **simile** is a comparison of two unlike things, typically marked by use of the words *like, as,* or *than*. Examples include "the snow was as thick as a blanket" or "she was as sly as a fox."

A **metaphor** uses an implied comparison or analogy to describe something. In the simplest case, a metaphor takes the form "The [first subject] is a [second subject]." We use metaphors regularly in daily life; "She's such a peach" is an example.

Just the Facts 2

The time and location of the story is called **setting**. There are several aspects to the setting of each story: the place or geographic location, the time or date, and the mood or atmosphere.

An **antagonist** is a character or sometimes a group of characters who actively oppose the main character, or **protagonist**, of a story. Usually, the antagonist represents a force that the main character must overcome.

The **plot** is the plan of action for a play, novel, poem, short story, or any other fiction book.

Just the Facts 3

Fairy tales are stories told to entertain and instruct about good and evil. They often include supernatural beings, magic, and royalty. They usually take place long ago and far away.

A **fable** is a fictitious story or tale, intended to teach about a truth, human emotion, or human behavior. Fables usually have a lesson or moral to be learned. Animals are often used in place of people as characters in fables.

A **mystery** is a fictional story in which a person solves a crime or explains a mysterious event. The person uses clues in the story to solve the mystery.

Just the Facts 4

Folklore is a collection of stories from a particular culture and time. Folklore often features exaggeration. A **myth** is a story about supernatural beings or events. A **legend** is a story handed down from earlier times and is often believed to be historical.

Fantasy is fiction that asks the reader to suspend reality and believe that elements of magic, wizardry, and supernatural events are possible. It often takes place in another world or time. **Science fiction** is a story that takes place in the future, where people use scientific and technological developments in amazing ways.

Just the Facts 5

Self-help books give advice to help people solve problems or accomplish things in their life.

Philosophy means "love of knowledge." Philosophers think about life and develop ideas or beliefs about life, knowledge, or behavior.

Nonfiction books are often based on true stories, history, facts, or ideas and are used to share information.

Types of nonfiction books:
- Poetry, plays, or narratives based on real life
- Biographies
- Photo documentaries
- How-to books
- Experiment and activity books
- Field guides and identification books

Just the Facts 6

A **theme** is a major message the author wants readers to have about an important issue or idea.

Most books have a theme, and in each theme are some important "big ideas."

Types of themes in books:
- Power
- Change or growth in life
- Interaction with nature
- Death
- Personal beliefs
- Relationships
- Loneliness and isolation
- Inhumanity

Character 1

Do any of the characters display the trait of honesty?

Were you surprised by the actions of any of the characters? How?

Describe a decision or choice made by one of the characters. Do you agree with this decision?

Who is the protagonist of the book? How do you know?

Character 2

Who is the antagonist of the book? How do you know?

What action of one of the characters confused you?

How would the book be different if told from another character's point of view?

Does the protagonist force the antagonist to change? If so, why and how?

Describe the appearance of your favorite characters.

Character 3

If you had to choose to be one of the characters, who would you chose? Why?

Does one of the characters remind you of someone whom you know? Why?

How would you feel if you were one of the characters in the book? Explain.

How do the actions of the character tell you about his or her personality?

Character 6

If you could change the behaviors of any character, which one would you change? Why?

Would you like the main character as a best friend? What qualities does the character display that lead you to that decision?

Did the main character (protagonist) change during the story, or did he or she stay the same throughout?

Would you want to read other books about these characters? Why?

Character 5

How does the setting of the book influence the characters?

Which character in the book faces the biggest problem? Why?

Tell one event of the story from another character's point of view (besides the narrator's).

What trait did you admire most in a character in the story? Why?

Character 4

Describe a scene in the book when a character's thoughts differ from his or her actions. Why do you think this happened?

How would the characters behave differently if the story were set in a different place or time?

Compare two characters in this book. Tell which one you think is a better person and why.

Plot 1: Basics

What do you think was the most important event in the story?

Where and when does the story take place?

Who are the main characters? What makes them the main characters?

What has happened in the story so far?

What is the problem or main situation in the story?

Character 8

If you could eliminate one character from the story, whom would you choose? What effect would that have?

What gift would you like to give the main character? Why?

How might you rewrite the story to include one of your friends as a character?

If you were the author, what future events or discoveries would you have the characters pursue?

How does the main character stand out from other characters?

Character 7

How does the personality of one character contribute to his or her eventual success or failure?

Who narrates the book? Why do you think the author made this choice?

Describe two events that portray the main character's personality.

Order the story characters from your favorite to your least favorite.

If you had been one of the characters, would you have done anything differently?

Plot 2

If you could choose one scene in the book to draw or illustrate, which would, you choose? What colors would you use? Why?

Summarize the story in
- 25 words or fewer
- 10 words or fewer
- 5 words or fewer

If you were to visit the setting of the story, what might you see there?

Plot 3

To whom might you recommend this book? Is there a particular group or population that you believe would enjoy this book?

Does the book have any value beyond entertainment?

How has the book influenced your viewpoint?

What one thing would you tell the author to change about the plot if you were to write to him or her?

Plot 4

What problem exists in this book? How is it solved?

Would this book work as a movie? What might have to be changed?

What do you consider the strongest part of the book? The weakest?

What did you learn from this book?

Plot 5

What do you think is the most important event in the story? What is the least important event in the story?

List the characteristics of a good story. Which ones apply to this story?

Could you sometimes predict what was going to happen next in the book? Did it help you to better understand the story?

Identify words in the story that the author used to help you create a picture of the story in your mind.

Plot 6

Would you change the ending if you could? If so, what changes would you make? Why?

Why do you think the author wrote this story?

How do you think the following people would react to this story?

- Someone in your family
- A friend
- Your teacher

Did you enjoy the way the story began? Explain.

Plot 7

Do you think the topic of this story is important?

What does the title mean? How is it important to the story?

How are the events in the story similar to the events in your own life?

Did the author of this book have an important point to make? Was this an interesting story?

Do you think there is any lesson to be learned from this story? Why, or why not?

Setting 2

In what way does the setting of this story relate to your life or to other books you have read?

Do you think the setting for this story was real or imaginary? Why?

How would the book change if it was set 100 years in the future or 100 years in the past?

What details does the author provide about the setting that help build the mood for the story?

Setting 1

What three words would you use to describe the setting of the story?

Why is the setting of this book an appropriate place for this story to take place?

What are some alternative settings that could have been used for this book?

How might the author have collected information about the setting for this book?

Plot 8

Explain a problem faced by one of the characters. How was it solved?

Describe any part of the plot that confused you.

Which scene would make a good preview, or trailer, for a movie?

What was the turning point of the story? How did it affect the plot?

Is the plot true to life (realistic)?

Did you feel any suspense in the plot? If so, what was the final outcome?

Illustrations

What media did the illustrator use? Did this help tell the story better?

Could the illustrations in the book tell the same story without the words? Why, or why not?

What colors does the illustrator use to tell the story? Why might he or she have chosen these colors?

Illustrations and Layout 1

How did the illustrations or diagrams help clarify the information?

How do the illustrations or page layouts differ from those of other books you have read? Which format is better? Why?

What information did you learn from the captions or illustrations?

What text features (diagrams, charts, tables) do you find most intriguing? Why?

Would this book be as good without the illustrations? Why, or why not?

Illustrations and Layout 2

Did the illustrations or page layout in this book make you want to read further? Why?

What part of the book first attracted your attention? Why?

What do the illustrations tell about the setting or time period?

What parts of the book or story might have inspired the illustrator? Why?

Do the illustrations make you think of a special place or event in your life? Explain.

Based only on the illustrations (not the words), what would you think the book is about?

Biography 1

What obstacles did this person face? How did these obstacles influence his or her life?

Who do you think influenced this individual's early years?

What ethical issues did the individual face?

What character traits did you admire most in this person? Why?

How much did a teacher influence this person? If you had been the teacher, how would you have wanted to influence this individual?

Biography 2

Why would an author write a biography about this individual?

What additional questions do you have about this person and his or her experience that this book did not answer?

How is this person's life different from your own? How is it similar?

What does the person about whom the biography is written value? Do you value similar things? Why, or why not?

Biography 3

How did the author organize events in this individual's life? What event do you believe was most significant in the individual's life?

Compare and contrast your family's culture with the culture of the main character.

In most biographies, the person has to overcome some difficulty. Describe an obstacle the person overcame.

What did you learn about yourself while reading this biography?

How would you describe the star of this biography? What traits did he or she possess that you relate to?

Biography 4

If you were going to write a biography, who would you write about? Why?

What details would you include in your biography, and why?

What characteristics of the person in the biography would you like to develop yourself? Why?

What do you think school was like for the person about whom this biography was written? Explain.

Theme 1: General Questions

Is the author trying to help you better understand some aspect of life?

Can you identify the author's message?

Explain how a theme in this book relates to your own life.

What lessons do the characters in the story learn from their experiences?

Describe an event in this book that helped you understand the "big idea" or theme in the story.

Does the theme affect the main character?

Theme 2: Personal Beliefs

Every individual has a set of personal beliefs. At some time in your life, you may have to stand up for what you believe is right. Sometimes we do not really know or understand our beliefs until we are confronted with a hard choice or a bad event.

Explain how the idea of personal beliefs is a theme in this book.

Do any of the main characters appear to have a strong set of personal beliefs? Explain.

Is there any belief that a character in this story would sacrifice for?

Theme 3: Interaction with Nature

Different people relate to nature in different ways. Some people, such as Native Americans, may have specific beliefs about their relationship with nature. Americans may relate differently to nature today than they did in the past.

Does the theme of people relating to nature appear in the book you are reading?

How do the characters in this book relate to nature?

Does the author use nature to represent something else in the book? If so, how?

Theme 4: Death

What big idea might be worth dying for? Examples could include freedom or the life of another person you love. Death may sometimes keep a character from understanding life. Some people think death is not the end but, rather, the beginning. Death certainly does not end a person's legacy or contribution to the lives of others.

How did the theme of death emerge in this book?

Do any of the main characters die? If so, what big ideas do you learn about death from the events in this book?

Theme 5: Personal Beliefs

One important theme relates to good and evil. Events in our history and culture suggest the existence of some good and some evil in most people.

How does the battle between good and evil play out in this book?

Does good triumph over evil in this book? How?

Do you think good usually triumphs over evil? Why?

Can you think of an event in your life or in the world in which evil seemed to triumph over good?

Theme 6: Power

The theme of power can relate to personal or individual power, institutional power (in work or government), or spiritual power to believe in forces that are bigger than ourselves.

Do authors have power? What is the power of the pen?

Do you think that authors have a responsibility to use their power to make positive changes? Why?

Does a person with personal or individual power have the right to use it for evil? Explain.

Does any character in this book use his or her power for good? Explain.

Theme 7: Change or Growth in Life

Challenges or difficulties can make people stronger. People who don't feel like they belong or fit in may face problems. However, some people become stronger and more resourceful when faced with challenges.

The only constant in life is change. Is that a theme in this book?

Does the theme of this book relate to the theme of a person's place in society?

Do any characters in this book feel as though they don't belong? Why?

Do any characters change in the course of the book? How?

Theme 8: Change or Growth in Life

People need internal strength (strength within themselves) to deal with sad or difficult times. Developing inner strength may take a lifetime of work. Many people find it difficult to develop inner strength.

Does a character in this book go through growth or a change in their life? How?

Do you think that any character in this book is stronger on the inside than on the outside? Who, and why?

Are any characters in this book who are weaker on the inside than on the outside? Who, and why?

Theme 9: Relationships

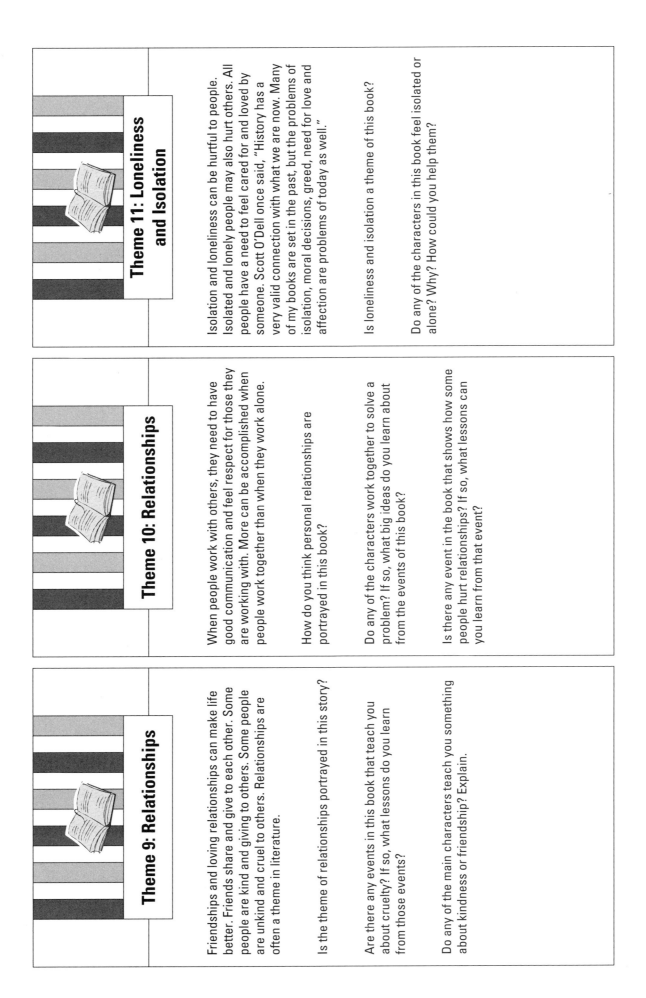

Friendships and loving relationships can make life better. Friends share and give to each other. Some people are kind and giving to others. Some people are unkind and cruel to others. Relationships are often a theme in literature.

Is the theme of relationships portrayed in this story?

Are there any events in this book that teach you about cruelty? If so, what lessons do you learn from those events?

Do any of the main characters teach you something about kindness or friendship? Explain.

Theme 10: Relationships

When people work with others, they need to have good communication and feel respect for those they are working with. More can be accomplished when people work together than when they work alone.

How do you think personal relationships are portrayed in this book?

Do any of the characters work together to solve a problem? If so, what big ideas do you learn about from the events of this book?

Is there any event in the book that shows how some people hurt relationships? If so, what lessons can you learn from that event?

Theme 11: Loneliness and Isolation

Isolation and loneliness can be hurtful to people. Isolated and lonely people may also hurt others. All people have a need to feel cared for and loved by someone. Scott O'Dell once said, "History has a very valid connection with what we are now. Many of my books are set in the past, but the problems of isolation, moral decisions, greed, need for love and affection are problems of today as well."

Is loneliness and isolation a theme of this book?

Do any of the characters in this book feel isolated or alone? Why? How could you help them?

Theme 12: Inhumanity

Some people are cruel and treat others very badly. Understanding others may help to reduce cruelty and inhumanity to others.

What does it mean to really understand others?

Where do inhumanity and cruelty exist in the world today? What could each of us do to reach out to prevent it?

Is inhumanity and cruelty to others a theme in this book?

Does anyone help the character who is treated unkindly? How?

Experiments 1

What would happen if you deleted a step or changed the order of the steps in the experiment?

Summarize this experiment for a friend in a way that would make him or her want to do it.

What variables could you manipulate to add to your knowledge of this topic?

Did the experiment have the results you expected? Why or why not?

Experiments 2

How could you apply the procedures of this experiment to a different subject for research?

How else could you modify the experiment to extend your learning?

What concepts in science does this experiment teach?

Do you think that you would get the same results each time if you repeated the experiment 25 times? Why, or why not?

Fairy Tales 1

Is this fairy tale similar to other fairy tales you have read? How are they similar?

A **fractured fairy tale** takes a traditional fairy tale and changes it in some way. For example, the main character may be changed from male to female, or the setting may be updated to modern times. If you were going to "fracture" this fairy tale, how would you do it? Why?

Have you read other versions of this fairy tale? Do any of them come from other cultures? How did they differ from this one?

Fairy Tales 2

How would this fairy tale be different if it was told from another character's perspective?

What lesson do you think the author is teaching with this tale? How do you know?

If this fairy tale was made into a movie, to whom would it appeal most? Why?

Fairy tales are usually about good versus evil. What two forces are contrasted in this story?

Fairy Tales 3

What other fairy tales does this story remind you of?

What is the problem in this fairy tale, and how do you think it will be solved?

Are there characters in this fairy tale that remind you of characters in other stories? Who and what traits make them similar?

If you could play one of the characters in the movie version of this fairy tale, who would you be? Why?

Fairy Tales 4

Fairy tales often feature the numbers 3 or 7 (the three billy goats, the seven dwarfs, the wolf who tries to blow down the pigs' houses three times). Do these numbers have any significance in this tale? If so, how do they influence the story?

Does any character have a magical power? What is the power? How would the story change if a different character had the power?

Does this fairy tale have any characters that are from royalty (for example, a king or a princess)? How are they different from other characters?

Fables

Think about the characters in this fable. What are the best and worst traits the main characters possess? Which trait wins in the end?

What moral or lesson is to be learned from this fable?

What can you learn about human feelings or behavior from the characters in this fable?

How does the setting influence or contribute to the conflict or its resolution in this fable? How would the story change if the fable was set in a different place or time?

Folklore, Myths, and Legends

Picture the main character from this story. How did the author help you create a visual image in your mind?

What traits of this character cause him or her to have super abilities or powers?

Is this story believable? What has been exaggerated?

In what way would the story be different without the exaggeration?

If you could meet the main character, what questions would you ask?

What would it be like to live in the place or during the time of this story?

Fantasy and Science Fiction

Do you think this kind of story could ever happen in real life? Why, or why not?

Imagine that we had the creatures, gadgets, or modes of transportation in our society that are in the book. How would your life be different?

If you could add a creature, gadget, mode of transportation, or something else to this story, what would it be? What would change in the story as a result?

Do you have any ideas for an invention that would make this story better? Describe your idea and how it would change the story.

Self-Help 1

What kind of useful self-help strategies does this book provide?

What kind of evidence does the author provide to suggest that his or her strategies are effective for others?

After reading this book, what other books would you like to read?

Did this book help you? Why, or why not?

Self-Help 2

Why did you select this book to read? What questions did you have when you started to read the book? Were your questions answered?

If you were going to write a self-help book for other kids, what would it be about?

Can you think of a fictional character who might benefit from reading this book? In what way would he or she benefit?

Did this book help you see things from a different perspective? Was it helpful?

Mysteries 1

Think about the protagonist in the story. What are his or her good and bad traits? How do these traits help or hurt the protagonist when he or she is solving the mystery?

How would reading this story be different if you knew the solution before you started reading?

Compare yourself to the character investigating the mystery. What traits do you have in common? What traits are different?

After you finish reading this book, think about the conclusion. Was the ending as you expected?

Mysteries 2

How do you know that this book is a mystery (besides the label on the book)?

What clues has the author given so far to help you solve the mystery at this point in the story?

Have you decided that any characters are innocent of any misdeeds? Why do you think so? Provide evidence from the story.

Do you think the author will reveal "who did it" by the end of the story, or will you have to be the one to decide? What information do you need in order to solve the mystery?

Mysteries 3

A **red herring** is a suspect (or object) that the author adds to take some of the suspicion away from the person who really committed the crime. Describe any red herrings in the story.

Have you decided that any characters are guilty of any misdeeds? Why do you think so? Provide evidence from the story.

If you were investigating this mystery, what steps would you take to uncover the truth?

Would you ever read the ending of a mystery first? Why, or why not?

Humor 1

What makes a story humorous or a comedy?

What would have made this story even funnier? Why?

Which character do you think has the best sense of humor? Why?

Is there one character who has no sense of humor at all? If so, how does that character interact with the other characters?

Does the use of humor make this story more enjoyable? Why, or why not?

Humor 2

If you could have a conversation with a character from the book, which character would it be? What would you talk about? What would you ask him or her?

What makes this comedy different from a joke book? What benefits or strengths does this book have over a joke book?

Is this book similar to other books you have read? How?

How would you respond if you witnessed one of the humorous scenes from this book?

How does the author use humor to define a character in the book? Why is this character funny?

Philosophy

Have you changed any of your ideas because you read this book?

Does the author have a main point in this book? What is it?

Did the author try to persuade you to agree with his or her beliefs? If so, how?

What kind of support does the author give for his or her arguments?

How is the information in this book the same or different from your own beliefs?

Poetry 1

From whose perspective is the poem written? Who might be narrating the poem?

What moves you in the poem? The language? The images?

Select a phrase from the poem that caught your attention while you were reading. Do you think the author used it on purpose? Why, or why not?

On the basis of this poem, what do you know about the narrator's or character's feelings?

What visual images come to mind when you read this poem?

Poetry 2

How would this poem change if the narrator were different?

If you turned this poem into a song, what kind of music would you use? Why?

What kind of illustration do you think would be appropriate for this poem?

What two emotions did you feel while reading any single poem in this book? Did your emotions change as you read other poems?

How would the impact of this poem change if it were written as prose?

Poetry 3

How does the poet's choice of words influence the visual images that come into your mind while you read?

How does the poet use rhythm to convey meaning in this poem?

How would this poem be different if it were written in a different poetic style? For example, as a limerick instead of a haiku?

Choose a poem to read aloud. What does it sound like?

Does the poem remind you of a book you have read?

Nonfiction 1

How could an idea in this book improve or change the world?

Describe some professions that relate to this topic. What kinds of work do these people do?

How is this book organized? By date, time of year, place, alphabetically, step by step? Why do you think the author organized the material this way?

How might this book change if it were written by an author of the opposite gender, a different age, or a different cultural heritage?

Nonfiction 2

Can you identify one cause-effect relationship among the events in the book?

Describe an interesting relationship in this book.

How effectively did the author present different perspectives on an issue?

How do the ideas in this book relate to your life?

What could have been done to improve this book? Why?

Nonfiction 3

Would this book be a good choice to include in a time capsule? Why, or why not?

Bias happens when the author presents only one point of view on a topic that has two or more important viewpoints. Do you think there is bias in how the material in this book was presented? Why, or why not?

How did the table of contents and index help you to use this book?

What improvements would you make to make the book easier to use?

What events in history did this book help you understand?

Nonfiction 6

If you had to make an advertisement about the topic of this nonfiction book, how would you do it?

Which sections of the book would you want to read first? Why?

What questions would you like to ask the author after reading the book? Why are these questions important?

What would you tell the author about a student's understanding of this topic?

How do you read a nonfiction book differently from a fiction book?

Nonfiction 5

Why might a nonfiction book have more than one author? Why is collaboration important in this type of writing?

What part of this book could the author have left out without changing your understanding of the topic?

Compare what you learned in this book with what you already knew or thought you knew about the topic.

What is one big question you still have after reading the book?

Nonfiction 4

How do you think the author learned the information presented in this book?

What is the most important idea the author is conveying about the topic?

What are three details the author used to stimulate readers' interest in this topic?

Why do you think the author chose to write about this topic? Do you think the topic is important?

After reading this book, do you want to delve into this topic more deeply? What other books might you find? Where would you find them?

Nonfiction 7

Is everything in the book based on fact? Does the author provide opinions? How can you tell the difference between facts and opinions?

How did the pictures and the words in the book help you create an image of the setting?

How would you find another book on the same topic? Would you want to read it? Why, or why not?

Nonfiction 8

Would you have wanted to live during the time that the book is set in? Why, or why not?

What elements of the author's writing help you understand the important facts or ideas in the book?

Have you read a book on this topic before? If so, how is this book different? How is it similar?

Is the author an expert on the subject? How do you know?

Nonfiction 9

Does the author of this book try to persuade you to believe anything? How?

Can you imagine how people dressed during the time or in the place in which the book is set? How would you describe the differences between the clothes in the book and what you wear?

Do you think people read nonfiction books to answer questions that they have? What steps might they take to find answers?

How-to-Books

Which sections of this book did you want to read first? Why? What would the other sections provide?

What recommendations would you give the author for improving this book?

What would be your greatest challenge in doing what the author recommends?

Do you need any special resources or tools to follow the directions in the book?

Nonfiction and Fiction

If you were to write a follow-up to this book, what part of this book would you like to research in more depth?

Who is the most memorable person in the book?

Describe the author's writing style. For example, what is his or her narrative style?

What questions do you now have about the time period in which the events in the book occurred?

What would the world be like if the events in this book had not happened?

Nonfiction 10

Have you visited any of the places in this book? How might visiting the places in the book improve your understanding of the events in the book?

What does this book make you think about? Do questions come to mind? Give an example of some of your thoughts or questions.

What about the setting of this book is different from the world we live in now?

Inventions and How-to-Books

How would this modern invention have affected another era in history?

How would your life today be different if this invention had not been created?

In this how-to book, what steps might you change to improve the process?

What would it have been like to experience the first successful trial of this invention?

How did this book help you learn a skill you are interested in pursuing?

Understanding Audience 1

What other topics or ideas might people who like this book be interested in?

Describe the type of person who might be most interested in this topic. How are you similar to the person you described?

Do you think people who read this book will be sympathetic to the main character? Why, or why not?

Understanding Audience 2

Would you recommend this book to a favorite fictional character? Which one? Why?

What was the author's purpose in writing this book? Was the author successful? Why, or why not?

Who is the intended audience of the book? How do you know?

Would you recommend this book to a friend? Why, or why not?

Exploration Books

Have you read any fiction books that deal with the topic of this book? After reading this book, do you think the fiction book treated the content accurately?

Look at the format of the book. What other topics could be covered using this format? What nonfiction topics would *not* be appropriately covered in this format?

Suggest a plot for a piece of fiction in which this information plays a pivotal role.

Is there any information presented in this book that looks like a fact but that you believe is really an opinion? How can you tell what is really accurate?

History and Current Events

How is this book's issue, problem, or topic relevant to your world today?

Compare your family's culture with the one you read about.

If you were to rewrite the ending of this book, how would you change history?

How might you feel about the events in this book if you were living in the time period in which it is set?

What person or group of people in this book faced the most challenges? Why?

What might have happened if the events in this book had happened 200 years later? How might the events have changed?

Reading Attitudes 1

Do you ever reread a book? If so, why do you read it again?

Imagine that reading had never been invented. Would this be a good thing or a bad thing? Why?

Do you like to get books as presents? Why, or why not? Have your feelings about receiving books changed at all since the beginning of the school year?

Reading Attitudes 2

Complete this sentence: Reading helps me . . .

For you, what is the most difficult thing about reading? Can the teacher or anyone else help you with it? How?

What do you like most about reading? What do you like least?

Is reading important to you? Why, or why not?

What new strategies are you using that have helped you become a better reader? How have they helped?

Describe how you feel when you are reading.

Reading Attitudes 3

Do you have a favorite author? If so, who is it and why do you like the books he or she writes? If not, why do you think you have not found an author you like?

Do you have a favorite genre? Which one, and why? If not, what would help you to like books more?

What do you know about yourself as a reader? How has this changed since last month? Last year?

Where and when do you like to read best? How does this information help you choose books to read?

What helps you to get interested in a book? How does this knowledge help you choose books?

Reading Attitudes 4

Complete this sentence: To me, reading is . . .

If you could choose anything to read about, what would you choose, and why?

Do you and your friends talk about books or reading? Why, or why not?

Have you ever seen a movie made from a book you read? If so, which did you enjoy more, the book or the movie? Why?

What helps you understand books better?

Make your own bookmark!

(Then leave it in the book to test your classmates.)

Book Title: _____

Author: _____

Easy Question:

_____
_____

Hard Question:

_____
_____
_____

Thought-Provoking Question:

_____
_____
_____

Make your own bookmark!

(Then leave it in the book to test your classmates.)

Book Title: _____

Author: _____

Easy Question:

_____
_____

Hard Question:

_____
_____
_____

Thought-Provoking Question:

_____
_____
_____

Make your own bookmark!

(Then leave it in the book to test your classmates.)

Book Title: _____

Author: _____

Easy Question:

_____
_____

Hard Question:

_____
_____
_____

Thought-Provoking Question:

_____
_____
_____

Weekly Teacher Log

A template for a weekly teacher log is provided to assist you in organizing and recording your implementation of the SEM-R framework as well as documenting your vision for student growth. If your school requires you to turn in lesson plans, you may want to consider using a copy of this form to reduce paperwork.

The teacher's log book provides space for you to develop your own lesson plans and record your reflections as well as your goals. The weekly log consists of two pages. The first page is the lesson plan itself. At the top of the page is a space to set a guiding theme for the week. The three main columns of the log allow you to record the various activities you plan to pursue during the three SEM-R phases each day. Space is also provided to record the time spent in each phase. Note that you may not pursue an activity in each phase every day due to time constraints or your own creative or instructional needs.

On the second page of the weekly log, space is provided for you to record your reflections about the week. You may wish to reflect on the week's successes or identify obstacles that prevented you from reaching your goal. As you reflect, you may think about a new strategy that you have tried or comment on observations that have surprised or concerned you. This is your space to evaluate, regroup, and plan for the next week. To help you focus the activities of your students and actively engage your process of implementing the SEM-R program, a space is provided at the bottom of the page for weekly goal setting.

Weekly Teacher Log

Teacher: _Miss Shirley_   Dates: _Week One_

Weekly goal:
To develop a positive classroom climate and introduce SIR and the reading logs.

	PHASE ONE	PHASE TWO	PHASE THREE
MONDAY	Books: _Matilda_ Introduce other books by Roald Dahl No. of minutes = 20	Student conferences with: Circulated to observe and encourage students No. of minutes = 15	Choices offered: Entire class completed the Reading Interest-a-Lyzer No. of minutes = 15
TUESDAY	Books: _The Librarian of Basra_ Discussion of care and use of classroom library No. of minutes = 19	Student conferences with: Worked with Carlos, Maria, and Jack to find books; circulated to observe and guide No. of minutes = 16	Choices offered: Continue to read book Audio books Buddy read Renzulli Learning No. of minutes = 15
WEDNESDAY	Books: _It Looks Like Spilt Milk_ Discussion of metaphors & similes No. of minutes = 18	Student conferences with: Yesica Milton No. of minutes = 17	Choices offered: Creativity in Language Arts whole-class lesson followed by activity (Way Out Words) No. of minutes = 15
THURSDAY	Books: _Thank you, Mr. Falker_ No. of minutes = 17	Student conferences with: Pedro Julissa No. of minutes = 18	Choices offered: Audio books Buddy read Renzulli Learning Creativity in Language Arts activity No. of minutes = 15
FRIDAY	Books: _Frindle_ Introduce other books by Andrew Clements No. of minutes = 15	Student conferences with: Ami Tania Arman No. of minutes = 20	Choices offered: Audio books Buddy read Renzulli Learning No. of minutes = 15

Weekly reflection:

I was surprised at how quickly my students got used to the idea of reading silently for an extended period of time. I expected that getting them settled would require much effort! When they started to lose interest on Thursday, I put a sticky note by the target stop time on the clock. It really helped to focus the most inattentive students.

What went well this week:

I am able to connect with students personally, and the bookmark questions are enabling me to ask conference questions even when I do not know the plot of the book.

What I will improve next week:

As I conference with individual students, I would like to bring their awareness to the text-to-self connections they are making, to improve their metacognitive skills.

Personal goal for next week:

Keeping conferences to five minutes

Goal for students for next week:

Get all students to understand a text-to-self connection and have my advanced readers understand the concept within the context of the conference

SEM-R Quality Indicator Checklists

Teachers who plan ahead and commit the time they need to implement the SEM-R have better outcomes in the classroom. During the years we have conducted this research, we have been able to identify the indicators of a high-quality implementation and have developed checklists for each phase that teachers can use to identify the highest level of implementation for each of the three phases of the SEM-R. When we work with teachers who are implementing the SEM-R, we always give them copies of these quality indicators because our experience has shown us that teachers who know what is considered the highest level of practice in any of the SEM-R phases have better levels of implementation. Accordingly, we have included these indicators to provide teachers with goals and standards to strive for as they implement the SEM-R.

While Phase One and Phase Two of the SEM-R have remained consistent with their original conception, Phase Three has evolved throughout the development and study of the SEM-R in accordance with teacher, classroom, and student needs and differences. While Phase Three focuses on individual student choices and interests, common characteristics of highly effective Phase Three interventions have been observed in multiple classrooms. The list of characteristics provided is intended to serve as a benchmark of successful implementation of Phase Three. Developing a quality Phase Three implementation is a process that takes time. By introducing the process gradually, teachers enable students to make a natural transition. Creating a structure and organization for the phase by clearly communicating expectations to students is critical to success.

Quality Indicators for Phase One: Hooking Kids on Reading

The most successful book hooks occur when . . .

- ☐ Teachers model book selection behaviors
- ☐ Book choices are effective in demonstrating the identified purpose
- ☐ Teachers engage students in a discussion of genre characteristics, including comparisons and contrasts with other texts
- ☐ Teachers use expression while reading aloud to enhance their listeners' connection to the text
- ☐ Most of the students regularly demonstrate visible excitement or emotional involvement with the book
- ☐ Teachers model higher-order thinking skills and encourage students to apply those higher-order skills as well as literary concepts to frame the discussion of the book
- ☐ Teachers frequently use open-ended questions or strategies that allow entry and challenge at multiple levels
- ☐ Students are helped to make multiple connections (text to text, text to self, and text to world) through modeling, direct questions, and ongoing discussion
- ☐ Over time, book hooks provide access to a wide variety of titles, authors, genres, and themes

Quality Indicators for Phase Two: Supporting Independent Reading

Students receive the highest levels of support for their independent reading when their classroom embodies the following practices:

- ☐ Most students start to read without any reminders beyond initial direction.
- ☐ The teacher conducts conferences without interruption throughout Phase Two.
- ☐ The teacher communicates a purpose for each student's oral reading before listening to the student read.
- ☐ The teacher extends discussion beyond the student's next book choice to address book selection habits in general.
- ☐ The teacher uses questions at multiple levels of complexity across conferences and uses at least one high-level question in every conference.
- ☐ The teacher diagnoses individual needs based on students' oral reading and helps students integrate varied reading strategies that are clearly connected to demonstrated reading behaviors.

☐ The teacher provides verbal guidance or environmental reminders on self-regulation strategies for reading (for example, verbal reminders on the use of sun and cloud cards to indicate when students need help or self-regulation strategies posted in classroom). All or most students can self-regulate their behavior throughout Phase Two.

Quality Indicators for Phase Three: Facilitating Interest and Choice

A highly effective Phase Three intervention exhibits the following characteristics:

☐ Most students start to work without any reminders beyond the initial directions.

☐ Activity choices include open-ended options and complex projects that extend the challenge of previous phases. Open-ended options enable children to choose work they want to do and to do that work in a preferred learning and product style. That is, we do not want all students to write a report or create a book jacket.

☐ Activity choices demonstrate responsiveness to specific student interests and students' varied preferences in expression styles in product development.

☐ The teacher provides verbal guidance or environmental reminders on self-regulation strategies (for example, verbal reminders at the start of Phase Three or self-regulation strategies posted in classroom), and all students self-regulate their behavior throughout Phase Three.

☐ Most students demonstrate visible enthusiasm for their chosen activity and show commitment to the tasks involved.

☐ The teacher enhances Phase Three activities through physical organization and procedures that ease student access to resources.

Phase One: Support Materials for Book Hooks

In Phase One of the SEM-R, teachers engage students in *book hooks* by reading selections of literature aloud and by inviting students to question and think about what has been read, thus building their skills in listening comprehension. Bookmarks with higher-order questions (included in the preceding section) are often used in this process. This section provides the following resources and tools:

Reading Comprehension Strategies in the SEM-R

Embedded in the SEM-R are cognitive reading strategies that distinguish the SEM-R as a reading program that supports increases in reading fluency and comprehension. In this resource, the strategies identified by top researchers in the field of reading instruction are synthesized and outlined. Example questions are provided that suggest how a teacher might effectively embed these strategies in Phase One book hooks. Teaching these strategies allows book hooks to move beyond being brief read-alouds to become targeted, high-interest lessons on applying high-level reading strategies.

Books That Act as Hooks

During our research on the SEM-R, we have observed some very effective book hooks. This list includes books that have been used to hook kids on new genres, encourage reluctant readers, and generally generate enthusiastic responses. When multiple students fervently request to read the book hook selection, then we know the book hook was a success!

Lists of Recommended Books

We are often asked for a list of books that we recommend for use in the SEM-R. Our goal in providing this list is to support your implementation of the SEM-R by providing a diverse repertoire of high-interest, high-quality texts.

Talented readers pose a unique challenge for teachers. Because of their advanced abilities in reading, it is often difficult to find books that provide a challenge yet present age-appropriate context, themes, and ideas. At times, complex themes with a less challenging reading level are the answer, and at other times, a high challenge level is necessary to provide continued growth. To address this conundrum, we have developed a book list for talented readers. Enjoy!

Frequently Asked Questions About Phase One

As we conduct our research on the SEM-R, several questions continue to recur, regardless of schools' demographics. We address those questions in this list. While the list may not answer every question you have, we hope that it will address the most imperative ones.

Reading Comprehension Strategies in the SEM-R

Essentially, any instruction that a teacher provides to connect a reader with a text for improved understanding can be considered instruction in a reading strategy. While the SEM-R endeavors to engage students with challenging and enjoyable reading materials, it is important that students also build an understanding of the strategies that readers use to understand what they read. Through explicit instruction and modeling of reading strategies, students learn to systematically apply strategies to increase their comprehension of the texts they encounter.

In this resource, we present the most widely accepted reading strategies as defined and researched by the top professionals in the field of reading instruction. We encourage you to use these strategies, teach them, and model them for your students.

Paris's Strategies (Adapted from Paris, 2004)	Mosaic of Thought Strategies (Keene & Zimmerman, 1997)	Strategies That Work (Harvey & Goudvis, 2000)
Making connections	Making connections	Making connections
Determining importance	Determining importance	Determining importance
Questioning	Questioning	Questioning
Visualizing	Visualizing, sensory images	Visualizing and inferring
Making inferences	Making inferences	
Summarizing	Synthesizing	Synthesizing
Metacognition		

Making Connections

When readers make connections, they relate the background knowledge they already have to information in the text. Making connections enables readers to achieve a deeper understanding of the texts they read. Three types of connections are presented here: text to self, text to text, and text to world.

Text-to-Self Connections

A text-to-self connection involves the reader making an authentic connection between a person, object, or event in the text and himself.

Example: How does this story relate to your own life?

Text-to-Text Connections

A text-to-text connection occurs when a reader sees a relationship between two texts. A text can be anything written—for example, a book, a poem, or a song.

Example: Does this book remind you of another book that you have read? What was similar about the two books?

Text-to-World Connections

A text-to-world connection happens when the reader associates a text with something that has happened or is happening in the world.

Example: Do you think your friends would enjoy meeting the main character? Why or why not?

Determining Importance

Students must evaluate material to figure out which parts are most important or valuable in building their understanding of the text.

Example: What were some of the most important parts of the story? Why?

Questioning

Readers ask themselves questions about the texts they read. Questions should occur naturally as a reader tackles increasingly challenging texts or concepts and ideas of increasing complexity.

Example: What is one big question you still have after reading this book?

Visualizing

Visualizing involves making pictures in one's mind of what is going on in a scene or story that is read or heard.

Example: Which scene would you most like to illustrate? Why?

Making Inferences

Inferences are conclusions that a reader draws from reading, based on assumptions that are implied but not directly stated in the text or deductions that can be made based on facts in the text.

Example: Why did the author write this book?

Synthesizing

Synthesizing is the process of sorting through information, choosing and combining the most salient or important details to describe a situation or create something new.

Example: Compare the main character's personality at the beginning of the story with her personality at the end.

Metacognition

Metacognition is thinking about one's own thinking. Enhancing metacognition during reading draws the reader's attention to the processes she is using as she reads so that she can be more cognizant of them. This information can be used to improve focus and develop better self-regulation skills while reading.

Example: Has any part of this book confused you? If so, which part? If not, has any part of the book surprised you? If so, which part? Was any part of the book different than what you might have expected? Please describe why it was confusing.

References

Harvey, S., & Goudvis, A. (2000). *Strategies that work: Teaching comprehension to enhance under-standing.* Portland, ME: Stenhouse.

Keene, E., & Zimmerman, S. (1997). *Mosaic of thought.* Portsmouth, NH: Heinemann.

Paris, S. G. (2004, July). *How to teach and assess reading comprehension.* Seminar conducted at the CIERA Summer Institute, Ann Arbor, MI.

Books That Act as Hooks

The Abracadabra Kid: A Writer's Life (1996) by Sid Fleischman

Alphaboat (2002) by Michael Chesworth

Ancient Egypt Revealed (2002) by Peter Chrisp

Art Fraud Detective (2000) by Anna Nilsen

As the City Sleeps (2002) by Stephen T. Johnson

Backyard Detective: Critters Up Close (2002) by Nic Bishop

Can You See What I See? Picture Puzzles to Search and Solve (2002) by Walter Wick

Carver: A Life in Poems (2001) by Marilyn Nelson

Charlie Bone and the Invisible Boy (2004) by Jenny Nimmo

The Cod's Tale (2001) by Mark Kurlansky, illustrated by S. D. Schindler

A Corner of the Universe (2002) by Ann M. Martin

Darby (2002) by Jonathan Scott Fuqua

Dear Mrs. LaRue: Letters from Obedience School (2002) by Mark Teague

The Dinosaurs of Waterhouse Hawkins (2001) by Barbara Kerley, illustrated by Brian Selznick

Don't Know Much About the Kings and Queens of England? (2002) by Kenneth C. Davis, illustrated by S. D. Schindler

Double Fudge (2002) by Judy Blume

Ella Minnow Pea (2001) by Mark Dunn

Frank O. Gehry: Outside In (2000) by Jan Greenberg and Sandra Jordan

Grandma Francisca Remembers: A Hispanic-American Family Story (2002) by Ann Morris, photos and illustrations by Peter Linenthal

The Great Pancake Escape (2002) by Paul Many, illustrated by Scott Goto

Handel, Who Knew What He Liked (2001) by M. T. Anderson, illustrated by Kevin Hawkes

Helen Keller: Rebellious Spirit (2001) by Laurie Lawlor

Henry Hikes to Fitchburg (2000) by D. B. Johnson

Hole in My Life (2002) by Jack Gantos

If the Shoe Fits: Voices from Cinderella (2002) by Laura Whipple, illustrated by Laura Beingessner

Jethro Byrd, Fairy Child (2002) by Bob Graham

The Lamp, the Ice, and the Boat Called Fish (2001) by Jacqueline Briggs Martin, illustrated by Beth Krommes

The Lewis and Clark Trail: Then and Now (2002) by Dorothy Hinshaw Patent, photos by William Munoz

Lives of Extraordinary Women: Rulers, Rebels (and What the Neighbors Thought) (2000) by Kathleen Krull, illustrated by Kathryn Hewitt

Love That Dog (2001) by Sharon Creech

Madlenka (2000) by Peter Sis

Midnight for Charlie Bone (2003) by Jenny Nimmo

Miss Alaineus: A Vocabulary Disaster (2000) by Debra Frasier

Molly Moon's Incredible Book of Hypnotism (2003) by Georgia Byng

The Mysteries of Harris Burdick (portfolio edition) (1996) by Chris Van Allsburg

Orwell's Luck (2000) by Richard W. Jennings

Out of the Ocean (1998) by Debra Frasier

Paul Revere's Midnight Ride (2002) by Stephen Krensky, illustrated by Greg Harlin

Rome Antics (1997) by David Macaulay

The Seeing Stone (2001) by Kevin Crossley-Holland

The Shakespeare Stealer Series (2004) by Gary Blackwood

Sitting Ducks (1998) by Michael Bedard

Smithsonian Visual Timeline of Inventions (1994) by Richard Platt

Squids Will Be Squids: Fresh Morals, Beastly Fables (1998) by Jon Scieszka, illustrated by Lane Smith

Stargirl (2000) by Jerry Spinelli

Stranger in the Woods (2000) by I. T. Sams, R. Carl, and Jean Stoick

The Thief Lord (2002) by Cornelia Funke

The Three Pigs (2001) by David Wiesner

The Weighty Word Book (2000) by Paul M. Levitt, illustrated by Janet Stevens

When Marian Sang (2002) by Pam Munoz Ryan, illustrated by Brian Selznick

William Shakespeare and the Globe (1999) by Aliki

The Word Eater (2000) by Mary Amato

The Year I Didn't Go to School (2002) by Giselle Potter

You Forgot Your Skirt, Amelia Bloomer (2000) by Shane Corey, illustrated by Chelsey McLaren

You Read to Me, I'll Read to You: Very Short Stories to Read Together (2001) by Mary Ann Hoberman, illustrated by Michael Emberley

Lists of Recommended Books

These lists of recommended books for use with the SEM-R are organized to facilitate use by teachers, parents, and students according to different search criteria. There are a variety of ways to search for books that might be appropriate choices for young talented readers. We have chosen six ways to categorize books:

1. Award winners
2. Choice winners
3. Classics
4. Author
5. Genre
6. Reading level

Award Winners

Our first choice is to look for books that are acclaimed for their writing or illustrations (or both). We want good readers to have the opportunity to read well-crafted text. Therefore, the following section is devoted to recent award-winning books. The Web sites provide lists of the award winners and other books considered for the awards, often honor books or runners up, for many years.

Book Awards and Web Sites

Lists of the most distinguished annual literary awards for children's books can be found at the Web site of the American Library Association at http://www.ala.org/ala/awardsgrants/booksprintmedia/childrenyngadults/index.cfm. The awards found at this site are shown in the following table.

Award	Recent Winners
Batchelder Award: Awarded to an American publisher for a children's book that has been translated from another language	2009: *Moribito: Guardian of the Spirit* written by Miyuki Miyabe, translated from Japanese by Cathy Hirano 2008: *Brave Story* written by Miyuki Miyabe, translated from Japanese by Alexander O. Smith 2007: *The Pull of the Ocean* written by Jean-Claude Mourlevat, translated from French by Y. Maudet 2006: *An Innocent Soldier* written by Josef Holub, translated from German by Michael Hofmann
Pura Belpré Medal: Honors a Latino or Latina writer and illustrator whose work best portrays the Latino cultural experience	2009: *The Surrender Tree: Poems of Cuba's Struggle for Freedom* by Margarita Engle 2008: *The Poet Slave of Cuba: A Biography of Juan Francisco Manzano* by Margarita Engle 2006: *The Tequila Worm* by Viola Canales 2004: *Before We Were Free* by Julia Alvarez
Caldecott Medal: Awarded for the most distinguished American picture book for children	2009: *The House in the Night* illustrated by Beth Krommes, written by Susan Marie Swanson 2008: *The Invention of Hugo Cabret* by Brian Selznick 2007: *Flotsam* by David Wiesner 2006: *The Hello, Goodbye Window* illustrated by Chris Raschka, written by Norton Juster
Theodor Seuss Geisel Medal: Given to an author or illustrator who has made a distinguished contribution to beginning reader books	2009: *Are You Ready to Play Outside?* by Mo Willems 2008: *There Is a Bird on Your Head* by Mo Willems 2007: *Zelda and Ivy: The Runaways* by Laura McGee Kvasnosky 2006: *Henry and Mudge and the Great Grandpas* by Cynthia Rylant
The Coretta Scott King Award: Presented to an African American author or illustrator for promoting understanding and appreciation of the culture of all peoples in pursuit of the American Dream	2009: *We Are the Ship: The Story of Negro League Baseball* by Kadir Nelson 2008: *Elijah of Buxton* by Christopher Paul Curtis 2007: *Copper Sun* by Sharon Draper 2006: *Day of Tears: A Novel in Dialogue* by Julius Lester

Newbery Medal: Given annually to the book that makes the most distinguished contribution to children's literature	2009: *The Graveyard Book* by Neil Gaiman 2008: *Good Masters! Sweet Ladies! Voices from a Medieval Village* by Laura Amy Schlitz 2007: *The Higher Power of Lucky* by Susan Patron 2006: *Criss Cross* by Lynne Rae Perkins
Odyssey Award (established in 2008): Awarded for the best audio book for children or young adults	2009: *The Absolutely True Diary of a Part-Time Indian* by Sherman Alexie, produced by Recorded Books, LLC 2008: *Jazz* by Walter Dean Myers, produced by Live Oak Media
Michael L. Printz Award: Honors an author of exemplary young adult literature	2009: *Jellicoe Road* by Marlina Marchetta 2008: *The White Darkness* by Geraldine McCaughrean 2007: *American Born Chinese* by Gene Luen 2006: *Looking for Alaska* by John Green
Robert F. Sibert Informational Book Medal: Recognizes authors and illustrators of informational books	2009: *We Are the Ship: The Story of Negro League Baseball* by Kadir Nelson 2008: *The Wall: Growing Up Behind the Iron Curtain* by Peter Sís 2007: *Team Moon: How 400,000 People Landed Apollo 11 on the Moon* by Catherine Thimmesh 2006: *Secrets of a Civil War Submarine: Solving the Mysteries of the H. L. Hunley* by Sally M. Walker
John Steptoe Award for New Talent: Recognizes new writers or illustrators whose work contributes to appreciation of the African American experience	2009: *Bird* by Shadra Strickland 2008: *Brendan Buckley's Universe and Everything in It* by Sundee T. Frazier 2007: *Standing Against the Wind* by Traci L. Jones 2006: *Jimi and Me* by Jaime Adoff
Wilder Medal: Awarded to a U.S. author or illustrator whose books have made a lasting contribution to children's literature	2009: Ashley Bryan 2007: James Marshall 2005: Laurence Yep 2003: Eric Carle 2001: Milton Meltzer 1998: Russell Freedman 1995: Virginia Hamilton 1992: Marcia Brown

State Book Awards

Many states have their own book awards or choice lists. Links to these state sites can be found at author Cynthia Leitich Smith's Web site at http://www.cynthialeitichsmith. com/lit_resources/awards/stateawards.html. Although not necessarily a comprehensive list of state awards, her site is a good place to start.

Choice Winners

Many worthy books are published each year that do not receive awards. Fortunately, these books are often compiled in lists that indicate their popularity, their appeal to children and young adults, or their notable writing, themes, or contributions to society. Each year, a number of organizations create book choice lists, which are developed by educators and teachers, children and young adults, or library professionals. Some of the most popular choice lists are listed in the following table.

Organization	*Choice List and Web Site*
The Assembly on Literature for Adolescents (ALAN)	Bill's Best Books http://alan-ya.org/index.php?option=com_magazine&Itemid=9999
Association for Library Service to Children (ALSC)	Notable Children's Books http://www.ala.org/ala/mgrps/divs/alsc/awardsgrants/ childrensnotable/pastchildrens/default.cfm
International Reading Association (IRA)	Children's Choices http://www.reading.org/Resources/Booklists/ChildrensChoices.aspx Teachers' Choices http://www.reading.org/Resources/Booklists/TeachersChoices.aspx Young Adults' Choices http://www.reading.org/Resources/Booklists/Young AdultsChoices.aspx
Young Adult Library Services Association (YALSA)	Best Books for Young Adults http://www.ala.org/ala/mgrps/divs/yalsa/booklistsawards/ bestbooksya/bbyahome.cfm

Classics

Classic children's literature is literature that has endured over time. Not all of the books on this list are strictly children's literature, but they have been determined to be appropriate for young readers who are reading at a high level of proficiency. Many of the authors have written additional books that would also be appropriate for young readers. The following table indicates the Lexile, or reading level, for each book. A detailed explanation of Lexile levels can be found in the Reading Levels section on page 71.

Title and Author	Lexile Level	Title and Author	Lexile Level
The Adventures of Sherlock Holmes by Arthur Conan Doyle	1080	*The Legend of Sleepy Hollow* by Washington Irving	770
The Adventures of Tom Sawyer by Mark Twain	950	*Little House in the Big Woods* by Laura Ingalls Wilder	930
The African Queen by C. S. Forester	na	*The Little Prince* by Antoine de Saint-Exupéry	710
Alice's Adventures in Wonderland by Lewis Carroll	890	*Little Women* by Louisa May Alcott	1300
Anne of Green Gables by Lucy Maud Montgomery	990	*My Friend Flicka* by Mary O'Hara	960
A Bear Called Paddington by Michael Bond	750	*The Old Man and the Sea* by Ernest Hemingway	940
Black Beauty by Anna Sewell	900	*Peter Pan* by J. M. Barrie	920
The Borrowers by Mary Norton	780	*Pippi Longstocking* by Astrid Lindgren	870
Charlotte's Web by E. B. White	680	*Rebecca* by Daphne Du Maurier	880
A Christmas Carol by Charles Dickens	1080	*The Red Pony* by John Steinbeck	810
The Count of Monte Cristo by Alexander Dumas	930	*Robinson Crusoe* by Daniel Defoe	1070
The Cricket in Times Square by George Selden	780	*The Secret Garden* by Frances Hodgson Burnett	970
Diary of a Young Girl by Anne Frank	1080	*The Story of Doctor Doolittle* by Hugh Lofting	580
Frankenstein by Mary Shelley	940	*The Swiss Family Robinson* by Johann Wyss	910
The Gift of the Magi by O. Henry	940	*To Kill a Mockingbird* by Harper Lee	870
Gone with the Wind by Margaret Mitchell	1100	*Treasure Island* by Robert Louis Stevenson	1070
Gulliver's Travels by Jonathan Swift	1210	*Twenty Thousand Leagues Under the Sea* by Jules Verne	1030

(Continued)

(*Continued*)

Title and Author	Lexile Level	Title and Author	Lexile Level
The Hobbit by J.R.R. Tolkien	1000	*The Velveteen Rabbit* by Margery Williams	820
The House at Pooh Corner by A. A. Milne	830	*The War of the Worlds* by H. G. Wells	1170
The Hunchback of Notre Dame by Victor Hugo	1340	*White Fang* by Jack London	970
The Indian in the Cupboard by Lynne Reid Banks	780	*The Wind in the Willows* by Kenneth Grahame	1140
Ivanhoe by Sir Walter Scott	1410	*The Witch of Blackbird Pond* by Elizabeth George Speare	850
Johnny Tremain by Esther Forbes	840	*The Wonderful Wizard of Oz* by L. Frank Baum	1000
The Jungle Book by Rudyard Kipling	1140	*The Yearling* by Marjorie Kinnan Rawlings	750

Author

There are a number of prolific contemporary authors whose work is diverse and appeals to many young readers. A few of those authors are listed here, along with a selection of some of their books. Note that some of these authors write books on a range of reading levels. This is important to remember because it means that some of the books at higher reading levels may also contain more mature content that may not be appropriate for young readers. The following tables indicate the Lexile, or reading level, for each book. A detailed explanation of Lexile levels can be found in the Reading Levels section on page 71.

Angela Johnson

Angela Johnson celebrates the African American experience through narratives and prose. Her books explore family relationships as well as historical events and are written for audiences of different ages.

Title	Lexile Level	Title	Lexile Level
Bird	710	*Looking for Red*	740
A Cool Moonlight	1060	*Maniac Monkees on Magnolia Street*	650
The First Part Last	790	*One of Three*	460
Heaven	790	*A Sweet Smell of Roses*	710
Just Like Josh Gibson	920	*Wind Flyers*	na

Gordon Korman

Gordon Korman's books are often humorous. Students will identify with the strong friendships in his books and will thrill at the adventures in the trilogies.

Title	Lexile Level	Title	Lexile Level
Dive trilogy	750	Kidnapped trilogy	760
Everest trilogy	710	*Maxx Comedy: The Funniest Kid in America*	770
Island trilogy	620	*No More Dead Dogs*	610
Jake, Reinvented	800	*Son of the Mob*	690

Lois Lowry

The characters in Lois Lowry's books are typically strong children. The themes of her novels often involve a utopian society, the main character's discovery that all is not as it seems, and his or her journey to discover real meaning or truth.

Title	Lexile Level	Title	Lexile Level
All About Sam	670	*Gooney Bird Greene*	590
Anastasia Krupnik	700	*Number the Stars*	670
Autumn Street	870	*The Road Ahead*	na
Gathering Blue	680	*A Summer to Die*	860
Gossamer	660	*The Woods at the End of Autumn Street*	na

Note: na = not available

Walter Dean Myers

Walter Dean Myers writes books for children and young adults. He explores experiences of African American characters, illuminating their struggles and triumphs. He writes realistic narratives, biographies, short stories, and poetry.

Title	Lexile Level	Title	Lexile Level
Autobiography of My Dead Brother	830	*Me, Mop, and the Moondance Kid*	640
Bad Boy: A Memoir	970	*Monster*	na
Fallen Angels	650	*Contributions to My Name Is America series*	920
Game	na	*Slam!*	750
The Greatest	na	*Somewhere in the Darkness*	640
Jazz	na	*Sunrise over Fallujah*	na

Note: na = not available

Katherine Paterson

Katherine Paterson creates strong young characters that often face difficult situations. The characters, often loners or orphans, learn to overcome their difficulties or adapt to their changed circumstances.

Title	Lexile Level	Title	Lexile Level
Bridge to Terabithia	810	The King's Equal	780
The Great Gilly Hopkins	800	Lyddie	860
Jacob Have I Loved	880	Of Nightingales That Weep	950
Jip: His Story	860	The Same Stuff as Stars	670

Richard Peck

Richard Peck's novels often feature characters who do not conform to a particular group or young adults who take on adult responsibilities. He writes in a variety of genres, including historical and realistic fiction, horror, and mystery.

Title	Lexile Level	Title	Lexile Level
Are You in the House Alone?	730	Lost In Cyberspace	550
Close Enough to Touch	690	On the Wings of Heroes	730
Ghosts I Have Been	830	Remembering the Good Times	690
The Great Interactive Dream Machine	580	Strays Like Us	650
Here Lies the Librarian	780	The Teacher's Funeral: A Comedy in Three Parts	750
A Long Way from Chicago	na	A Year Down Yonder	610

Note: na = not available

Jerry Spinelli

Jerry Spinelli's books span a range of reading levels. He creates recognizable characters and chronicles their navigation through typical joys, trials, and tribulations of growing up. Many of his characters exhibit courage or admirable traits.

Title	Lexile Level	Title	Lexile Level
The Bathwater Gang	420	Maniac Magee	820
Crash	560	Night of the Whale	na
Jason and Marceline	620	Stargirl	590
Knots in My Yo-Yo String: The Autobiography of a Kid	980	Who Put That Hair in My Toothbrush?	600
Loser	650	Wringer	690

Note: na = not available

Laurence Yep

Laurence Yep's stories represent a range of genres (fantasy, realistic fiction, science fiction) and draw on different cultural traditions, especially his Chinese American heritage. The themes of his books often explore conflict and tolerance.

Title	Lexile Level	Title	Lexile Level
American Dragons	990	The Lost Garden	1110
Child of the Owl	920	Mia	860
Dragon's Gate	730	The Rainbow People	680
The Earth Dragon Awakes	510	The Serpent's Children	770
Hiroshima	660	Tiger's Apprentice	740

Genre

Knowing the type of book or genre a student likes to read can facilitate book recommendations by adults or book selection by the student. Avid readers often have a genre preference. Here are some suggestions within different genres. The following tables indicate the grade or Lexile level, for each book. The grade levels indicate the grades at which the book is recommended for SEM-R programs. A detailed explanation of Lexile levels can be found in the Reading Levels section on page 71.

	Biography	
Title	Author	Lexile Level or Grade Level
Different Like Coco	Elizabeth Matthews	grades 4–6 and higher
First Flight: The Story of Tom Tate and the Wright Brothers	George Shea	460
Hatshepsut, His Majesty, Herself	Catherine Andronik	1080
Helen Keller	Margaret Davidson	520
I am Scout: The Biography of Harper Lee	Charles J. Shields	grades 4–6 and higher
Lady Liberty: A Biography	Doreen Rappaport	grades 2–5
Lincoln: A Photobiography	Russell Freedman	1110
Living Up the Street	Gary Soto	1140
Mother Teresa: Sister to the Poor	Patricia Reilly Giff	720
Odd Boy Out: Young Albert Einstein	Don Brown	grades 1–5
A Picture Book of Jackie Robinson	David Adler	890

(Continued)

(Continued)

Title	Author	Lexile Level or Grade Level
A Restless Spirit: The Story of Robert Frost	Natalie Bober	grade 6 and higher
Run, Boy, Run	Uri Orlev	570
Shark Lady: True Adventures of Eugenie Clark	Ann McGovern	750
Surviving Hitler: A Boy in the Nazi Death Camps	Andrea Warren	820

Fantasy

Title	Author	Lexile Level or Grade Level
Artemis Fowl series	Eoin Colfer	620
Children of the Red King series	Jenny Nimmo	700
Eragon series	Christopher Paolini	710
The Golden Compass	Philip Pullman	930
Inkspell series	Cornelia Funke	890
Redwall series	Brian Jacques	800
The Spiderwick Chronicles	Tony DiTerlizzi	570

Fiction

Title	Author	Lexile Level or Grade Level
Are You There God? It's Me, Margaret	Judy Blume	570
Babe, the Gallant Pig	Dick King-Smith	1040
The Bears on Hemlock Mountain	Alice Dagliesh	490
Because of Winn-Dixie	Kate DiCamillo	610
Big Mouth and Ugly Girl	Joyce Carol Oates	grade 6 and higher
The Cay	Theodore Taylor	860
Clementine	Sara Pennypacker	790
A Dog's Life: The Autobiography of a Stray	Ann M. Martin	870
Foundling	D. M. Cornish	970
Hoot	Carl Hiaasen	760
Julie of the Wolves	Jean Craighead George	860
Lemony Snicket: The Unauthorized Autobiography	Lemony Snicket	1270

Lily's Crossing	Patricia Reilly Giff	720
Poppy	Avi	670
The Tale of Despereaux	Kate Dicamillo	670
Tornado	Betsy Byars	500

Autobiography

Title	*Author*	*Lexile Level or Grade Level*
Bad Boy: A Memoir	Walter Dean Myers	970
Rosa Parks: My Story	Rosa Parks	970
Through My Eyes	Ruby Bridges	860
26 Fairmount Avenue	Tomie DePaola	760
Up from Slavery: An Autobiography	Booker T. Washington	1320
The Wall: Growing Up Behind the Iron Curtain	Peter Sis	grade 6 and higher

Fairy Tales/Fables/Folklore

Title	*Author*	*Lexile Level or Grade Level*
Aesop's Fables	Jerry Pinkney	760
Alladin and Other Tales from the Arabian Nights	translated by J. J. Dawood	970
Arrow to the Sun: A Pueblo Indian Tale	Gerald McDermott	480
The Complete Brothers Grimm Fairy Tales	Wilhelm Karl Grimm and Jacob Ludwig Carl Grimm	grades 4–6 and higher
Dragonology: The Complete Book of Dragons	Dugald A. Steer	1220
Giants, Monsters, and Dragons: An Encyclopedia of Folklore, Legend, and Myth	Carol Rose	grades 4–6 and higher
The Girl Who Loved Wild Horses	Paul Goble	670
Hans Andersen's Fairy Tales	Hans Christian Andersen	1060
Little Firefly: An Algonquin Legend	Terri Cohlene	490
Perrault's Fairy Tales	Charles Perrault	grades 4–6 and higher
Russian Fairy Tales	Aleksandr Afanasev	grades 2–5

(Continued)

(*Continued*)

Title	Author	Lexile Level or Grade Level
Strega Nona's Magic Lessons	Tomie DePaola	290
Tales of Brothers Grimm	retold by Peg Hall	400
The True Story of the Three Little Pigs	Jon Scieszka	570
Yeh-Shen: A Cinderella Story from China	Ai-Ling Louie	840

Historical Fiction

Title	Author	Lexile Level or Grade Level
The Adventures of Robin Hood	Howard Pyle	1270
Beyond the Divide	Kathryn Lasky	900
Bull Run	Paul Fleischman	810
Caddie Woodlawn	Carol Ryrie Brink	890
Catherine, Called Birdy	Karen Cushman	1170
Egyptology	Emily Sands	1180
A Lion to Guard Us	Clyde Robert Bulla	360
Listening for Lions	Gloria Whelan	900
The Midwife's Apprentice	Karen Cushman	1240
Morning Girl	Michael Dorris	980
My Brother Sam Is Dead	James Lincoln Collier and Christopher Collier	770
Skylark	Patricia MacLachlan	470
Summer of My German Soldier	Bette Greene	800
Torchlight	Carol Otis Hurst	640
Working Cotton	Sherley Anne Williams	600

Informational Text

Title	Author	Lexile Level or Grade Level
Actual Size	Steve Jenkins	1080
Afghanistan to Zimbabwe: Country Facts That Helped Me Win the National Geographic Bee	Andrew Wojtanik	grades 2–6 and higher
Animals in Winter	Henrietta Bancroft and Richard G. Van Gelder	380

Danger! Earthquakes	Simon Seymour	710
Dinosaurs (Encyclopedia Prehistorica series)	Robert Sabuda	grades K–3
Flood: Wrestling with the Mississippi	Patricia Lauber	850
Magic School Bus Inside the Earth	Joanna Cole	500
The New Way Things Work	David Macaulay	1180
Owen and Mzee: The True Story of a Remarkable Friendship	Isabella Hatkoff, Craig Hatkoff, and Paula Kahumbu	920
Prairie Visions: The Life and Times of Solomon Butcher	Pam Conrad	1090
Secrets of a Civil War Submarine: Solving the Mystery of the H. L. Hunley	Sally M. Walker	1060
Trains	Gail Gibbons	470
What Do You Do with a Tail Like This?	Steve Jenkins and Robin Page	740
You Can't Smell a Flower with Your Ear!	Joanna Cole	390
Zoo	Gail Gibbons	630

Myths and Legends

Title	Author	Lexile Level or Grade Level
Andy and the Lion	James Henry Daugherty	510
Ariadne Awake!	Doris Orgel	grades 4–6 and higher
Black Ships Before Troy: The Story of the Iliad	Rosemary Sutcliff	1300
Celtic Gods and Heroes	John Green	grades 2–5
Dateline: Troy	Paul Fleischman	860
Goddesses, Heroes, and Shamans: The Young People's Guide to World Mythology	Cynthia O'Neill, editor	1000
The Gods and Goddesses of Ancient China	Leonard Everett Fisher	960
The Gods and Goddesses of Ancient Egypt	Leonard Everett Fisher	grades 2–6 and higher

(Continued)

(*Continued*)

Title	Author	Lexile Level or Grade Level
The Gods and Goddesses of Olympus	Aliki	grades 2–5
The Golden Fleece and the Heroes Who Lived Before Achilles	Padraic Colum	980
Greek Gods and Goddesses	Robert Graves	990
King Arthur and the Knights of the Round Table	M. C. Hall	390
The Mists of Avalon	Marion Zimmer Bradley	1120
The Norse Myths	Kevin Crossley-Holland	830
The World of King Arthur and His Court	Kevin Crossley-Holland	1200

	Poetry, Verse	
Title	Author	Lexile Level or Grade Level
Blue Lipstick: Concrete Poems	John Grandits	grades 2–6
Brown Angels: An Album of Pictures and Verse	Walter Dean Meyers	grades K–5
A Child's Garden of Verses	Robert Louis Stevenson	grades K–3
Frenchtown Summer	Robert Cormier	1380
Jabberwocky	Lewis Carroll, adapted by Christopher Myers	grades 4–6 and higher
Joyful Noise: Poems for Two Voices	Paul Fleischman	grades 2–5
I'm in Charge of Celebrations	Byrd Baylor	700
The Light in the Attic	Shel Silverstein	grades K–5
Love That Dog	Sharon Creech	1010
The Nonsense Verse of Lewis Carroll	Lewis Carroll	grades K–6
Poetry for Young People: Langston Hughes	David Roessel and Arnold Rampersad, editors	grades 4–6
Science Verse	Jon Scieszka	grades K–3
The Tell-Tale Heart and Other Writings	Edgar Allen Poe	1350
Walking on the Boundaries of Change	Sara Holbrook	grade 6 and higher
A Writing Kind of Day: Poems for Young Poets	Ralph Fletcher	grades 3–6 and higher

Reading Level

The reading level of a book is another way to search for books that are a good match for a reader. It is important to remember that a student's background knowledge and level of interest in a topic influence how easily he can read a book. Reading levels are meant to be a guide or jumping-off point and should not be used to restrict a student's reading choices.

Lexile Levels

The books selected for this list represent a variety of topics and genres and, within a particular grade level, different reading levels as indicated by the Lexile level. The Lexile measure is a score assigned to a book to indicate the readability level based on the frequency of certain words and the length of sentences in the text. More information on Lexile levels can be found at www.lexile.com. Within the SEM-R, talented readers are defined as children who read two levels above their chronological grade. The books on this list have therefore been selected to represent a range of one to two levels above a child's current grade placement. The left side of the following table illustrates typical Lexile reading levels by grade. The right side shows the Lexile ranges recommended for SEM-R book choices at several grade levels.

Standard Lexile Levels		*Lexile Levels for Talented Readers*	
Grade	*Lexile Range*	*Grade*	*Lexile Range*
Kindergarten	less than 200	Kindergarten–first grade	200–700
First grade	200–400		
Second grade	300–500	Second grade–third grade	400–900
Third grade	500–700		
Fourth grade	650–800	Fourth grade–fifth grade	800–1000
Fifth grade	750–950		
Sixth grade and higher	850–1050	Sixth grade and higher	900 and higher

A student who is highly motivated or interested in a topic may be able to read books about that topic at a more advanced level than she typically can with other books. The topic, content, or theme should also be considered when students choose books. While the reading level may not be challenging, the content or events presented in a book may be beyond the developmental or emotional level of a child and should be factored in when making book recommendations to children. All of these factors have influenced the books selected for specific grade levels on the lists of recommended books.

Recommended Books by Reading Level

KINDERGARTEN–FIRST GRADE BOOKS

Title	Author	Genre	Lexile Level
The Adventures of Sparrowboy	Brian Pinkney	Fiction	540
Amelia Bedelia	Peggy Parish	Fiction	140
The Bears on Hemlock Mountain	Alice Dalgliesh	Fiction	490
The Best-Loved Doll	Rebecca Caudill	Fiction	na
Bravest Dog Ever: The True Story of Balto	Natalie Standiford	Historical fiction	330
Cam Jansen and the Chocolate Fudge Mystery	David Adler	Mystery	560
The Case of the Fidgety Fox	Cynthia Rylant	Mystery	240
Cryobiology	Cherie Winner	Nonfiction	na
Days with Frog and Toad	Arnold Lobel	Fiction	320
The Desert Is Theirs	Byrd Baylor and Peter Parnall	Poetry	520
Diary of a Spider	Doreen Cronin	Fiction	510
The Dust Bowl	David Booth and Karen Reczuch	Historical fiction	620
Eloise	Kay Thompson	Fiction	na
Fancy Nancy	Jane O'Connor	Fiction	420
Fantastic Mr. Fox	Roald Dahl	Fantasy	600
The First Strawberries: A Cherokee Story	Joseph Bruchac	Fairy tale, folk tale	320
Flatfoot Fox and the Case of the Missing Eye	Eth Clifford	Mystery	300
Frederick	Leo Lionni	Fiction	500
George's Secret Key to the Universe	Lucy and Stephen Hawking	Fiction	na
Girl Wonder: A Baseball Story in Nine Innings	Deborah Hopkinson	Nonfiction	380
Henry and Mudge	Cynthia Rylant	Fiction	420
I Was a Third Grade Spy	Mary Jane Auch	Fiction	510
Jamie and Angus Together	Anne Fine	Fiction	740

Keeper of the Doves	Betsey Byars	Fiction	590
The Log Cabin	Ellen Howard	Historical fiction	570
Martin's Big Words	Doreen Rappaport	Nonfiction	410
Matisse: The King of Color	Laurence Anholt	Historical fiction	600
My Father's Dragon	Ruth Stiles Gannett	Fantasy	990
One City, Two Brothers	Chris Smith	Fiction	na
Owen	Kevin Henkes	Fiction	370
Pale Male: Citizen Hawk of New York City	Janet Schulman	Realistic fiction	na
The Polar Express	Chris Van Allsburg	Fiction	520
Previously	Allen Ahlberg	Fairy tale, folk tale	na
The Puzzle of the Platypus and Other Explorations of Science in Action	Jack Myers	Nonfiction	na
Samsara Dog	Helen Manos	Fiction	na
Serengeti Journey: On Safari in Africa	Gare Thompson	Nonfiction	na
The Seven Treasure Hunts	Betsy Byars	Fiction	380
The Silver Spoon of Solomon Snow	Kaye Umansky	Fiction	600
Snow	Uri Shulevitz	Fiction	270
The Snow Leopard	Jackie Morris	Fantasy	na
Squids Will Be Squids	Jon Scieszka and Lane Smith	Fiction	610
Stone Fox	John Reynolds Gardiner	Historical fiction	550
Stone Soup	Marcia Brown	Fiction	480
Tornado	Betsy Byars	Fiction	500
The True Story of the Three Little Pigs	Jon Scieszka	Fairy tale, folk tale	570
Where Does Electricity Come From?	Susan Mayes	Nonfiction	na
Young Cam Jansen and the Baseball Mystery	David A. Adler	Mystery	260

Note: na = not available

SECOND GRADE–THIRD GRADE BOOKS

Title	Author	Genre	Lexile Level
Amazing Grace	Mary Hoffman	Fiction	680
Ballerina Dreams	Lauren Thompson	Fiction	860
The BFG	Roald Dahl	Fiction	720
A Boy Called Slow	Joseph Bruchac	Fiction	690
Candyfloss	Jacqueline Wilson	Fiction	740
Chasing Vermeer	Blue Balliett	Mystery	770
Clementine	Sara Pennypacker	Fiction	790
The Cricket in Times Square	George Selden	Fiction	780
The Dangerous Book for Boys	Conn Iggulden and Hal Iggulden	Nonfiction	na
The Daring Book for Girls	Andrea J. Buchanan and Miriam Peskowitz	Nonfiction	na
Diary of a Wimpy Kid	Jeff Kinney	Fiction	860
A Dinosaur Named Sue	Pat Relf	Nonfiction	910
Eleven: A Mystery	Patricia Reilly Giff	Mystery	600
Ella Enchanted	Gail Carson Levine	Fairy tale, folk tale	670
Encyclopedia Brown and the Case of the Sleeping Dog	Donald Sobol	Mystery	610
Escape! The Story of the Great Houdini	Sid Fleischman	Nonfiction	940
The Facts and Fictions of Minna Pratt	Patricia MacLachlan	Fiction	650
Firegirl	Tony Abbott	Fiction	670
From the Mixed-up Files of Mrs. Basil E. Frankweiler	E. L. Konigsburg	Fiction	700
Harry Potter and the Sorcerer's Stone	J. K. Rowling	Fantasy	880
Holes	Louis Sachar	Fiction	660
How Nearly Everything Was Invented	Jilly MacLeod	Nonfiction	na
The Hundred Dresses	Eleanor Estes	Fiction	870
I, Freddy	Dietlof Reiche	Fiction	710
The Invention of Hugo Cabret	Brian Selznick	Fiction	820
Joey Pigza Loses Control	Jack Gantos	Fiction	800

Letting Swift River Go	Jane Yolen	Historical fiction	860
The Liberation of Gabriel King	L. L. Going	Fiction	780
Lily's Crossing	Patricia Reilly Giff	Historical fiction	720
Maniac Magee	Jerry Spinelli	Fiction	820
Marie Curie: Brave Scientist	Keith Brandt	Nonfiction	630
The Miraculous Journey of Edward Tulane	Kate DiCamillo	Fiction	700
Mrs. Frisby and the Rats of NIMH	Robert O'Brien	Fantasy	790
My Name Is Henley: My Life and Times as a Rescued Dog	Judith Kristen	Fiction	na
My Side of the Mountain	Jean Craighead George	Fiction	810
The Mysterious Benedict Society	Lee Stewart	Fiction	840
Phineas L. MacGuire Erupts!	Frances O'Roark Dowell	Fiction	810
Please Write in This Book	Mary Amato	Fiction	na
Poppy	Avi	Fiction	670
Redwall	Brian Jacques	Fantasy	800
Roxie and the Hooligans	Phyllis Reynolds Naylor	Fiction	930
Rules	Cynthia Lord	Fiction	780
Shelter Dogs: Amazing Stories of Adopted Strays	Peg Kehret	Nonfiction	940
Six Million Paper Clips	Peter Schroeder	Nonfiction	na
The Snake Scientist	Sy Montgomery	Nonfiction	930
Snow Treasure	Marie McSwigan	Historical fiction	690
Snowflake Bentley	Jacqueline B. Martin and Mary Azarian	Nonfiction	830
Strega Nona	Tomie DePaola	Fairy tale, folk tale	800
The Tale of Despereaux	Kate Dicamillo	Fiction	670
The Tree of Life: A Book Depicting the Life of Charles Darwin	Peter Sis	Nonfiction	890
Walk Two Moons	Sharon Creech	Fiction	770
Where the Red Fern Grows	Wilson Rawls	Fiction	700

Note: na = not available

FOURTH GRADE–FIFTH GRADE BOOKS

Title	Author	Genre	Lexile Level
Armageddon Summer	Jane Yolen and Bruce Coville	Fiction	820
Art Fraud Detective: Spot the Difference, Solve the Crime	Anna Nilsen	Mystery	970
The Bad Beginning	Lemony Snicket	Fiction	1010
Beardance	Will Hobbs	Fiction	890
Birchbark House	Louise Erdrich	Historical fiction	970
The Book Thief	Markus Zusak	Fiction	730
The Boys' Book: How to Be the Best at Everything	Dominique Enright and Guy Macdonald	Fiction	1040
Broken Song	Kathryn Lasky	Fiction	750
Bud, Not Buddy	Christopher Paul Curtis	Fiction	950
The Cabin Faced West	Jean Fritz	Historical fiction	860
Captains Courageous	Rudyard Kipling	Fiction	1020
Code Talker: A Novel About the Navajo Marines of World War II	Joseph Bruchac	Fiction	910
Crime Scene: The Ultimate Guide to Forensic Science	Richard Platt	Nonfiction	1190
Cross My Heart and Hope to Spy	Ally Carter	Fiction	na
Dear Mr. Henshaw	Beverly Cleary	Fiction	910
Destination Unexpected	Donald R. Gallo	Fiction	680
Discovering Great Artists: Hands-on Projects for Children	MaryAnn Kohl	Nonfiction	na
Dragonflight	Anne McCaffrey	Fantasy	940
Edgar Degas	Mike Venezia	Nonfiction	860
Eragon	Christopher Paolini	Fantasy	710
Esperanza Rising	Pam Munoz Ryan	Fiction	750
Ever	Gail Carson Levine	Fiction	
Geronimo	Joseph Bruchac	Historical fiction	900
The Ghost's Grave	Peg Kehret	Mystery	790
The Girls' Book: How to Be the Best at Everything	Juliana Foster	Fiction	na

The Great Art Scandal: Solve the Crime, Save the Show!	Anna Nilsen	Mystery	na
Harry Potter and the Chamber of Secrets	J. K. Rowling	Fantasy	940
Harry Potter and the Goblet of Fire	J. K. Rowling	Fantasy	880
Harry Potter and the Order of the Phoenix	J. K. Rowling	Fantasy	820
Harry Potter and the Prisoner of Azkaban	J. K. Rowling	Fantasy	880
A History of US: All the People	Joy Hakim	Nonfiction	940
Isaac Newton (Giants of Science Series, no. 2)	Kathleen Krull	Nonfiction	1000
The Kid Who Named Pluto	Marc McCutcheon	Nonfiction	1020
Leonardo da Vinci	Diane Stanley	Nonfiction	1010
Let the Circle Be Unbroken	Mildred Taylor	Historical fiction	850
The Lion, the Witch and the Wardrobe	C. S. Lewis	Fantasy	940
Lord of the Flies	William Golding	Fiction	770
My Brother Martin	Christine King Farris	Biography	970
Old Yeller	Fred Gipson	Fiction	910
Rebecca of Sunnybrook Farm	Kate Douglas Wiggins	Fiction	960
Roll of Thunder, Hear My Cry	Mildred Taylor	Historical fiction	920
Shh! We're Writing the Constitution	Jean Fritz	Historical fiction	950
Shiloh	Phyllis Reynolds Naylor	Fiction	890
The Watsons Go to Birmingham	Christopher Paul Curtis	Fiction	1000
When Zachary Beaver Came to Town	Kimberly Willis Holt	Fiction	700
Who Can Open Michelangelo's Seven Seals?	Thomas Brezina and Laurence Sartin	Mystery	na
Who Can Save Vincent's Hidden Treasure?	Thomas Brezina and Laurence Sartin	Mystery	910
Witness	Karen Hesse	Historical fiction	700
A Year Down Yonder	Richard Peck	Fiction	610

Note: na = not available

BOOKS FOR SIXTH GRADE AND HIGHER

Title	Author	Genre	Lexile Level
And Then There Were None	Agatha Christie	Mystery	570
Animal Survivors of the Arctic	Barbara Somervill	Nonfiction	1050
Boy	Roald Dahl	Biography	1090
Bud, Not Buddy	Christopher Paul Curtis	Fiction	920
Built to Last	George Sullivan	Nonfiction	950
Career Ideas for Kids Who Like Art	Diane Lindsey Reeves	Nonfiction	na
Clarice Bean Spells Trouble	Lauren Child	Fiction	980
Diary of a Young Girl	Anne Frank (translated by B. M. Mooyaart)	Biography	1080
Eleanor Roosevelt: A Life of Discovery	Russell Freedman	Biography	1100
Every Living Thing	James Herriott	Fiction	1100
Farewell to Manzanar	Jeanne Wakatsuki	Biography	1040
47	Walter Mosley	Fiction	860
Galileo's Daughter: A Historical Memoir of Science, Faith and Love	Dava Sobel	Historical fiction	1530
Girl with a Pearl Earring	Tracy Chevalier	Historical fiction	na
Habibi	Naomi Shihab Nye	Fiction	850
Harry Potter and the Deathly Hallows	J. K. Rowling	Fantasy	1000
Harry Potter and the Half-Blood Prince	J. K. Rowling	Fantasy	930
Hatchet	Gary Paulsen	Fiction	950
The Higher Power of Luck	Susan Patron	Fiction	1010
I Have a Dream	Martin Luther King, Jr.	Speech	1130
The Incredible Journey	Sheila Burnford	Nonfiction	1320
Introduction to Art Techniques	Ray Smith	Nonfiction	na
Island of the Blue Dolphins	Scott O'Dell	Fiction	1020
The Joy Luck Club	Amy Tan	Fiction	930
Kokopelli's Flute	Will Hobbs	Fiction	870

Last of the Mohicans	James Fenimore Cooper	Fiction	1350
Life of Pi	Yann Martel	Fiction	830
Longitude: The True Story of a Lone Genius Who Solved the Greatest Scientific Problem of His Time	Dava Sobel	Historical fiction	1320
Looking at Art	Laurie Schneider Adams	Nonfiction	na
Out of the Dust	Karen Hesse	Fiction	na
The Outsiders	S. E. Hinton	Fiction	750
Parrot in the Oven: Mi Vida	Victor Martinez	Fiction	1000
The Phantom Tollbooth	Norton Juster	Fiction	1000
Photo by Brady: A Picture of the Civil War	Jennifer Armstrong	Nonfiction	1200
Shabanu: Daughter of the Wind	Suzanne Fisher Staples	Fiction	970
A Single Shard	Linda Sue Park	Historical fiction	920
The Sisterhood of the Traveling Pants	Ann Brashares	Fiction	600
Sounder	William Armstrong	Fiction	900
Stotan!	Chris Crutcher	Fiction	1020
To Kill a Mockingbird	Harper Lee	Fiction	870
Uncle Tom's Cabin	Harriet Beecher Stowe	Fiction	1050
Under the Persimmon Tree	Suzanne Fisher Staples	Fiction	1010
The Voice That Challenged the Nation	Russell Freedman	Fiction	1180
The Water Horse	Dick King-Smith	Biography	910
The Well	Rebecca Scaglione	Fiction	na
Whale Talk	Chris Crutcher	Fiction	1000
The Winter Room	Gary Paulsen	Fiction	1170
Wizardology	Dugald Steer	Fiction	1180
The Wonderful Wizard of Oz	L. Frank Baum	Fiction	1000

Note: na = not available

Frequently Asked Questions About Phase One

Are book hooks synonymous with read-alouds?

Yes, Book hooks are our version of very exciting read-alouds that hook students into liking reading and reading more often! They are our nickname for Phase One read-alouds, which also incorporate bookmark questions. So the read-alouds are used as book hooks to get students involved (or hooked!) on reading.

Can we integrate reading skills such as comparing and contrasting in Phase One?

Yes. Skills like comparing and contrasting as well as other reading skills and literary skills (for example, analyzing theme, character, setting, or narrative styles) can be integrated into both your Phase One read-alouds and your Phase Two conferences.

Should we use the SEM-R bookmarks at the beginning or the end of our Phase One read-alouds?

Some teachers use the bookmarks at the beginning of the session in order to prepare or focus students' listening skills. Some teachers prefer to use them at the end of their Phase One session to ensure that students have listened actively and can respond.

How can we use the SEM-R bookmarks in Phase One and in Phase Two?

The bookmarks are usually used to scaffold comprehension skills during discussions after Phase One read-alouds as well as with individual students during Phase Two conferences. The questions were formulated to develop higher-order thinking skills that are aligned with curriculum standards. The bookmarks have also been used to stimulate students to move into Phase Three if an interest develops! Keep in mind that you can always use your own creativity to come up with questions and ways to motivate students to read. Think of the bookmarks as easy ways to ask questions that will stimulate higher-order thinking about most children's books. You can also modify bookmark questions for students with special needs and for those who are reading well above grade level.

Tell us again how to use the student writing prompts. Can they be used as part of Phase One?

Once a week, we would like you to have students react to what they are reading by using a brief writing prompt to enable them to practice writing the kinds of critical reading strategies that they are developing as part of Phases One and Three in the SEM-R. Writing helps them to reflect using different analyses and evaluation skills than merely thinking or offering an idea in class. This reflection exercise can be done during Phase Three, but you can introduce the writing prompt as part of your read-alouds in Phase One in order to give students time to think about their brief written response.

Phase Two: Support Materials for Independent Reading

The second phase of the SEM-R emphasizes supported independent reading (SIR). Phase Two develops students' self-regulation skills through silent independent reading of self-selected books coupled with individualized reading conferences. Teachers coach students to select books that are slightly above their current reading level; the appropriate match is continually assessed through conferences with each student two to three times each week. Students record their daily progress in a reading log that features the book title and number of minutes read. Once each week, all students write a response to a teacher-generated higher-order question, which is often taken from the SEM-R bookmarks that are provided in this book.

Teachers track individual students' progress by monitoring their reading logs, reading and responding to students' writing, and keeping records of individual conferences. Initially, teachers find that the majority of their students select books that are too easy. Students are told that they can take easier books home to read but that during class, they are required to select books that challenge them. Challenge is defined as students' encountering some words that they do not know and some ideas that encourage them to reflect on what they are reading. In the beginning of any implementation of the SEM-R, our classroom observations have indicated that most students can read appropriately challenging books for five to fifteen minutes a day without losing concentration or focus. Teachers add a minute or two each day during the SEM-R intervention, extending the time of their daily sessions within three to four weeks to thirty-five to forty-five minutes. During in-class reading time, teachers circulate to provide individual, differentiated instruction and support. For struggling readers who read below grade level, teachers provide support for skills such as decoding difficult words and model strategies for inferring challenging vocabulary from context. With more advanced readers, teachers discuss higher-order themes and ask critical questions that focus on synthesis, evaluation, and discussion, as well as use of more advanced reading strategies. Eventually, teachers begin to ask all students these higher-order questions, and low-achieving students learn how to respond through coaching during Phase Two and through listening to their teacher scaffold these strategies as a part of Phase One book hooks.

Choosing Books for Independent Reading: Making the Right Match

In the SEM-R, individualized book selection requires teachers to help students choose books that are one to one and a half levels above their current reading level. This resource will provide you with the information you need to make sure that students are reading at appropriate levels of challenge and that their books are highly interesting to them.

Supporting Students in Selecting Books

In this lesson, we summarize a number of strategies to help teachers work with students to select the right level of challenge for their SIR books. We suggest that the match between student and book be discussed in class with all students first and then as a part of the individual conferences. We include helpful hints for this important part of the SEM-R and discuss the critical role played by interest in making the right selection.

Conferencing Strategies

During our research on the SEM-R, we have observed many successful conferences, and this resource synthesizes the strategies that have been effectively used with students to increase reading fluency comprehension and to engender a love of reading.

One of the most challenging aspects of the SEM-R is providing students with meaningful differentiated instruction while assessing their current reading level, all during five minutes of conference time. We provide specific strategies for limiting the time you spend with each student while providing targeted and explicit instruction in reading strategies.

Management Tips for Supporting Independent Reading

Clearly stating the processes, procedures, and expectations associated with the SEM-R will set a standard for students and help create a classroom of focused and engaged readers. This resource provides some specific management ideas that you can use from the first day of implementation.

Progress Assessment Rubric

Many teachers have asked how they might use student assessment within the parameters of the SEM-R. While high-stakes assessment runs contrary to creating a love of reading, it is helpful for students to receive feedback and participate in the assessment process. This rubric is just one example that can be used as an assessment tool by students or teachers. Use it in its current form, or modify it to suit your needs.

Providing a Purpose for Reading

Teachers help their students clarify the purpose for their reading during the individual student conferences. A teacher may discuss the need to read a poetry book differently, for instance, than a realistic fiction text and would then share specific strategies for reading poetry. In another conference, the teacher would help a student learn that it is common practice to read sections of a nonfiction book rather than the entire book. Alternately, teachers may also discuss that the purpose of reading self-selected books during reading class is to make sure that every student is reading something of challenge and interest to him or her in order to further develop as a reader.

Using Student Reading Logs

Student logs provide students with a powerful tool for tracking their progress, setting goals, and reflecting on their understanding of texts while increasing their use of self-regulated learning strategies. The "Watch Your Reading Grow" chart, Books I Have Read, and Books to Read in the Future are an important part of the SEM-R log and have been used effectively throughout our research. A template for a daily student log is provided, along with a partial sample of how it might be filled in.

"Watch Your Reading Grow" Chart

Another way to help students appreciate their individual increase in time spent reading each day is to encourage them to chart the progress they make each day when they read. Ask students to use the "Watch Your Reading Grow" chart to list the days or weeks that they read in the space along the bottom of the chart and then plot the number of minutes they read each day, using the numbers on the left of the chart. Students who need more support can use this chart on a daily basis to chart increases that will encourage them to continue reading. Others may plot the mean of the week in which they are reading and watch their progress over months, as opposed to days and weeks. In our study, teachers reproduced the "Watch Your Reading Grow" chart to encourage students who needed more visible signs of progress; however, it can, of course, be used by all students.

Frequently Asked Questions About Phase Two

Throughout our research, several questions have been regularly asked about Phase Two. We address those questions and a few more. We hope that by sharing these questions and responses, we will answer some of the questions you may have.

Choosing Books for Independent Reading: Making the Right Match

An essential feature of supported independent reading (SIR) is that students select books that are sufficiently challenging. SIR is based on the premise that students will benefit more from the experience of reading independently if they are challenged by complex content, ideas, and language. This premise is especially true if the book is of personal interest to the student and she is highly motivated to read it. However, if books are too challenging, students may become frustrated or unmotivated and fluency and comprehension will not improve. Evaluating the appropriateness of student book selections is challenging, yet it is one of the most critical aspects of ensuring the success and effectiveness of SIR.

There are two ways to think about the level of challenge of a book selection for an individual student.

Word-Reading Level

Word-reading level refers to whether a student can read the words in a book. Students should be able to automatically read most of the words on any page. In addition, students should read with a high degree of fluency (that is, smoothly and quickly). However, in an appropriately challenging book, students should encounter some words that are unfamiliar and new to them, especially seldom-used words or words with complex meanings that they may not have been exposed to in everyday conversation. Students learn to read new words by encountering them in a supportive context in which they can read the surrounding words fluently.

Complexity of Content

Complexity of content refers to whether students can understand, appreciate, and think critically about the content of a book. Students should be able to answer basic questions about character, setting, and plot. In addition, students should be able to interact with text at a more complex level by making inferences, analyzing and synthesizing information, and relating content to their own experiences. However, the content, ideas, and language in a book should challenge students. In other words, the content should challenge the boundaries of what students can understand easily. Books should encourage students to use and develop critical thinking skills, expand their knowledge and understanding, and think about ideas differently.

Linking Students to Appropriate Books

Deciding whether a book is an appropriate choice for SIR will be a different process for different students. For example, a talented reader may choose a book with a word-reading level at or above grade level. However, the student may not be sufficiently challenged by the book's content. Given the student's high degree of word-reading fluency, he should be encouraged to choose a more advanced book with a greater complexity of content.

On the other hand, a struggling reader may choose a book in which the content and ideas are sufficiently challenging. However, because of less-developed reading skills, the student may have to expend so much energy just to read the words that he is unable to understand or even access the content. This student should be supported in choosing a book with equally challenging content but with a word-reading level that is more matched with his reading ability and thus that he can read fluently.

Because students in your class will all have very different reading skills, there are no exact rules for deciding whether a book is an appropriate choice for SIR. However, the following general procedures are helpful guidelines:

- Listen to the student read a page of the book. The student's reading should be smooth and fluent, and most words should be read correctly and automatically. The student's reading should not sound halting or labored.

- It is hoped that some words will be unfamiliar to the student, especially if they are seldom-used words or words with complex meanings that the student may not have been exposed to in daily conversation. If the student can easily read and understand every word, it is likely that the book is not providing enough challenge.

- After listening to the student read, you should ask a few basic comprehension questions about what the student just read. The student should be able to answer these questions easily.

- Next, you should ask a few more difficult, probing questions that require the student to make inferences or think about broader themes. These will help you assess whether the student understands the book at a more complex level.

The student should be able to offer reasonable responses to these questions. On the other hand, if the student is able to answer these questions too easily, the book content may not be appropriately challenging.

- Most important, use your knowledge of your student, her reading ability, and her level of understanding, and ask yourself, "Does the book seem like a good fit? Does the book seem too difficult or too easy? Should this student be challenging herself more?"

- Our research has demonstrated that high levels of student interest can provide the stimulus for students to tackle more challenging reading material. In fact, some students' reading fluency and comprehension have dramatically increased because of their high levels of interest. The task is to find **the right match**.

Supporting Students in Selecting Books

Our experiences have enabled us to watch as students try to find books that are both interesting and challenging. We have also had the opportunity to watch insightful teachers guide students in their book selections and in this section we summarize some of the strategies that work best.

Goal
To improve the quality and quantity of student engagement time with a book

Objective
To provide students with strategies for choosing a challenging, enjoyable book to read

Supplies Needed
A collection of books representing a variety of genres and styles from the library, classroom collections, or sources outside of school

Activities
1. To begin the discussion, choose a high-interest book and show it to your students. Ask your students some questions such as the following:

   - What clues tell you about this book?

   Writing student responses on a board or overhead transparency will enable the class to refer to their ideas throughout the lesson. The goal is to help students identify

   - Illustrations
   - Information on book jacket
   - Information on the title page
   - Subject focus
   - Information about the author

Select a couple of exciting pages to read aloud to your students. The selection does not necessarily need to come from the beginning of the book. Then ask students,

- What interests you about this book?

- Is there anyone interested in reading this book or one like it during supported independent reading (SIR)?

2. Have each student work with a partner or in a small group to discuss his personal preferences for selecting a book. Ask them,

- What clues (from the preceding discussion) do you find most useful for making choices about what to read?

For example, some students may find the information on the book jacket helpful in choosing a book because it tells them about the characters, while other students may glean the most information from the illustrations on the cover or inside pages because those tell them where and when the story is taking place.

3. Provide a number of different books for small groups of students to preview. Encourage them to rely on their recently discussed criteria for selecting a book. To facilitate student discussion, guiding questions can be asked, such as

- What do you think is the subject of this book?

- What clues did you use to decide what the book is about?

- Do you know anything about the book's author?

- Is this book a work of fiction or nonfiction?

- Why would someone read this book?

- Who do you think would enjoy this book?

Ask each group to present its book recommendations to the class.

4. Introduce the ten-page chance strategy by discussing the following guidelines for book selection:

- Read the first ten pages of the book to see if you like it. Remember, you must read at least ten pages.

- After ten pages, if you don't like the book, explain your reasons to your teacher and then select another book. You can ask your teacher or a friend to help you select another book.

- If you are not sure whether you like the book after ten pages, read another ten pages to help you decide.

- When reading for pleasure, it is important to find a book that you like!

5. As the students prepare to read, review the rules for SIR:

   • Make sure that you have a book to read that is challenging for you. If you don't have a book, choose one from the class library or ask an adult to help you find one.

   • Reading logs will be completed after SIR is finished.

Possible Extensions

1. If students seem to be struggling to find appropriately challenging books, you may want to assemble three or four different-colored bins or crates of books leveled for below average, average, or above average readers and then provide students with guidance about selecting a book from a particular bin.

2. During a regularly scheduled library time or at a specially arranged time, this lesson provides a perfect opportunity to visit the school library and invite the librarian to share some tips for finding a good book.

3. To ensure that your students have ample opportunities to read at home as well as at school, encourage each child to have a public library card. One teacher using the SEM-R went so far as to take her entire class to the local public library for a tour!

Conferencing Strategies

During the regularly scheduled supported independent reading time, the teacher should meet with students individually. The purpose of these individual conferences is to

- Evaluate the appropriateness of the student's book selection in terms of comprehension and sophistication of ideas and content

- Provide support for students in developing reading fluency and comprehension by helping them acquire reading strategies and by asking them high-level questions about their independent reading

- Make connections with students' interests

- Suggest possibilities for further reading and study

Each individual conference should take about four or five minutes (so teachers should be able to meet with each student at least once or twice each week). Individual conferences should take place in a quiet area of the classroom where students will feel comfortable reading aloud and talking openly. Although conferences should be informal, remember that they are a crucial component of the SIR intervention.

Effective Five-Minute Conferences

1. When you begin a conference, sit down with the student and ask her to tell you a little bit about her book. Keep in mind that you are asking the student to synthesize information from the book rather than recount every detail. Give the student limits to enable her to more effectively summarize—for example,

   - "Tell me about the story in three sentences or less."
   - "Take thirty seconds to tell me about the book."

2. Ask the student to describe whether she likes the book so far, and why.

3. Ask the student to read a little bit of the book aloud to you, starting wherever she stopped when you dropped in. Have the student read about a page

or for about a minute. Again, give the student limits so that you will not have to interrupt her as she is reading—for example,

- "Pick up where you left off. Read me a couple of paragraphs."
- "Read me a page."

4. If the student comes to a word she does not know, wait a few seconds and then tell her the word. Allow the narrative flow to keep going, rather than interrupting it with too much time spent trying to figure out the word.

5. If the student is missing so many words that it is impossible for a narrative flow to occur, stop her and suggest that maybe this book should be saved to read later on, after she has had time for more reading practice. Have the student write the name and author of the book on the sheet "Books to Read in the Future," and then help her choose a new book.

6. Pay careful attention to how the student reads the passage. Listen for the number of words that are difficult for her, for expression, and for other indications of comprehension.

7. When the student finishes reading, offer some comments that reflect praise. Try to be specific (for example, "I really liked how you used different voices for the characters!" or "I liked how you went back and corrected yourself on a word that you missed!"). Then ask the student a couple of open-ended follow-up questions about the reading. You may want to use one of the bookmarks as a guide, or you may want to ask some questions that are more specific to the passage itself.

8. The questioning portion of the conference should take only about three minutes. The overall conference should take only five to six minutes at the most.

9. Try to ask questions that go beyond simple recall of what happened in the text. Ask "why" questions, and remind the student to support her answers with evidence from the book.

10. Try to ask questions that are challenging for that particular student. Varying questions will help to differentiate conference discussions.

11. A good source of questioning is the connections that can be made with the text. Remember to ask questions about connections of the text with other texts, with the student and her experiences, and with what is going on in the world.

12. The follow-up questioning time is also a good time to review words that the student missed. Go back and point out some words that were challenging, and ask the student how she might have tried to figure out the words. Talk about strategies for figuring out words, such as using clues from the context, using pictures, or looking for parts of the word that are familiar.

13. In some cases, the reading and discussion portions of the conference, together or separately, might indicate that the book is too hard or too easy for the student. If this is the case, encourage her to try a different book. In the case of books that are too easy, talk to the student about the importance of reading challenging books while at school, where someone can help her, and encourage her to read the easy book at home.

14. Initial the student's conference record on the appropriate date to show that the conference was conducted. You may want to list any major strategies that you worked on or difficulties the student had. Thank the student for sharing some reading time with you.

Management Tips for Supporting Independent Reading

Establish a routine with clear expectations. In a world filled with standards and accountability, few elementary or middle school students (or teachers) regularly enjoy the academic autonomy that independent reading time provides, so it is important to provide students with boundaries that will ensure productive independent reading time. The following ground rules have been used in classes in which the SEM-R has been implemented:

- You must have a book to read.

- If you aren't enjoying a book and have given it a fair chance (read at least ten pages), ask the teacher to help you choose a new one.

- Select and remain in one reading area during independent reading time.

- Only reading is happening. (You may talk quietly during conferences.)

- Do your best reading the whole time.

When it comes to the environment, think comfort! You may find that beanbag chairs, cozy couches, rockers, carpet squares, or even your teacher's chair offer appealing spaces in which students can read. However, if a more relaxed classroom configuration seems like it might be disruptive for the majority of your students, introduce these special reading spaces as a reward for good reading behavior or as part of a special class celebration after reaching a target number of minutes of independent reading.

Provide self-regulation tools. As we have implemented the SEM-R across the United States, we have watched students gain self-regulation strategies. Some students already have strong skills in this area, others learn to focus and read very quickly, and still others need a great deal of help, support, and guidance as they try to learn to read for twenty, thirty, and forty-five minutes each day. This section includes a number of suggestions that have helped teachers help students gain self-regulation strategies.

- Encourage students to focus on one particular bookmark or bookmark question, to provide a purpose as they begin their reading for the week. As students find evidence in their book to help them answer a question, they can either mark the spot with the bookmark or make a note of the page in their reading log. They will then be prepared to discuss their ideas with you during their reading conference.

- Provide students with sticky notes or scratch paper on which to jot down questions, concerns, or unfamiliar vocabulary so that they can continue to read until an adult is available for a discussion.

- Share your SIR target time with your students, and celebrate the days when everyone exceeds expectations. Younger students in particular have a difficult time gauging the amount of time that they are actually reading silently. Providing students with a visual reminder of their goal (like a stop time written on the board, a timer, or a sticky note placed on the clock marking the end of independent reading time) may help them to sustain a focus on their reading.

- Many teachers have remarked that during self-directed activities, few students can raise their hand and continue to be productive at the same time. We have found that providing students with an unobtrusive cue to indicate that they need adult assistance benefits everyone. One of the teachers during the pilot study used a creative method. She gave each student a card showing a sun on one side and a rain cloud on the other. While the student was reading without a problem, the card is was kept beside him with the sunshine facing up; however, as soon as a problem occurred, the student could flip over the card, displaying the rain cloud and indicating to the teacher that assistance was needed. A template for such a conference cue is provided for you at the end of this chapter.

Make a plan for how to help struggling students. It takes time and practice to develop the self-regulation skills that enable a student to engage in an extended period of independent reading, and not all students can or will progress at the same pace. It is important to recall that in many cases, students who have difficulty maintaining focus during independent reading may also struggle with other barriers to their reading fluency or comprehension. Offering a few creative alternatives for these students may provide them with the support they need to progress during SIR. Some of our favorite strategies include providing audio books, access to a computer, an adult reading partner, buddy reading, or a reading reward contract.

Record student progress. Keeping an accurate record of student conferences is an easy way to assess student learning during a SEM-R program. Two types of records have been useful to teachers in implementing the SEM-R.

1. **Which students are due for conferences.** One goal of the SEM-R is that all students participate in at least two individual conferences each week during Phase Two. Setting up a class roster in a simple grid will allow you to assess at a glance who needs to meet with you. Employing a "deli" system is another way to track student conferences for both you and your students. Simply provide each student with a numbered card on which they write their name and then post the cards for the students with whom you will be conferencing at the front of the room each day. As you have a reading conference with each student, remove the card, allowing others to see who is up next.

2. **Notes.** During an individual conference, notations about book selection and preferences, reading strategies, or comprehension questions can be made in the student's reading log or on a separate record sheet for future reference. We have included a rubric that was designed and used by a group of third-grade teachers who based their criteria on those already existent in their school's report card.

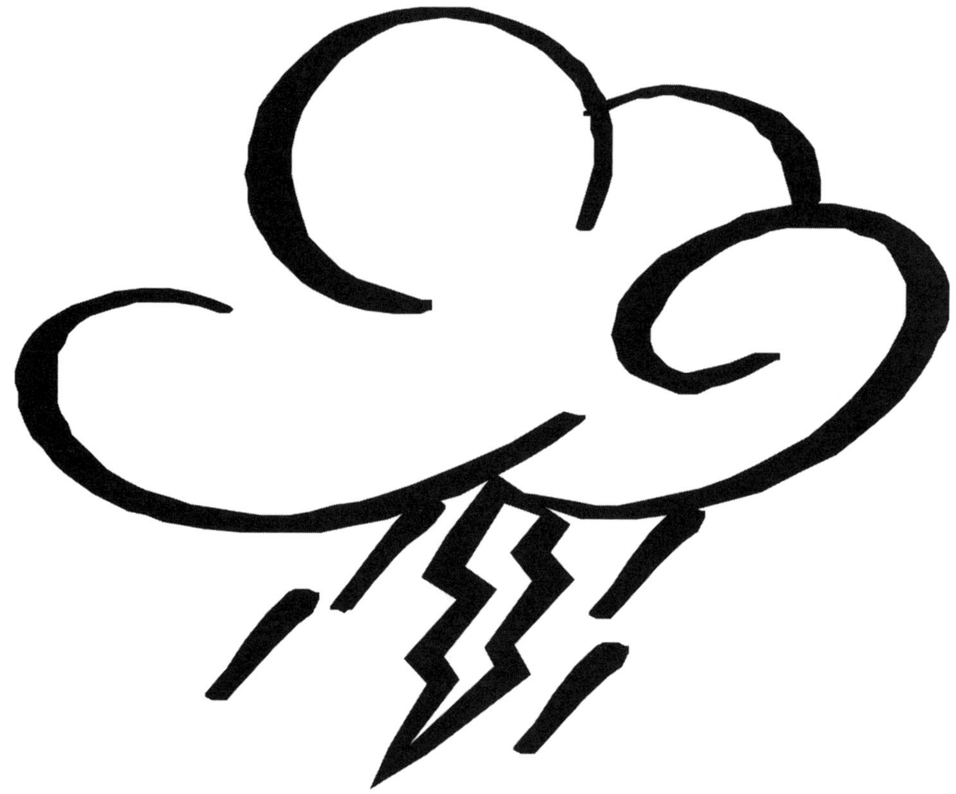

Progress Assessment Rubric

Student Name: _____

Date: _____ Teacher Initials: _____

	Never	Rarely	Usually	All the Time
Self-Regulation: Chooses to read independently without prompts from teacher *Comments:*	0	1	2	3
Fluency: Learning new vocabulary in context *Comments:*	0	1	2	3
Comprehension: Uses reading strategies to make meaning of the text and responds critically to bookmark questions *Comments:*	0	1	2	3
Book Selection: Selects books that are challenging and personally interesting *Comments:*	0	1	2	3
Reading Reflection: • Relevance: 1 point • Complete sentences: 1 point • Paragraph (3–5 sentences): 1 point • Two specific details: 1 point *Comments:*	1	2	3	4

Total Score /16

Providing a Purpose for Reading

As the students begin their independent reading, it is helpful for them to have a purpose or a focus for their attention as they read. You might encourage your students by saying, "When you are reading today, I want you to think about how you would describe the characters in your book and whether they are realistic or not."

Writing prompts are also a way to provide students with a purpose for their reading. To help students write an insightful reflection or determine what should be written in their log, provide a set of criteria. Here is an example of one teacher's criteria:

- You need to write complete sentences.

- There should be three to five sentences (to make a paragraph).

- You need at least two specific details.

- Your reflection has to be relevant! Your answer should be about the story you are reading.

- Plot summary doesn't always mean that you have answered the question.

Writing Prompts: Text-to-Self Connections
1. What qualities do you share with the main character in the story?

2. How does this story relate to your own life?

3. How has the book influenced your viewpoint?

4. What did you learn from this book?

5. How are the events in the story similar to the events in your own life?

6. Do the characters remind you of someone in your family? In what way?

7. Why do you like or dislike one of the characters?

8. If you were to choose a friend from the characters in the book, which one would you select? Why?

9. List the characteristics necessary for you to like someone. How do they apply to the story characters?

10. If you were one of the characters, would you do anything differently? Why?

11. What would you do if one or more of the characters moved into your neighborhood?

12. What did you learn from the main character that could be useful or harmful in your own life?

13. To whom might you recommend this book? Is there a particular group or population that you think would enjoy this book? Why?

14. What might you tell this author if you were to write to him or her?

Writing Prompts: Story Elements

15. Which of the story's events reminds you of things that are happening right now?

16. Do you think the plot is true to life?

17. Why did the story end the way it did?

18. Would you like to have the main character as a friend? Why or why not?

19. How does the personality of a person in the book contribute to his or her success or failure?

20. Compare the main character's personality at the beginning of the story with his or her personality at the end of the story.

21. If you could change the behavior of any character, which one would you change? Why?

22. What character in the story has the biggest problem? Why? How did you arrive at that decision?

23. How would the problem change if the story took place elsewhere?

24. How does this particular setting help to develop the character?

25. Describe a journey in the story.

26. Do you think the setting of this story is real or imaginary? Why?

27. Is the author trying to leave the reader with an increased understanding of some aspect of life? If so, what is it?

28. Do the ideas of kindness, helping, and making the world a better place emerge in this book? In what ways?

29. Some books provide examples of goodness conquering evil. Does this book provide any?

30. What lesson does one or more of the characters learn that will help improve their lives?

31. How is this book like another book that you have read?

Writing Prompts: Nonfiction

32. How could an idea in this book improve the world?

33. What new information did you learn that made you curious about this topic?

34. How effectively did the author present different perspectives on an issue?

35. What would you suggest to improve this book? Why?

36. Do you think this book is biased in any way? If so, what advice would you give the author to reduce the bias?

37. What events in history did this book help you understand?

38. What is the most important idea that the author conveys about the topic?

39. After reading this book, do you want to delve into this topic more deeply? What other books might you find? Where would you find them?

40. Why might a nonfiction book have more than one author? Why is collaboration important in this type of writing?

41. Compare what you learned from this book with what you already knew about the topic.

42. What is one big question you still have after reading the book?

43. How do you read a nonfiction book differently from a fiction book?

44. What sections of the book did you want to read first? Why?

Other Writing Prompts

45. What gift would you like to give the main character? Why?

46. Describe some of the similarities between two or more characters in the story.

47. How might you rewrite this story to include one of your friends as a character?

48. If you were the author, what further episodes, events, or discoveries would you have the characters participate in?

49. Why did the author place the story in this location?

50. What were some of the problems or situations the characters encountered?

51. Describe two events that portray the main character's personality.

52. Describe the main character. Does the character seem real to you?

53. Explain the title.

54. How well might this book work as a movie?

55. What do you consider the strongest feature of the book? The weakest?

56. How might your parents or friends react to living in the story's setting?

57. Explain a problem that one of the characters had. How was it solved?

58. Might there have been a better solution to the problem that the main character faced than the one given in the book? If not, why? If so, what is it?

59. Which scene from the book would make a good preview, or trailer, for a movie?

60. What situation aroused your greatest feeling of suspense? What happened?

61. List details about the setting that might help determine where the story takes place.

62. Does the book have any value beyond entertainment?

Using Student Reading Logs

The purpose of the Student Reading Log is for teachers to learn which books students are reading and the amount of time they have spent reading silently in class each day. Students should complete the log every day at the end of Phase Two independent reading. Many teachers have found that the accuracy of the amount of time recorded improves when they write on the board the start time and end time of students' independent reading. Teachers with older students can model subtracting the start time from the stop time to calculate a total reading time, while those with younger students can simply write the number of minutes on the board. Students should compute the number of minutes they read and record it in their reading log.

One day each week, students should use the space provided in the Reflection section to write about the previous week's reading experiences. Most often, teachers ask students to complete this section at the end of the week on Friday. A list of potential writing prompt questions has been provided in the "Providing a Purpose for Reading" section of this book so that teachers can choose an appropriate topic for their students and then write it on the board or explain it orally. Many teachers also use bookmark questions for this purpose. Students need not necessarily copy the question into their log; they only have to write a thoughtful response. The questions should vary and should be selected to encourage students to reflect about reading and the strategies that are embedded in their conferences. To assist in record keeping, a box has been provided at the bottom of the daily log sheet on the first page of the log for teachers to record the question selected each week in their teacher logs. A completed sample of the daily log sheet and the Reflection section are provided for you to review.

Following the Reflection section of the student log is a Conference Information box. The teacher can complete this box at the end of each individualized conference held with the student. The Conference Information Box is a convenient way for a teacher to track the progress of each individual student. In addition, the student can read the information from the weekly conferences and use it as a reminder of the strategies to focus on in upcoming weeks.

If you wish to have your students keep track of the titles they have completed, they can list them in the "SEM-R Books I Have Finished" section. This section is a convenient way for teachers to monitor the books that students have read. Finally, we have included a "Books to Read in the Future" section of the log. The ultimate goal of each book hook is to have students in your classroom ask to read the book you have introduced, especially if it is in their area of interest and in their challenge zone. We realize that it is not reasonable to have twenty-five copies of the same book in each classroom. By providing a space for students to keep track of books they wish to read, you are modeling ways in which more mature readers use the public library as well as their own reading wish lists. This helps students to plan for future reading and develop good habits. In addition, if a book you have introduced is too far above the reading level of a student, the student can jot the title of the book in this section, with the goal of working hard in reading so that they can read that book later in the school year as a reminder of how much they have improved in reading.

Schoolwide Enrichment Model for Reading Student Reading Log

The University of Connecticut

Name:	
Teacher:	
School:	

Dates:_____ through _____

Book Title		
MONDAY		Pages read	
		Minutes read	
		Conf. Y/N	
TUESDAY		Pages read	
		Minutes read	
		Conf. Y/N	
WEDNESDAY		Pages read	
		Minutes read	
		Conf. Y/N	
THURSDAY		Pages read	
		Minutes read	
		Conf. Y/N	
FRIDAY		Pages read	
		Minutes read	
		Conf. Y/N	
This week's writing prompt:		

Reflection

_____

_____

_____

_____

_____

_____

_____

_____

_____

_____

_____

_____

_____

_____

Conference Information

Date:	Book:	
	Did the student read aloud? Y / N	Is this book a good match? Y / N
	Conference focus:	Focus for next time:
Length:	Notes:	

Date:	Book:	
	Did the student read aloud? Y / N	Is this book a good match? Y / N
	Conference focus:	Focus for next time:
Length:	Notes:	

Date:	Book:	
	Did the student read aloud? Y / N	Is this book a good match? Y / N
	Conference focus:	Focus for next time:
Length:	Notes:	

SEM-R Books I Have Finished

Date		Title, Author, and Genre (Type of Book)
Started	Completed	

Books to Read in the Future

Title	Author

Sample Student Reading Log

Name:	Alex
Teacher:	Ms. Jonas
School:	Center Street Elementary

Dates: _September 18_ **through** _September 22_

	Book Title		
MONDAY	*Surviving the Applewhites by Stephanie Tolan*	Pages read	*166 – 186*
		Minutes read	*35*
		Conf. Y/N	*Y*
TUESDAY	*Surviving the Applewhites by Stephanie Tolan*	Pages read	*187 – 216*
		Minutes read	*35*
		Conf. Y/N	*N*
WEDNESDAY	*City by David Macaulay*	Pages read	*1 – 58*
		Minutes read	*40*
		Conf. Y/N	*N*
THURSDAY	*City by David Macaulay*	Pages read	*58 – 112*
		Minutes read	*40*
		Conf. Y/N	*N*
FRIDAY	*Inkspell by Cornelia Funke*	Pages read	*1 – 15*
		Minutes read	*20*
		Conf. Y/N	*Y*

This week's writing prompt:

If you could change the behavior of any character, which one would you change? Why?

Reflection

At first when I started writing this, I thought that I would say that Jake in Surviving the Applewhites was the character whose behavior I would change. Now, however, I think his behavior was tied to the plot too much. After all, if he had never been as naughty as he was, like lighting fires and skipping school and stuff, then no one would have tried to help him. Instead, I wish that the father would have paid more attention to Jake because it really seemed like he needed a dad during lots of this story. He is the character that I would change to make him pay more attention to Jake. I think that if the author had done this Jake would have a better attitude for more of the story. This part of the story made me think about my relationship with my father. I am very grateful that my own father pays attention to me and I know how lucky I am. This book made me realize that all kids are not as fortunate as I am.

Conference Information

Date:	Book: *Inkspell*	
9/22	Did the student read aloud? (Y)/ N	Is this book a good match (Y)/ N
	Conference focus: *Inferences*	Focus for next time: *Still working on inferences*
Length: *5 min*	Notes: *Alex will write down on a sticky note at least 2 inferences about the book before the next conference.*	

SEM-R Books I Have Finished

Date		Title, Author, and Genre (Type of Book)
Started	Completed	
9/5	9/19	*Surviving the Applewhites* by Stephanie Tolan Fiction
9/20	9/21	*The City* by David Macaulay Historical Fiction

Books to Read in the Future

Title	Author
The Way Things Work	*by David Macaulay*
Artemis Fowl	*by Eoin Colfer*
Midnight for Charlie Bone	*by Jenny Nimmo*

Frequently Asked Questions About Phase Two

Tell us about the typical Phase Two conference with a student.

In Phase Two conferences, students usually read a few paragraphs and then the teacher provides individualized instruction in reading skills (for example, discussion of themes, decoding, or reading strategies). This brief instruction period is when the SEM-R bookmarks can be used and when basic reading skills can be reinforced, depending on individual students' needs. Teachers can also use this time to personalize and differentiate discussions of literary concepts such as characterization, plot, theme, settings, and narrative style.

Can I or should I have more conferences with struggling readers?

You should try to arrange similar numbers of conferences with all students in your class; all students deserve the opportunity to make continual progress in reading. If you think some students need much more help, try to get some parents to volunteer to come in and read with struggling readers, or consider involving students from different grade levels as reading buddies. If some students are not making progress, you may have to provide them with more help during conferences.

Tell us again about the challenge level of Phase Two books?

All students should be encouraged to read slightly above their current level of reading. We believe that teachers need to honor every child's attempt to improve. So if we have students in fourth grade who are reading at a kindergarten or first-grade level, we will still try to find high-interest books that are slightly above their current level of reading. Interests should also be taken into account. If students have an interest in a book, they may be encouraged to read books that are slightly more challenging than they may initially be able to tackle. We are looking for a match of book that enables each student to be stretched in fluency and comprehension.

Should we use Lexile levels as the primary basis for book selections?

The short answer is no. Here is our explanation. Lexile scores and other leveling systems are meant to be a guide or a starting point. Leveling systems use different criteria to determine the reading level of a book. Sentence structure, the length of sentences, the sophistication of words used, the author's writing style, the way the pictures support the story, the content, the genre, the concepts presented, and other factors influence the way a book level is determined. The first consideration when choosing a book for a student to read should be the student—interests, background knowledge, and motivation to read will influence success with any text. Once those factors are understood, the level of a book, such as the Lexile level, will help guide the student and teacher to books that are of an appropriate level of difficulty. Each book should be considered according to the content or topic, genre, and concepts or theme presented. Because Lexile scores and other leveling systems represent a range of books within any one level, one book in that level may be more challenging for a student to read than another, depending on the content, genre, writing style, and the student's interest in that topic. In our experience, it is clear that nothing does as good a job as teachers who conference with children and determine the appropriateness of their book selections on an individual basis over time. Our motivation for developing the SEM-R was to move beyond formulas that predetermine the books that students can read and toward allowing children to explore books that they want to read. The best way to find an appropriate match is for teachers to work individually with students, discover their interests, and then help them to read slightly above their current level.

Should we use the SEM-R bookmarks at every conference?

You may use them, or if you feel comfortable with the use of differentiated instructional strategies and the application of reading strategies to students' needs, you may develop your own questions.

Do we have to use the rubric in the book for every conference we have with each student?

No, the rubric that is available in this book can be used occasionally to track a student's progress for your records, or it can be used if you need to grade students during the SEM-R intervention. The rubric can also help you assess how best to help students improve their reading during your conferences. It can also be adapted to reflect the priorities of your own curriculum and state and district standards, as well as students' strengths and deficits in reading.

What about students who can only read for a few minutes? What do we do with them in Phase Two?

Students who can only read for a few minutes each day lack self-regulation, which we define as a set of constructive behaviors that guide how students learn. There is a set of self-regulation strategies that is common to most or all students, as well as an *individual* set of skills that each student must develop in order to maximize their effectiveness at learning and be successful in school and in life. Self-regulation skills can be taught by teachers, and those skills can be learned and controlled by students. As a teacher, you can help students increase their self-regulation and thus increase their reading time by a few minutes each day if you are consistent in your efforts. You can teach some of the self-regulation practices that we describe in *Joyful Reading,* and you can continue to encourage and engage students by using high-interest books and helping them to select books that they find appealing.

How can we encourage students to become more self-regulated and to read for longer periods?

We have included a series of strategies in *Joyful Reading* that respond to this question—for example, using challenges to consistently increase self-regulation time, tracking progress by recording the time that students spend on their reading, managing classroom procedures to help students stay on track, and motivating students to read by using several methods to help them find high-interest books. The best way we have found to encourage students to read longer is to be consistent in your high expectations that all of your students can read independently (with your support) and in helping them increase the time they read by a few minutes each week. Each student has to learn individual strategies that fit her own reading style.

What about students who never seem to find a book to read? If we encourage them and let them start by reading ten pages but they quit reading after twenty pages every time, what can we do?

You can try to find more exciting book hooks specifically geared to those students; you can try to have students do some reading while listening to books on CD; or you can simply tell students that they must choose from a selection of two or three books that you have chosen based on their interests! Students, however, must understand that they must have a book that they will continue reading. If they keep quitting after reading ten pages of several books, you might consider telling them that they must write a one-page explanation of why they did not like the book. This requirement has succeeded in motivating some students to focus on reading one book.

Should we let students take their Phase Two books home to read?

While you will want to encourage students to read at home, at the beginning of the SEM-R program, you may want to limit this practice until you learn which students are responsible enough to bring their book back to school for Phase Two reading time. Students can take a different book home to read; many students do well reading more than one book. If you have a difficult time with helping students find an appropriately challenging reading book and then they take their book home and lose it, you will have to start the process all over again. We recommend that you ask each student to keep the book they are currently reading during Phase Two in their log. As you begin to understand which students really enjoy reading and can be responsible about their work, you can encourage those students to take their book home. If they forget to bring the book back, they can begin another that they have thought about reading.

Phase Three: Support Materials for Student-Selected Activities

The ultimate goal in Phase Three of the SEM-R is to help students progress from teacher-directed reading opportunities to independent, self-directed activities over the course of a few months. To promote students' enjoyment of reading while continuing to develop their reading fluency and comprehension, teachers encourage students to select projects to pursue in areas of interest. Activities may include continuation of self-selected reading or other projects such as book discussion groups, activities that develop creative thinking and critical thinking, Web site visits, or special explorations. This section provides a variety of reading enrichment resources and tools that can be used to support students as they learn how reading can open doors to discovery.

Reading Interest-a-Lyzer

The Reading Interest-a-Lyzer is an instrument to help you identify student interests. A brief introduction to the Interest-a-Lyzer is provided, along with a reproducible copy of the instrument for use in your classroom.

Renzulli Learning

Renzulli Learning is a computer-based approach to enrichment teaching and learning. The Renzulli Learning System helps teachers and students identify, organize, and provide suggestions for student activities based on students' individual needs.

Creativity Training Activities

To introduce your students to the idea of open-ended responses, a selection of creativity training activities is presented. These activities are designed to promote dynamic thinking and focus on flexibility, originality, and elaboration.

Reading on the Internet

The Internet has changed the way in which we access information. This list includes a multitude of Web-based resources, including e-books. These resources combine the best literature and twenty-first-century technology.

Take a Test Drive! Exciting Web Sites for Students to Try

The Internet holds the answers to many students' burning questions, but before surfing the Web, students must learn to read for information. This series of links provides students with interest-based resources and a purpose for their Internet searches.

SEM-Xplorations: Enrichment Projects

We provide ten SEM-Xploration projects that are designed to scaffold students' investigations in areas of interest and their development of the skills necessary to conduct independent investigations.

Frequently Asked Questions About Phase Three

We address several questions that continue to recur during our research.

Reading Interest-a-Lyzer

One of the most important goals of the Schoolwide Enrichment Model for Reading is to improve students' attitudes toward reading and their enjoyment of it. One way to achieve this goal is to build on student interests. The Reading Interest-a-Lyzer should be completed by your students during the first week of the intervention to help you identify and encourage student interests through reading. Students will need approximately twenty minutes to complete the Reading Interest-a-Lyzer. Once the forms have been completed, we encourage you to review them and note any classroom trends or unexpected discoveries. This information might affect the books that you choose or recommend for your students; students should also be encouraged to reflect on their own responses and interests.

READING INTEREST-A-LYZER

Based on the Interest-a-Lyzer by Joseph S. Renzulli

Name _____ Grade _____ Age _____

1.   **Are you currently reading a book for pleasure?**   ❑ **Yes**   ❑ **No**

2.   **Do you ever read a book for pleasure?**   ❑ **Yes**   ❑ **No**

3.   **When I read for pleasure, I pick the following (check all that apply):**

❑ Novels or chapter books   ❑ History books   ❑ Picture books

❑ Newspapers   ❑ Sports books   ❑ Mystery books

❑ Poetry books   ❑ Fantasy books   ❑ Fiction books

❑ Cartoons or comic books   ❑ Science books   ❑ Biographies

❑ Humorous books   ❑ Scary books   ❑ Nonfiction books

❑ Magazines   ❑ Poetry books   Other:

4.   **I am more likely to read a book for pleasure that**

❑ a teacher suggests   ❑ my friend suggests

❑ a librarian suggests   ❑ has won an award

❑ is by an author whose books I have read   ❑ I just happened to see (hear about) in _____

5.   **Three favorite books that I would take on a month-long trip are**

1. _____
2. _____
3. _____

6.   **In the past week, I read for at least half an hour (30 minutes) on**

❑ No days   ❑ 1–2 days   ❑ 3–5 days   ❑ 6–7 days

7. **In the past month, I have read _____ for pleasure.**

❑ No books   ❑ 1 book   ❑ 2 books   ❑ 3 books   ❑ More than 3 books

8. **My favorite time to read for pleasure is:**

❑ Never   ❑ In the morning before school
❑ During school   ❑ During the midmorning
❑ Lunchtime   ❑ After school
❑ In the evening   ❑ Before falling asleep
❑ Whenever I can   ❑ _____

9. **When I read I like to** ❑ read one book   ❑ read more than one book at a time

10. **I like to receive books as presents.**   ❑ **Yes**   ❑ **No**

11. **I have a <u>public</u> library card.**   ❑ **Yes**   ❑ **No**

12. **I borrow books from the <u>public</u> library:**

❑ Once a week   ❑ Twice a week   ❑ A couple of times a month
❑ Every few months   ❑ A few times a year   ❑ Hardly ever
❑ Never

13. **I borrow books from the <u>school</u> library:**

❑ Once a week   ❑ Twice a week   ❑ A couple of times a month
❑ Every few months   ❑ A few times a year   ❑ Hardly ever
❑ Never

14. **The number of books I have at home is**

❑ None   ❑ 0–9   ❑ 10–19
❑ 20–29   ❑ 30–50   ❑ More than 50

15. **If I could meet any literary character (for example, Hermione from** *Harry Potter* **or the dog from** *Because of Winn-Dixie*)**, I would want to meet**

_____

_____

16.   The last three books that I read are

1. _____

2. _____

3. _____

17.   I would like to read a book about

_____

Renzulli Learning

Students today are turned on, plugged in, and tuned in to technology in ways that amaze most adults. From cell phones to iPods, text messages to blogs, simultaneous use of instant messaging while doing homework and listening to iPod music, and searches on Google, students are embracing technology and propelling technology companies toward record sales. According to Macintosh News Network, iPod sales alone are projected to exceed 8 million devices in 2008. Although most students are tech savvy, are most teachers able and ready to help students apply their technological skills to enhance their learning?

According to the CEO Forum on Education and Technology (2000), more than 95 percent of U.S. schools and 72 percent of classrooms had access to online Internet technology in June 2000. Educators across the country have varying levels of ease with the use of technology in classrooms. Some teachers do not use computers at all. Others use them occasionally and may enable students to access canned programs that provide a series of structured activities. Other teachers use a computer to access e-mail. And in some classrooms, teachers support every student's use of a laptop and encourage use of the World Wide Web and creation of multimedia work products. The use of laptops, PDAs, iPods, MP3 players, digital cameras, scanners, SmartBoards, and digital video cameras are among the most common devices used in classrooms today. This technology, however, is only as powerful as the skill of the users, and many teachers have not had in-depth training on how to use technology to enhance student achievement.

As students become more and more reliant on technology, especially for entertainment, many educators worry that they will become less engaged and bored by traditional instruction in the classroom. In any objective examination of this issue, it is clear that the use of technology will continue to expand in our personal lives, the workplace, the marketplace, and the classroom. Given mounting evidence of the need for students to be technologically literate, teachers need to be ready to adopt available technological tools. The use of technology in the classroom, like any resource, requires good teaching practices.

Where do teachers start? Many teachers have begun by using the World Wide Web as an educational resource to assist students with research. Some teachers find that incorporating the Internet into classroom pedagogy is fraught with a trilogy of recurring problems. First, resources can be unreliable, and many Web sites are blocked by school filters. Also, site content may be inappropriate for students' age level or objectionable for student use. Finally, searching the Web is time-consuming for students and teachers who are attempting to locate quality resources. Renzulli Learning is a new tool that minimizes these problems and offers individualization for student use. This Internet-based system takes the research and work behind the Enrichment Triad Model and the Schoolwide Enrichment Model (Renzulli & Reis, 1997) and moves it into a technology-based platform that is easily used by both students and teachers.

Helping Teachers Provide Enriched, Differentiated Learning for All Their Students

Renzulli Learning has been used by many teachers who have implemented the SEM-R. Renzulli Learning is an interactive online program that matches student interests, expression styles, and learning styles with a vast array of educational activities and resources. Using Renzulli Learning, students can explore, discover, learn, and create, using the most current technology resources, independently and in a safe environment.

Renzulli Learning consists of six major components:

- **The Renzulli Profiler:** an interactive assessment tool that identifies students' talents, strengths, interests, and preferred learning and expression styles, providing a comprehensive student learning profile

- **The Renzulli Enrichment Database:** an information warehouse containing over 35,000 carefully screened, grade-level appropriate, child-safe enrichment opportunities that are regularly monitored, updated, and enhanced and are expanding at a rate of over 500 per month

- **The Renzulli Enrichment Resource Search Engine:** a specialized data search facility that matches individual student profiles to the most appropriate enrichment activities from our database

- **The Renzulli Talent Portfolio:** a complete record of a student's online learning activities and academic progress

- **The Wizard Project Maker:** an online tool that helps students create their own high-interest projects and store them in their own talent portfolio

- **The Renzulli Reports:** a series of management tools for teachers, administrators, and parents, designed to help them follow individual students' learning progression, analyze group usage patterns, formulate lesson plans, and improve classroom organization

Collectively, these components provide both students and teachers with unique educational experiences that are directly suited to each student's unique learning profile while simultaneously providing parents with insights about their child's enrichment needs. Renzulli Learning also helps teachers get to know their students and better meet their diverse needs.

The Renzulli Learning System

The Renzulli Learning System (RLS) is based on the Enrichment Triad Model, which was developed by Joseph Renzulli (1977). It represents more than thirty years of research conducted by Renzulli and by Sally Reis (Renzulli & Reis, 1997) of the University of Connecticut's Neag School of Education and has been cited as the most widely used plan for enrichment and talent development in the world. Their work demonstrates that students achieve at higher levels when they pursue topics and activities of personal interest and that enrichment can be provided to all students through the use of this system. In its original paper-based format, this product had been field-tested and perfected for more than twenty years in approximately 5,000 classrooms.

The RLS helps teachers meet the diverse needs of all of their students through differentiated content and instruction. Differentiation is a process that addresses variations among learners in the classroom through multiple approaches that modify instruction and curriculum to meet the individual needs of students. The Renzulli Learning System helps teachers access a wealth of opportunities in order to provide appropriate differentiation activities for students of all levels of achievement and abilities, and it allows teachers to accomplish this differentiation in minimal time.

Perhaps the most significant aspect of the RLS is its emphasis on a student's strengths. Many other educational programs focus on finding and correcting weaknesses and liabilities. The RLS celebrates and builds on students' strengths, abilities, and interests.

The Profiler

The RLS Profiler is a computerized assessment tool that creates a unique profile for each student. It consists of carefully selected, user-friendly, research-based questions related to a student's particular interests. The system assesses students' **interests:** everything from athletics to zoology—whatever excites and inspires the student. The Profiler groups interests into thirteen major categories: performing arts, writing and journalism, mathematics, history, fine arts, sciences, athletics and sports, photography and video, social action, business, technology, literature and reading, and foreign language.

The Profiler also assesses students' preferred **expression styles,** which could be writing, oral debate, stage performance, sculpture, dance, or a host of other expressive techniques. The student shares how she most enjoys interacting with the world. The Profiler considers ten specific expression styles: written, oral, hands-on, artistic, audio-visual or display, dramatic, service, technological, musical, and commercial.

Preferred **learning styles**—the ways in which students like to learn new information—are also assessed in Renzulli Learning. Preferred learning styles range from individualized study to large-group engagements, paper-based review to digital technology. The Profiler focuses on nine learning styles: lecture, programmed instruction, discussion, peer tutoring, group work, learning games, technology, simulations, and independent study. Students' **abilities** are also measured using Renzulli Learning; students complete a self-evaluation of their performance in mathematics, reading, science, and social studies.

Students answer the Profiler questions in thirty to fifty minutes, and the Profiler produces an accurate, printable assessment of each student's interests, abilities, and learning preferences. Even better, the Renzulli Profiler reflects the world of learning from the students' perspective, not necessarily that of their parents or teachers. This makes it possible to provide enrichment based on the Enrichment Triad Model with optimal effectiveness and efficiency. By representing the student's view, the Profiler assessment becomes a major productivity tool for teachers, placing them months ahead in their efforts to understand how each child learns best and their ability to respond to and incorporate those preferred learning styles as part of an effective learning plan.

The Enrichment Database

The RLS Enrichment Database provides teachers with a vast storehouse of over 35,000 differentiated enrichment materials and resources for students with varying ability levels, interests, learning styles, and preferred styles of expression. Teachers using the RLS have easy access to a large supply of enrichment activities and resources that makes it possible to truly individualize and differentiate for students with varying needs.

The content of the RLS Enrichment Database is organized into fourteen separate categories that represent a wide range of educational activities. The categories are virtual field trips, real field trips, creativity training activities, training in critical thinking, independent study options, contests and competitions, Web sites based on personalized interests, high-interest fiction books, high-interest nonfiction books, how-to books for conducting research and creative projects, summer program options in special talent areas, online activities and classes, research skills, videos and DVDs.

All entries in the RLS Enrichment Database are carefully researched by Renzulli Learning educational specialists, screened for grade-level applicability, and coded into one or before of the fourteen enrichment categories. Items in each activity category are selected automatically by the Renzulli Enrichment Resource Search Engine to match students' grade level, ability level, interests, learning styles, and product styles, providing each student with a unique personalized selection of enrichment opportunities.

The Enrichment Resource Search Engine

The RLS Enrichment Resource Search Engine includes three specialized database search options, each geared to a specific application. The search automatically links each student's profile (interests, learning styles, and expression styles) with the RLS Enrichment Database to generate a customized list of activities designed to appeal to that student's grade level, interests, and abilities, as well as his or her learning and expression styles. A secondary self-directed search enables students and teachers to enter one or more self-selected keywords in order to locate specific database entries for interests, learning styles, and expression styles within their individual activity list. This feature is particularly useful for selecting a particular topic for project work or for in-depth study.

A global search capability enables students and teachers to access the entire RLS Enrichment Database, across all interests, expression styles, learning styles, or even grade levels. This permits students with capabilities above grade level to locate and pursue new activities and threads of interest, all within the safety of a prescreened information environment. It also helps teachers research possible projects and other curriculum enhancements within the same space their students explore. The combined search facilities of the RLS offer students an extensive, expanding menu of learning opportunities and offer teachers a new and valuable resource for classroom preparation.

The Talent Portfolio

The RLS Talent Portfolio includes of a series of open-ended student responses related to their thought processes, learning projects, and products. The Talent Portfolio includes

- "My Talent Portfolio"—an online portfolio where students can create and post writings, Internet links, images, and other work on projects or areas of interest

- Student responses to a series of unique and specially crafted open-ended questions focusing on thought-provoking areas of inquiry

- Student optional responses to the self-assessment questionnaires in the fourteen enrichment categories

- Student selections of "My Favorite" resources and their ratings of enrichment database entries

These services help personalize a student's learning experience and provide all students with outstanding opportunities to express their views, needs, experiences, and aspirations.

Management Tools for Teachers, Administrators, and Parents

The RLS features a collection of administrative reports designed to help make the process of enriching each student's learning process more efficient. These tools enable teachers, parents, and other mentors to learn more about students and to make grouping and enrichment easier. Reports include printable listings of

- Interests of individual students
- Interests of a group of students (summary)
- Expression styles of individual students
- Expression styles of a group of students (summary)
- Learning styles of individual students
- Learning styles of a group of students (summary)
- Grouping combinations of students' interests, learning, and product styles
- Individual student profiles

Also available are reports and documents associated with

- Registration information, along with the ability to edit student records (at the teacher level) and teacher records (at the manager level)
- Learning maps for enrichment differentiation activities
- Downloadable enrichment projects
- Downloadable creativity training activities
- Background articles by leading educational practitioners
- Lesson plans for using the RLS effectively
- Outstanding Web sites for teachers

The Renzulli Learning System is a stimulating tool for students, teachers, and parents. This unique Web-based program matches students' interests, learning styles, expression styles, abilities, and grade level with thousands of opportunities designed to provide enriching, challenging learning. This process can help improve students' test scores and fuel students' commitment to their educational pursuits.

For teachers, using the state-of-the-art technology provided by the RLS can help to raise classroom productivity and dramatically improve efforts to differentiate class activities during Phase Three of the SEM-R. The RLS can give teachers the virtual equivalent of multiple teaching assistants in their classroom every day. With Renzulli Learning, teachers can find articles on offering differentiated, enriching learning opportunities for students, and they can also access exciting Web sites in order to help their own teaching and download creative activities to use in their classroom. They can chart their students' progress by accessing their profiles and viewing all of the activities and assessments that they have completed. Teachers using this system can even submit their own ideas for activities and interact with other teachers, enrichment specialists, curriculum coordinators, and administrators from around the country. Finally, parents have their own Web site on which to view their child's progress and his or her profile. Renzulli Learning provides articles selected for parents, as well as helpful links to Web sites that are updated on a regular basis. In our work with the SEM-R, Renzulli Learning has been a perfect resource for Phase Three activities. In our research, we watched with amazement as reluctant readers who previously had had difficulty focusing when reading a book spent hours reading independently on the Internet when using Renzulli Learning on a regular basis.

References

CEO Forum on Education and Technology. (2000, June). The power of digital learning. In *The CEO Forum school technology and readiness report* (pp. 6–13). Washington, DC: Author.

Renzulli, J. S. (1977). *The Enrichment Triad Model: A plan for developing defensible programs for the gifted and talented.* Mansfield Center, CT: Creative Learning Press.

Renzulli, J. S., & Reis, S. M. (1997). *The Schoolwide Enrichment Model: A how-to guide for educational excellence* (2nd ed.). Mansfield Center, CT: Creative Learning Press.

Creativity Training Activities

General Strategies for Creativity Training

These materials from *New Directions in Creativity* (Renzulli & Callahan, 2000) have been designed to encourage creative development. They require minimal preparation time and teach techniques that facilitate creative thinking across disciplines and build a classroom atmosphere that supports creativity.

Brainstorming and the Fluency Principle

Fluency can be defined as the ability to produce several ideas or possible solutions to a problem situation and is an important condition for creative production. The greater the number of answers generated, the higher the probability of producing an original response (original in the sense that fewer students come up with similar responses). For example, if we asked a group of students to list all the utensils that people might use for eating, their initial responses would no doubt include common utensils such as forks, spoons, and knives. But if we encouraged the students to lengthen their list by using their imagination ("Suppose you didn't have any forks or spoons. What *could* you use?"), students would begin to explore some possible alternatives. They might suggest such items as sharpened sticks, shells, or bottle caps. If we then compared the lists of several youngsters, we would find that most of the initial answers were quite similar. As the lists grew longer, we would find more divergence, and the probability of a youngster producing an original response would increase. In other words, quantity breeds quality, and research has shown that individuals who produce a large number of ideas are more likely to produce ideas that are more original.

General strategies for creativity training, Lesson 1, and Activities 1–10 are all from Renzulli, J. S., & Callahan, C. M. (2000). *New directions in creativity: Mark 3.* Mansfield Center, CT: Creative Learning Press. The questions to guide brainstorming sessions are adapted from Arnold, J. E. (1962). Useful creativity techniques. In S. J. Parnes & H. F. Harding (Eds.), *Source book for creative thinking* (pp. 251–268). New York: Charles Scribner's Sons.

Brainstorming is a basic technique for increasing fluency of expression. Brainstorming can be carried out individually or in group sessions. The first step is to provide students with a problem that has many possible solutions. During the early stages of a brainstorming activity, students should write or verbalize *all* thoughts and ideas that come to mind, no matter how silly or wild the ideas may be. The best way to promote freewheeling and offbeat thinking is to value quantity and withhold criticism and evaluation until students have exhausted their total supply of ideas related to a given problem. Brainstorming, acknowledged as conceived by Alex Osborn, also came up with a series of questions that Bob Eberle later combined into SCAMPER to help both adults and children to generate ideas (Osborn, 1953).

Questions to Guide Brainstorming Sessions

These are only some of the questions that teachers and students can use to stimulate creative thinking during brainstorming activities:

Other Uses
- Can it be put to other uses as is?
- Can it be put to other uses if it is modified?

Adaptation
- What else is like it?
- What other ideas does it suggest?
- What could you copy?
- Whom could you imitate?

Modification
- What new twist can you make?
- Can you change the color, size, shape, motion, sound, form, odor?

Magnification
- What could you add?
- Can you add more time, strength, height, length, thickness, value?
- Can you duplicate or exaggerate it?

Minification
- Can you make it smaller, shorter, lighter, lower?
- Can you divide it up or omit certain parts?

Substitution
- Who else can do it?
- What can be used instead?
- Can you use other ingredients or materials?

- Can you use another source of power, another place, another process?
- Can you use another tone of voice?

Rearrangement
- Can you interchange parts?
- Can you use a different plan, pattern, or sequence?
- Can you change the schedule or rearrange cause and effect?

Reversibility
- Can you turn it backward or upside down?
- Can you reverse roles or do the opposite?

Combination
- Can you combine parts or ideas?
- Can you blend things together?

Strategies for Successful Creativity Explorations

- The success of any creativity training program depends on the amount of freedom and flexibility that exists in the classroom.
- When students are engaged in creativity training activities, you should encourage them to play with ideas, laugh, and have fun without worrying about being graded or evaluated.
- The most effective way to open up the classroom atmosphere is to minimize formal evaluation and lead students in the direction of self-evaluation.
- Show generous praise for quantity and inventiveness of responses, and students will quickly recognize the types of behavior that you value and will strive to achieve these types of behaviors.
- Try to avoid using phrases or expressions that are natural killers of creativity. Examples of such phrases include
  - Don't be silly.
  - Let's be serious.
  - That's ridiculous.
  - Quiet down.
  - The principal won't like it.
  - Let's be practical.
  - You should know better.
  - That's not our problem.

- We've tried that before.

- That's not part of the assignment.

- That's childish.

- A good idea, but . . .

- It won't work.

- Don't be so sloppy.

- An underlying purpose of these sample activities from *New Directions in Creativity* (Renzulli & Callahan, 2000) is to help youngsters learn how to evaluate their own creative products.

- Encourage students to reflect on their creative thinking processes by asking questions such as

  - What do *you* think about it?

  - Do you feel good about it?

  - Would you like to work on it some more?

  - Why do you like (or dislike) it?

  - What things (criteria) are important to you?

- Creativity time should be a fun time, and playfulness, impulsiveness, humor, and spontaneity are all part of having fun.

References

Arnold, J. E. (1962). Useful creativity techniques. In S. J. Parnes & H. F. Harding (Eds.), *Source book for creative thinking* (pp. 251–268). New York: Charles Scribner's Sons.

Osborn, A. F. (1953). *Applied imagination: Principles and procedures of creative thinking.* New York: Scribner.

Renzulli, J. S., & Callahan, C. M. (2000). *New directions in creativity: Mark 3.* Mansfield Center, CT: Creative Learning Press.

Further Reading

Cray-Andrews, M., & Baum, S. (1996). *Creativity 1, 2, 3* (2nd ed.). Unionville, NY: Royal Fireworks Press.

Davis, G. A. (1999). *Creativity is forever* (4th ed.). Dubuque, IA: Kendall/Hunt.

Von Oech, R. (1990). *A whack on the side of the head* (rev. ed.). New York: Time Warner Books.

Introductory Lessons in Creative Thinking

Following are three introductory lessons in creative thinking. Lesson 1 is suitable for students in all grades. Lessons 2 and 3 are aimed at sixth graders.

The three introductory lessons are followed by ten more creativity activities. These activities include teaching suggestions and templates for student activity sheets for students in elementary or even middle school.

Lesson 1: Encouraging Creative Thinking (All Grades)

As a precursor to this lesson, you may want to consider sharing with your class a read-aloud that focuses on a creative idea, a creative character, or a difficult situation requiring an unusual solution, like *Archibald Frisby* by Michael Chesworth or *It Looks Like Spilt Milk* by Charles Shaw.

To prepare students for using the creativity activities on their own, the basic strategy for this lesson consists of freeing the classroom atmosphere from the usual constraints often associated with convergent production. It is important for students to learn to appreciate questions and activities for which there are no right answers. You can introduce this concept by contrasting a convergent type of question with a divergent one. Before distributing the first activity sheet, you may say something like the following:

> Today we are going to begin practicing a new kind of thinking. This kind of thinking will help us learn how to explore many different kinds of solutions to a given problem. Some problems and questions have only one right answer, but there are also many problems and questions that have hundreds of possible answers.
>
> Suppose I asked you, "In what year did Columbus discover America?" [Wait for an answer, and write it on the board.]
>
> Are there any other possible answers to this question? [General conclusion should be negative.]
>
> Now suppose I were to ask you, "What are all of the possible ways that you might have come to school this morning?" [Call on youngsters, and list responses on the board. Students will probably give some fairly common responses such as walk, bus, car, bicycle.]

At this point, you might say,

> Remember, I said all of the **possible ways** that you might have come. Use your imagination. Let your mind wander, even if you think the method for coming to school is silly. How about by donkey or pogo stick? [Add these to the list on the board.]

This point is crucial to introducing the creativity training program. By suggesting the donkey and the pogo stick, you have accomplished three very important objectives:

1. You have conveyed the idea that answers need not be feasible, practical, or realistic.

2. You have let youngsters know that you will accept these kinds of answers.

3. You have let the youngsters know that you are capable of some way-out ideas.

You can emphasize this last point by grabbing a yardstick (conveniently placed nearby beforehand) and pretending it is a pogostick while you take a few hops. Students will no doubt become a little noisy, but it is very important to tolerate this reaction. If you hush them, the whole atmosphere of freedom will be lost, and they will feel that this new kind of thinking is the same old game—the teacher asks questions and students must answer only in the way the teacher believes to be right.

After your examples, students may give a wide variety of answers. Let them call out their answers (rather than having to raise their hand) as you quickly write them on the board. If necessary, prompt your students:

> Any other animals that you might come to school on? How about an airplane or a rocket? Or being dropped from a plane with a parachute?

A second crucial factor at this point is the generous use of praise on your part. Enthusiastic comments such as "good!" "great!" and "fantastic!" will help youngsters open up. Do not call on students who are not taking part. It takes some youngsters longer than others to trust the teacher and their classmates in this type of situation. The main idea is to let students know that you like what is going on and that you are having fun. When the flow of responses begins to slow down, say,

> Let's go one step further. Suppose you could change your size or shape. Can you think of some other ways that you might possibly come to school?

If no one responds, you might ask:

> Could you make yourself very tiny and come in your brother's lunch box? Or could you change to a drop of water and come in through the drinking fountain?

Continue to fill the board as long as the youngsters are generating responses. When you finally call a halt, say,

> I guess there really are many questions and problems that have several possible answers. Do you think this kind of thinking is fun?
>
> From time to time, we are going to be working on some activities like the one we just did. The main purpose of these activities will be to practice answering questions and solving problems that have many possible answers. We will be using our imaginations to come up with some clever new ideas.

At this point, distribute the first activity sheet, "Way-Out Words," (Activity 7, provided later in this resource) and read the directions with the students. If you have any doubts about youngsters' understanding of the directions, ask whether there are any questions. Then ask the students to complete the first exercise.

After they have finished, allow some students to discuss their responses. Ask, "How many had that idea?" and after a few students have shared their entire list, ask whether anyone has any responses that have not yet been mentioned. Praise unusual responses from individuals, and praise the entire group for catching on.

Lesson 2: The Overused Word Game (Grade 6)

1. Begin by reviewing previous discussions about thinking creatively. Help students to recall the basic concepts of brainstorming:

   - Think of many ideas.

   - Think of unusual ideas.

   - Don't be afraid to add to someone else's ideas.

   - Accept all answers.

2. Ask students to name some common or overused words. Then ask students what they would expect to happen if they applied the rules of brainstorming to their choice of vocabulary words.

3. Organize your class into teams of three or four members. Each team will need something on which to brainstorm (for example, scrap paper, chart paper, a small chalkboard, or marker boards).

4. Explain the rules of the Overused Word Game:

   - Everyone will be given a common and overused word. The word will also be given as an example in a sentence.

   - Each team will then generate a list of synonyms, using the brainstorming techniques that they have been practicing.

   - Each team must then circle the four most unusual synonyms on their list.

   - All teams will have five minutes to work with each word.

   - Each team will receive a score based on these criteria:

     - For each synonym: $+4$ points

     - For each synonym that no other team used: $+4$ points

     - For a word that is not a synonym of the overused word: -4 points

5. Examples:

   - It was a **bad** day.

     Synonyms: abominable, atrocious, awful, dreadful, heinous, horrific, miserable

   - She was **happy**.

     Synonyms: content, delighted, elated, ecstatic, joyful, overjoyed, thrilled

Lesson 3: Weighty Words (Grade 6)

1. Begin by writing the following definition from *Merriam-Webster's Collegiate Dictionary* on the board: "A **pun** is 'the humorous use of a word, or words that are formed or sound alike but have different meanings, in such a way as

to play on two or more of the possible applications; a play on words.'" Ask students to explain what a pun is in their own words. (You may wish to have a few examples readily available, like "reading between the *lions*.")

2. Explain that the stories in *The Weighty Word Book* use puns and word play to help people remember the definitions of difficult words. Then read one of the tales from *The Weighty Word Book* by Paul Levitt, Douglas Gurger, and Elissa Guralnick.

3. Ask students to define the word featured in the story. Discuss how the authors used a pun to help people remember the definition of the word.

4. Distribute writing paper. Students may wish to work alone or in a group to write their own weighty word story. Be sure to remind students that brainstorming and word webbing may be a useful way to develop an original tale.

5. Encourage students to share their tale with the rest of the class. As you discuss and compare student responses, the following discussion questions may be useful.

   • Which story do you find unusual? Why?

   • Which story do you find creative? Why?

   • How did you develop such an unusual idea?

   • What clues in the story helped you to determine the meaning of the word?

Reference

Levitt, P., Gurger, D., & Guralnick, E. (1985). *The weighty word book.* Longmont, CO: Bookmakers Guild, Inc.

Activities for Exploring Creativity

The goal of creativity training activities is for children to become more fluent, flexible, and original thinkers. Too often in these test-prep environments in which children attend school, teachers believe they must focus on lessons designed to help students do better on state assessments. Too little time is spent on creative learning activities. The activities in this section are designed to have children play with ideas and increase their ability to come up with new and unusual ideas.

Activity 1: If I Wrote the Book (Transforming Figures)
Objectives

- To develop the ability to alter characteristics of known objects
- To increase nonverbal originality and flexibility

Teaching Suggestions

1. Introduce this activity by reading the poem "The Purple Cow" by Gelett Burgess aloud.

   The Purple Cow[1]

   I never saw a purple cow,
   I never hope to see one;
   But I can tell you anyhow,
   I'd rather see than be one!

2. The poem will probably provoke giggles from the students; ham it up, if you wish. The children will be more likely to be creative on this exercise if they are feeling a bit silly. Explain how the authors of children's books often take ordinary animals and make them unusual or funny in some way in order to make the animal character more outstanding and memorable. Good examples of such characters that children may be familiar with include Walt Disney's Dumbo (an elephant that can fly) and any of Dr. Seuss's strange animals.

3. Draw a very simple dog on the chalkboard, and have your class suggest alterations that would make it funny, different-looking, or able to do a special thing. Give it strange colors or patterns, funny features, or strange clothes.

4. Distribute the activity sheets. Tell the students to imagine that they are writers of stories about animals that are very different. Tell them to change the animals on the sheets to make them unusual. Point out that their animals

---

1. "The Purple Cow" is from *The Burgess Nonsense Book* by Gelett Burgess. Copyright © 1901, renewed 1929 by Gelett Burgess. Reprinted by permission of J. B. Lippincott Company.

should be able to do different things, and ask them to label the animals and then talk about them. Suggest that they may wish to give their animals names that are relevant to their special characteristics.

5. Allow students to show their work to the class, and encourage them to talk about their ideas for funny animals. Be sure to praise their drawings, pointing out particularly unusual or clever ideas. Exposure to the ideas of others may provoke additional responses. It is important, therefore, to give students an opportunity to add new responses after discussing the pictures. Display the activity sheets on the bulletin board or in the hallways, if your students do not object. This type of exercise is one that other students in the school will enjoy sharing.

Follow-up Activities

*   Encourage your students to think up their own animals to alter in an original way. Or have them play a musical art game in which each student draws an animal while music plays. Stop the music at intervals and ask them to pass their papers to the person behind or beside them. That person then adds on to his or her neighbor's drawing as the music plays once again. When the music stops, the students pass their papers on as before. The animals resulting from this joint effort are sure to be unusual.

*   The class might also enjoy working on one large, mural-sized picture of an animal. Or two teams might compete in drawing two huge animals. Students could also construct three-dimensional animals out of found materials, fabric scraps, or papier-mâché.

*   Have the class discuss the problems such an animal might experience (such as the social ostracism Dumbo encountered because of his ability to fly). Considering the special abilities of such animals will lead students to a better understanding of their attitudes toward others who are different.

Name _____ Date _____

1a. If I Wrote the Book

How can you change these animals?

Name _____   Date _____

1b. If I Wrote the Book

How can you change these animals?

Activity 2: Rhyme Time (Creating Rhymes)
Objectives
- To develop the ability to create simple rhymes
- To develop verbal flexibility

Teaching Suggestions

1. Introduce this lesson after exposing the class to poetry. Read selections that you feel are appropriate for the age group. If the poems relate to units of work that you are doing in the classroom, so much the better. Poetry that deals with the season at hand, that relates to special events that the children have celebrated, or that is just for fun would be especially suitable. Common nursery rhymes work well. Because of the nature of the activity sheets, choose only rhyming poetry. Point out the words that rhyme in each poem, and list them on the board. Emphasize that rhyming words have the same ending sounds.

2. Distribute the activity sheets. On the first activity sheet, ask students to think of all the words they know that rhyme with the last word in the first line. They should write the words or draw pictures of them in the blank spaces. On the second activity sheet, have the class finish the first and second lines using words that rhyme. Point out that the poems will change meaning if the children change the rhyming words. It may be necessary to read the couplets to the class as they work. After they have finished the work, have them share some of their responses and display the activity sheets.

3. If individual students have difficulty thinking of rhyming words, have the class as a whole work together on the activities. List on the board (with students' help) all the words that rhyme for each couplet in the first activity. Then have students choose words from this list to complete their couplets. If this procedure is followed, be sure to emphasize that there is no one correct answer and that you will accept any new word that rhymes with the last word in the first line.

4. Some students may want to create new, original rhyming words. If so, read some Dr. Seuss poems in which he makes up his own words, or read the following poem, "Eletelephony," by Laura E. Richards.

Eletelephony[2]

Once there was an elephant,

Who tried to use the telephant—

---

2. "Eletelephony" is from *Tirra Lirra: Rhymes Old and New* by Laura E. Richards (Little Brown and Company, 1955). Reprinted by permission of John Richards and of Little Brown and Company.

No! No! I mean an elephone

Who tried to use the telephone—

(Dear me! I am not certain quite

That even now I've got it right.)

Howe'er it was, he got his trunk

Entangled in the telephunk;

The more he tried to get it free,

The louder buzzed the telephee—

(I fear I'd better drop the song

Of elephop and telephong!)

Follow-up Activities

- You might follow work on these activity sheets with a unit on poetry writing. If you feel that the class is ready, introduce other forms of poetry. Read a short story to the class, and ask students to summarize it in simple poetic form. In some classes, this activity works best when the entire class participates (with the teacher writing suggestions on the chalkboard) in order to produce a final poem on a large piece of chart paper.

- Invite students, as individuals or as a class, to add verses to poems you read.

Resource

Tucker, S. (1997). *Word weavings*. Glenview, IL: Good Year Books.

Name _____   Date _____

2a. Rhyme Time

Can you finish these rhymes?

The rain was falling down.

It covered all of my _____ .

This morning it was cold.

I put on a hat that was _____ .

You gave me a baseball bat.

Now hand me my new _____ .

I opened the door and ran.

After I saw the _____ .

Name _____   Date _____

2b. Rhyme Time

While I was looking down
I saw a funny down _____.

Please fill the _____.
With something that is _____.

Here is a big _____.
I'll take it into the _____.

While heading for the _____.
I found a red _____.

Activity 3: The Doodler (Elaborating)
Objectives

- To increase elaboration skills
- To increase the ability to integrate parts into a whole

Teaching Suggestions

1. Following is an example of a droodle. (A droodle is a doodle that is also a riddle.)

   Place the droodle on the chalkboard and ask, "What could this be?" List the responses. Say that all the responses are good and that the droodle could be any of them; however, *your* idea was that it was the neck of a very tall giraffe.

2. Now draw several droodles on the board and say that each droodle represents only part of a picture. Ask individual students to come to the board and draw additions on the droodles that will change them. Have the children label their droodles. Then talk to the class about *doodles,* which are aimless drawings. Put four doodles on the chalkboard and present them in a manner similar to your presentation of the droodles.

3. Distribute the activity sheets. Call attention to activity "a," and tell your students to make the doodle a part of a picture. Encourage them to elaborate on their drawing, suggesting that they put in as many details as possible. Have them give their picture a name. Some students may wish to discuss their picture with the class, explaining what the doodle made them think of and how they incorporated the doodle into the final picture.

4. Activity "b" presents several doodles. Direct students to make each of the doodles a part of a separate picture. Again, encourage elaboration and have students give their pictures titles. Have students volunteer to have their activity sheet displayed. You may wish to design a bulletin board with a large central doodle and then arrange student worksheets around that figure.

Follow-up Activities

- Have students close their eyes and start doodling. Have them doodle to music, and encourage them to have a good time with the bizarre results. Hold a doodling contest, and select the strangest doodles as the winners.

- Have the class play a doodling game in which each person draws for five minutes (or less), until the sound of a bell (or a clap of your hands). All doodlers must immediately pass their drawings on to the person behind or on one side of them, and that person must then continue drawing on the same sheet, elaborating on the picture. For interesting results, have the class pass the drawings four or five times. Be sure to display the doodles.

- Make string paintings. Give each child a piece of manila or white paper and a twelve-inch string. Place metal pie plates containing mixed powder paints or poster paints on a table at the front of the room. Ask the children to come forward one at a time and dip their string into the color they prefer. Tell them to place the wet string on one half of the paper in an interesting pattern and then fold the other half of the paper over the string pattern. Tell them to press down and then open the paper and throw away the string. Point out that this process makes two identical doodles. Have the children complete the pictures with crayons after returning to their seat.

- Glue loose string, yarn, or elbow macaroni to a sheet of paper, arranging them to form part of a picture. Ask students to complete the picture.

Name _____   Date _____

3a. The Doodler

Make this doodle part of a picture.

Give your picture a title.

Name _____   Date _____

3b. The Doodler

Make this doodle part of a picture.

Give each picture a title.

Activity 4: Spin a Story (Developing Fluency)
Objectives
- To develop verbal fluency
- To develop the ability to produce an original story based on given information.

Teaching Suggestions

1. With the help of the class, recall the stories of *Red Riding Hood, Snow White,* and *Hansel and Gretel.* Ask the children what might have happened if Red Riding Hood had set out for her grandmother's house, met a wicked witch, and was rescued by a handsome prince. Point out that you are combining aspects of three different stories to create a new story. Discuss your new story.

2. In front of the room, place three boxes: one labeled *People;* one, *Places;* and one, *Actions.* Have each class member write the name of a person from a story on a sheet of paper and place it in the box labeled *People.* Do the same for *Places* and *Actions.* Now mix up the papers in each box. Choose one student to select a paper from the *People* box, then from the *Places* box, and then from the *Actions* box. Make up a class story on the chalkboard from the three selected items. Save the boxes for a follow-up activity.

3. Before passing out the activity sheets, show the class the spinner they will use in this activity. (Directions for constructing a spinner are given after the follow-up activities.) Be sure the children understand its function and operation. Then distribute the activity sheets. Ask each class member to write three different items under each of the three category titles on the sheet for activity 4a. Emphasize that each person's sheet will be different. Once the students have completed activity 4a, have one person come forward and spin the spinner. Call out the number on which the pointer stops. Ask each class member to circle the item following that number in the *Animals* column. Select another person to spin for the *Actions* column and another for *Places.* Next, tell the class members to put the three circled items together and elaborate on them to form a story.

4. Present activity 4b in a similar manner, sharing the resulting stories.

Follow-up Activities
Use the three boxes of labeled items that served as an introduction to this activity to create new stories. Each class member could select three items, place them together, and create a story, or you might leave the three boxes in the room and suggest that students make selections and then write stories in their free time. You could have students file the stories in a central place and share them at a later date.

Change the topics on the boxes periodically to make new story generators. Suggest that students illustrate their stories and place them in the library corner. If it's feasible, have students dramatize their stories as plays or puppet shows.

Directions for Making a Spinner

Cut out two figures like those illustrated in this section, and paste them on cardboard. The circle should be about six inches in diameter and the arrow should be about five inches long. Trim the cardboard to the shape of the figures and place the arrow on the number wheel. Pass a thumbtack through the bottom of the number wheel and through the arrow so that it passes through the dot in the center of the wheel and the dot in the arrow. A paper fastener can serve the same purpose as the tack.

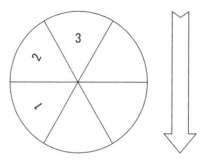

Name _____   Date _____

4a. Spin a Story

Write the names of three animals, three actions, and three places. Be sure to put them in the correct box. With the help of a spinner, choose one idea from each box and write a story.

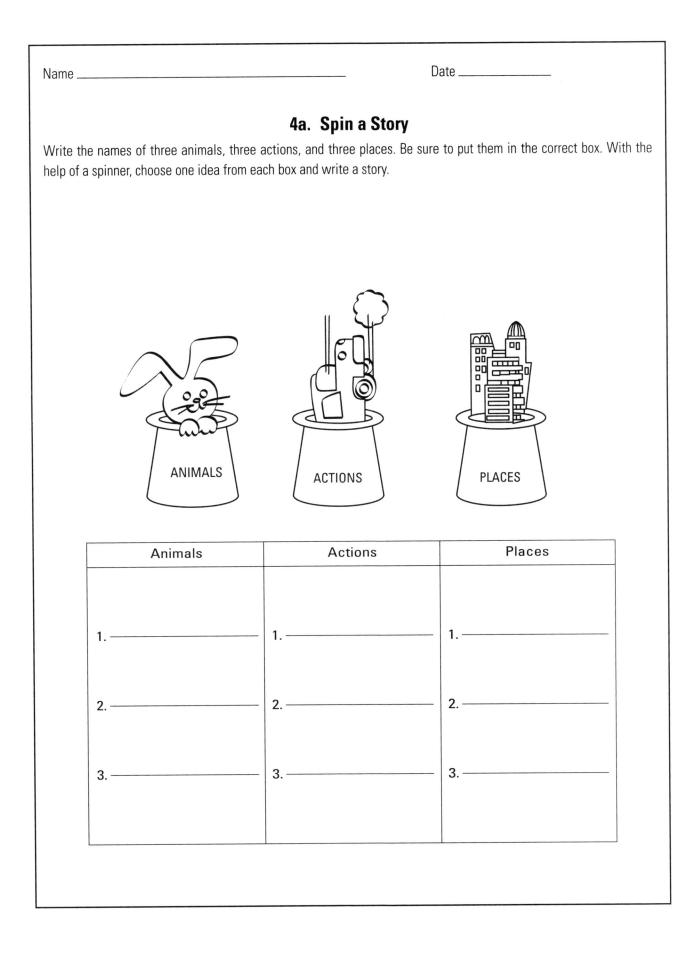

Animals	Actions	Places
1. _____	1. _____	1. _____
2. _____	2. _____	2. _____
3. _____	3. _____	3. _____

Name _____ Date _____

4b. Spin a Story

Write the names of three jobs, three machines, and three actions. Be sure to put them in the correct box. With the help of a spinner, choose one idea from each box and write a story.

JOBS   MACHINES   ACTIONS

Jobs	Machines	Actions
1. _____	1. _____	1. _____
2. _____	2. _____	2. _____
3. _____	3. _____	3. _____

Activity 5: Consequences (Speculating and Imagining)

Objectives

- To develop ideational fluency and originality
- To develop the ability to speculate and to imagine

Teaching Suggestions

A goal of education should be to encourage children to think more creatively. Too few teachers take the time in school to develop creative thinking skills and encourage children to use their creativity and imagination.

Since most of the situations in th is activity are improbable, it allows students to exercise a playful imagination. You can encourage this playfulness by adding your own unusual suggestions to the discussion. Humor is a very important part of creativity, and students will make an extra effort to be clever and humorous if they feel that their teacher values these traits. Humor also has its own built-in feedback mechanism. If students' ideas result in spontaneous laughter or comments, they will be getting an immediate peer evaluation of their work.

Follow-up Activities

- Encourage students to devise their own improbable situations, and allow them to ask their classmates to think of possible consequences. Newspapers and magazines occasionally print articles and pictures that record unusual happenings. You might post some on the bulletin board and suggest that students write a possible consequence beneath a picture or article whenever they have a good idea.

- Pose hypothetical questions based on history. Allow students to speculate on what would have happened if the South had won the Civil War or if the Louisiana Purchase had never taken place.

Name _____   Date _____

5a. Consequences

Sometimes it is fun to let your mind wander and imagine all the things that would happen if an unusual situation were to occur. For each of the following situations, list as many possible consequences as you can.

What would happen if there were no such thing as darkness or night? Two examples are given.

_____
_____
_____
_____
_____
_____
_____
_____

Cars would not need headlights. People who stayed up late would not be called "night owls."

_____
_____
_____
_____
_____
_____
_____
_____

_____

What would happen if automobiles were completely banned tomorrow because of pollution?

_____

_____

_____

_____

_____

_____

_____

Name _____   Date _____

5b. Consequences

For each of the following situations, list as many possible consequences as you can.

What would happen if everyone in the world suddenly became twelve inches tall?

_____
_____
_____
_____
_____
_____
_____
_____
_____
_____
_____
_____

_____

What would happen if there were no such thing as a mirror?

_____
_____
_____
_____
_____
_____
_____
_____
_____
_____
_____
_____

Activity 6: Cartoon Captions (Writing Humor)

Objectives

- To develop the ability to produce varied implications based on given figural material

- To show relationships between figural and semantic material

Teaching Suggestions

1. A good way to introduce this activity is to show students a cartoon that conveys a humorous situation without a caption. Then show them a captioned cartoon with the caption removed or covered and ask whether the cartoon brings out the humor in the situation. Ask the class what words might be written below the cartoon to make it humorous. Try to elicit several responses from students, and allow them to decide which caption they like the best. It is important to emphasize that there are many possible captions. After several students have had an opportunity to suggest captions, you might reveal the caption that was written by the cartoonist.

2. After students have completed each activity sheet, ask them to read their captions aloud or display their activity sheets on the bulletin board. Exposure to each other's responses may provoke additional ideas, so give students a chance to add new responses.

3. This activity provides an opportunity to help students appreciate peer evaluation. The class will exhibit varying amounts of laughter in relation to the degree of humor that a caption brings out. Students may choose to submit their best cartoons to the school newspaper for possible publication.

Follow-up Activities

- Ask students to cut out and bring to class cartoons that they think would be good for this activity. They can mount the cartoons on poster paper and display them on a bulletin board with space for students to add their own captions.

- Introduce youngsters to political cartoons and the special types of messages that they attempt to convey. Be sure to point out the symbolic nature of political cartoon characters (Uncle Sam, donkey, elephant, and so on). Famous political cartoons such as those by Thomas Nast allow students to see the way that editorial opinions of historical events can be communicated. Invite students to draw political or editorial cartoons about past or current events.

- One game-like activity might involve matching cartoons with appropriate captions. Break the class into workable groups, giving half of each group some cartoons and the other half the corresponding captions. Have students try to find the right caption for each cartoon.

- An exciting variation of the "Cartoon Captions" activity is to ask youngsters to draw their own cartoons and exchange them with their classmates so that the classmate can add the caption. Or you might give students a caption and ask them to produce a sketch that brings out the humor implicit in the caption. As a final exercise, you can synthesize figural and semantic activity by asking children to draw cartoons and then write captions for their own cartoons.

Name _____   Date _____

6a. Cartoon Captions

For each cartoon on this page, write two captions to help make the cartoon humorous.

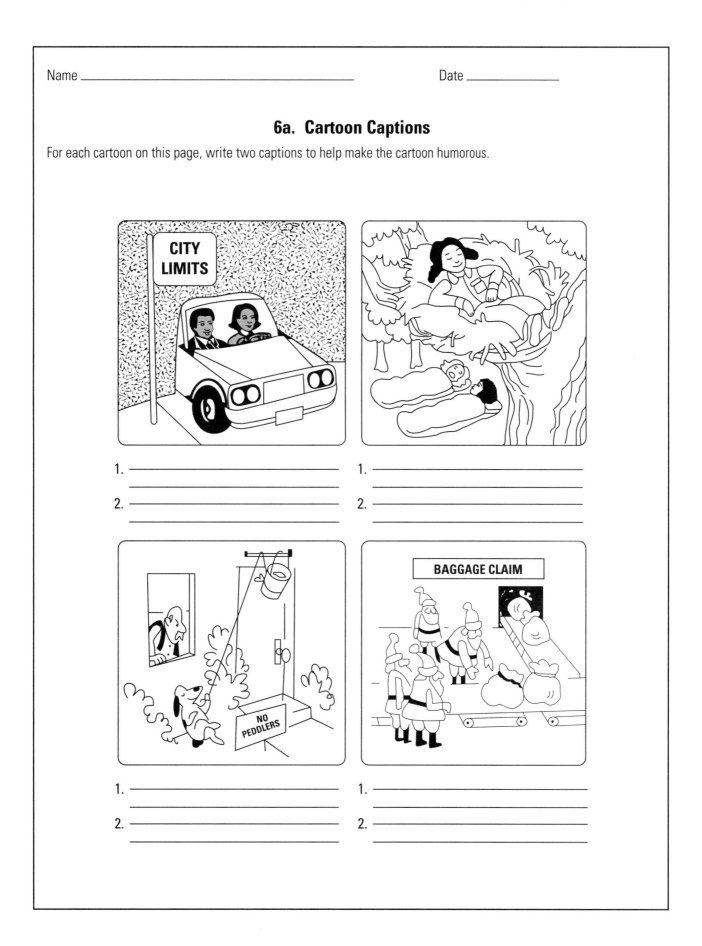

1. _____   1. _____
   _____   _____
2. _____   2. _____
   _____   _____

1. _____   1. _____
   _____   _____
2. _____   2. _____
   _____   _____

Name _____   Date _____

6b. Cartoon Captions

For each cartoon on this page, write two captions to help make the cartoon humorous.

1. _____

2. _____

1. _____

2. _____

1. _____

2. _____

1. _____

2. _____

Activity 7: Way-Out Words (Linking Words and Symbols)

Objective

To develop the ability to produce a symbolic relationship between the meanings of words and the way they are written.

Teaching Suggestions

1. Write the word *look* on the chalkboard and ask, "How can I make the word *look* look like *look*?" If students do not get the idea, fill in the two o's so that they look like eyes and draw eyebrows above them. Before distributing the activity sheets, ask students whether they can think of any other words that look like their meanings and invite them to write the words on the board. When students are working on these exercises, allow them to use colored pencils or crayons at their desk.

2. After students have completed their activity sheets, ask them to reproduce their responses on the board. As you review the responses with the class, ask, "Did anyone write this word differently from the way it is written on the board?" Allow all major variations of each word to be reproduced on the chalkboard, and let the class decide which variation they like best. You may want to reserve a section of the bulletin board for students to display their original versions of "way-out words."

Follow-up Activities

- Ask students to compile lists of words that they could use for additional "Way-Out Words" activities.

- Students who show an interest in this type of activity may want to refer to "Wacky Wordles," a section in *Classic Brainteasers* by Martin Gardner (Salt Lake City: Sterling, 1995). It shows how well-known sayings can be expressed in a symbolic fashion. Students may want make their own "Wacky Wordles."

Name _____   Date _____

7a. Way-Out Words

Words can sometimes be written in ways that make them look like their meanings. See if you can write each of the following words so that it will look like its meaning. Examples of how the first words might be written are shown below.

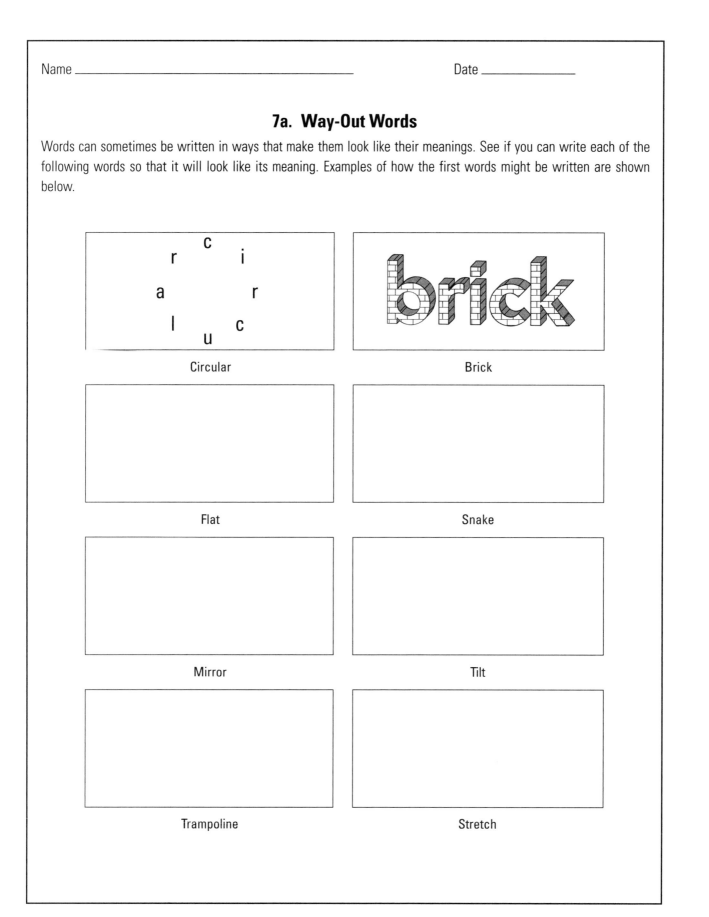

Circular

Brick

Flat

Snake

Mirror

Tilt

Trampoline

Stretch

Name _____   Date _____

7b. Way-Out Words

See if you can write each of the following words so that it will look like its meaning.

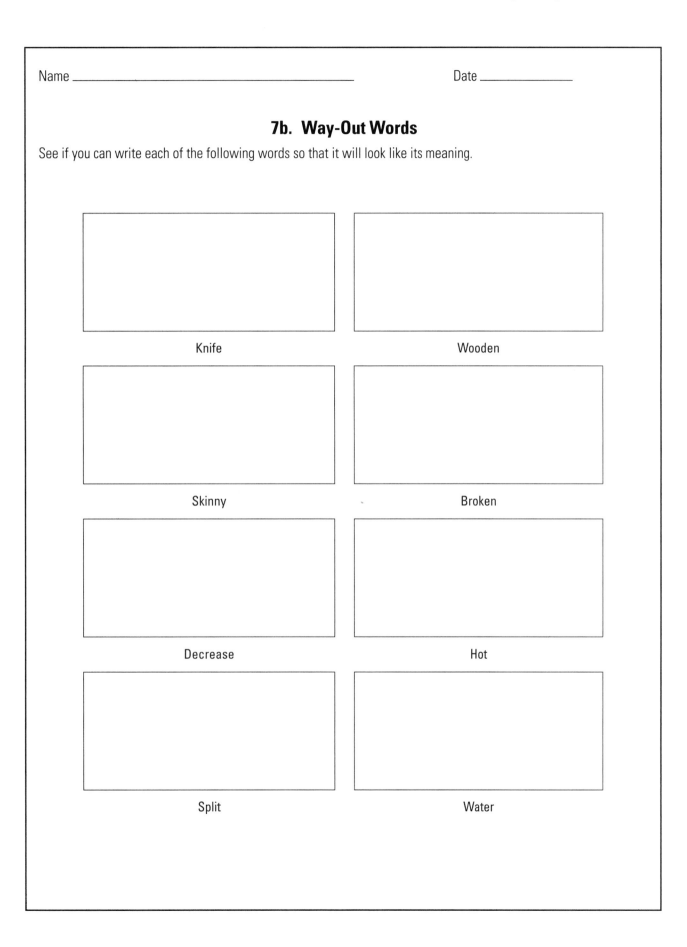

Knife	Wooden
Skinny	Broken
Decrease	Hot
Split	Water

Activity 8: Make-a-Sentence (Creating Ideas from Words)
Objectives
- To develop expressional fluency and flexibility

- To develop the ability to organize words into meaningful, complex ideas

Teaching Suggestions
Words for the "Make-a-Sentence" activities have been purposefully selected because of their limited logical relationship to each other. This limited relationship is essential to achieving the creativity objectives listed. Because students sometimes have difficulty starting this activity, encourage them to persevere by being very receptive to their early responses. These early responses may be somewhat awkward and often humorous, but students will quickly realize that by using clauses and compound sentences, they can construct meaningful thoughts. After students have caught on to the activity, you can increase the level of difficulty by asking them to construct sentences with a minimal number of words. This slight modification, perhaps carried out under mildly competitive conditions, will require a reorientation of their thinking.

Follow-up Activities
- Many variations can be introduced into the "Make-a-Sentence" activity: the number of specified words can be increased; the number of connecting words (that is, nonspecified words) can be limited; and the specified words can be "loaded" with various parts of speech, words from spelling lists, or words from social studies units. When selecting words, choose ones that do not logically go together. Students will write very ordinary sentences if you select words such as *little, lost, dog,* and *boy.*

- Students can develop dictionary and vocabulary skills by working in teams to prepare sets of words for a "Make-a-Sentence" competition. They will undoubtedly seek out unusual words, thus inspiring their classmates to look up words in the dictionary.

- You can also use this activity to develop vocabulary and syntax skills in a foreign language if students have already begun study in this area.

Name _____   Date _____

8a. Make-a-Sentence

See how many sentences you can write, using the four words listed below in each sentence. Do the same for the second set of words. You may change the nouns by making them plural and the verbs by changing their tense. You may also change some words by adding suffixes such as **-er, -est,** or **-ness.** Use the back of this page if you need more space.

tiger   leaves   wet   number

_____
_____
_____
_____
_____
_____
_____

A number of tigers dashed through the wet leaves.
"The wet tiger is sleeping in Cage Number 5," said the man who was raking leaves.

_____

puppet   tissue   how   stop

_____
_____
_____
_____
_____
_____
_____
_____
_____

Name _____   Date _____

8b. Make-a-Sentence

See how many sentences you can write, using the four words listed below in each sentence. Do the same for the second set of words. You may change the nouns by making them plural and the verbs by changing their tense. You may also change some words by adding suffixes.

instrument   smoke   explain   busybody

_____
_____
_____
_____
_____
_____
_____
_____
_____

sell   teenagers   bread   statue

_____
_____
_____
_____
_____
_____
_____
_____
_____
_____
_____

Activity 9: Changing Things (Brainstorming)
Objectives

- To develop ideational fluency

- To give practice in brainstorming

Teaching Suggestions

1. To introduce this activity, call attention to items that are functional and designed to appeal to the eye (for example, automobiles, toasters, furniture). To help students understand the difference between works of art and products that have been beautified for aesthetic rather than functional reasons, ask students whether a modernistic design of a clock makes it any more useful.

2. After students have completed the exercises, invite students to read aloud some of their lists and suggested changes. Give special praise to unusual items and to ideas that are unique in the group. Ask students to draw on their own experience in explaining why they would like to have certain things made more attractive or durable.

Follow-up Activities

You can develop similar activities around other possible modifications. For example, things can be made softer, quieter, safer, or less expensive. Ask students to set the specifications and try them out on their classmates. You can also ask students to suggest functional or aesthetic changes in other common objects, such as telephones, bicycles, playgrounds, highways, and/or eating utensils.

Name _____ Date _____

9a. Changing Things

Many things that serve a useful purpose in our daily lives are more appealing because they have been made more attractive or beautiful. For example, dishes have been beautifully designed and decorated so that they are attractive as well as useful. In the spaces below, list all the things you can think of that might be made more beautiful or attractive. Try to think of things that no one else has thought of. A few examples are given to help you get started. Use the back of this page if you need more space.

pencils _____   _____   _____

garbage cans _____   _____   _____

_____

Select one of the things from your list and tell how you would go about making it more beautiful or attractive. Use the back of this page if you need more space. On a separate piece of paper, make a sketch of the thing you designed.

_____
_____
_____
_____
_____
_____
_____
_____
_____
_____
_____
_____
_____
_____
_____

Name _____   Date _____

9b. Changing Things

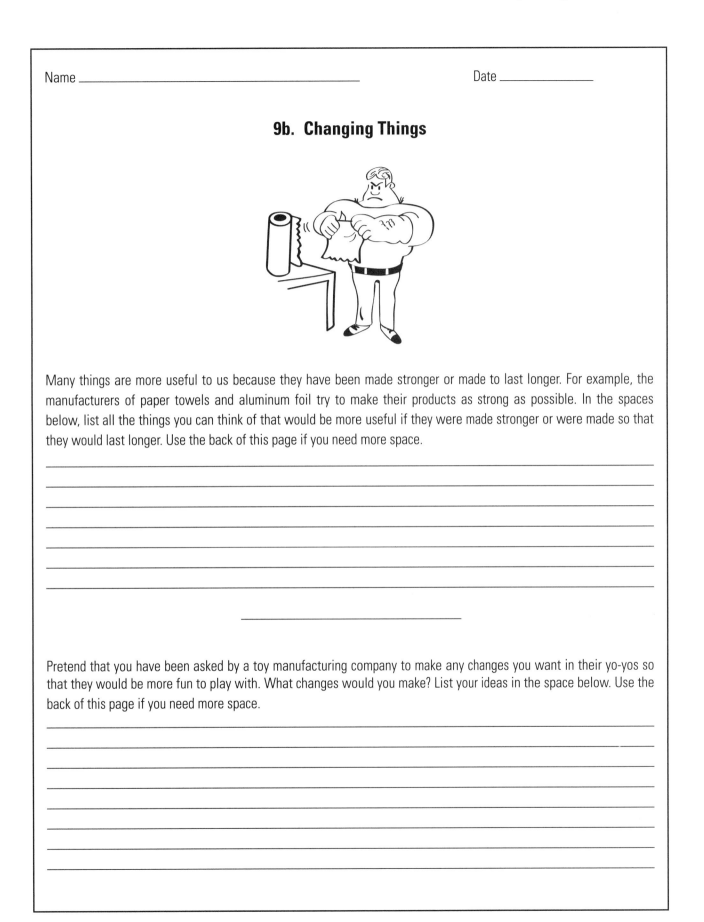

Many things are more useful to us because they have been made stronger or made to last longer. For example, the manufacturers of paper towels and aluminum foil try to make their products as strong as possible. In the spaces below, list all the things you can think of that would be more useful if they were made stronger or were made so that they would last longer. Use the back of this page if you need more space.

_____
_____
_____
_____
_____
_____
_____

_____

Pretend that you have been asked by a toy manufacturing company to make any changes you want in their yo-yos so that they would be more fun to play with. What changes would you make? List your ideas in the space below. Use the back of this page if you need more space.

_____
_____
_____
_____
_____
_____
_____
_____

Activity 10: Can You Design It? (Planning)
Objectives

- To develop nonverbal elaboration and originality

- To produce an organized plan arranged in unique ways that anticipate consequences

- To write a description that translates figural information into verbal information

Teaching Suggestions

1. Before students begin this activity, ask them to brainstorm a list of things that they want to include in their plan. If they have had some experience in scale drawing, you might suggest that they devise a scale for their drawing and use a ruler to convert objects to a given scale.

2. After students have completed each exercise, have them develop a comprehensive list on the board of all the things that are included in the drawings. Use a tally mark to record each time an object is repeated. Call attention to objects that are relatively unique in the group.

3. Display students' plans on the bulletin board, and compare them with pictures and plans that might be available from magazines or actual blueprints. (Maps of parks and recreation areas are sometimes made available so that users can easily locate equipment and facilities. Ask youngsters who might visit parks or recreation areas to look for such maps and descriptive literature.)

Follow-up Activities

- You can relate language arts activities to this activity by asking students to write descriptions and specifications for their classroom and recreation area plans. Technical writing is a highly valuable skill that youngsters seldom get a chance to develop. Encourage students to be imaginative by reminding them that descriptive writing should create a mental image that accurately represents the object being described and, at the same time, makes the object sound attractive. You can use this follow-up activity with students who are especially interested in writing or with students who like to draw but are somewhat reluctant to write. For the latter group, emphasize the drawing but use the figural work as a basis for getting them to do some writing about their drawings.

- Other design activities can be based on a variety of objects. Entire schools, rocket ships, houses, traffic systems, and various types of stores, banks, and zoos are some of the things that youngsters can design. For those who express a high degree of interest in this area, you might want to obtain some blueprints or books on design and drafting and arrange for them to talk with an architect or draftsman.

Resources

Miller, L. (1998). *KidTech.* New York: Dale Seymour.

Slafer, A., & Cahill, K. (1995.) *Why design?* Chicago: Chicago Review Press.

Name _____   Date _____

10a. Can You Design It?

Have you ever wished that you could change the design of your schoolroom? Imagine that you are an architect and that you have been asked to develop a creative design for a classroom. The room can be any size or shape you want, but it must be able to accommodate about twenty-five students. How would you design your classroom? What furniture, equipment, and other things would you include? Draw your floor plan in the space below.

Name _____   Date _____

10b. Can You Design It?

Pretend that you have been asked by your city to design a playground or recreational park. The park should have recreational facilities for both children and adults. What types of playing fields and equipment would you have in your park? Draw a ground plan for your recreational park in the space below. Try to include facilities for as many types of activities as possible.

Reading on the Internet

Books and literature are readily available on the Internet as well as from classroom or school libraries. Electronic literature can be particularly attractive to students who are interested in a topic but have already exhausted classroom and library resources. Kids may also be attracted to the novelty offered by Web sites with illustrations and sound files, and they can gain computer skills while navigating the Web.

Because so much information is available, we have included only a small, introductory portion of what the Internet offers. For more information on a topic, start surfing!

Authors' and Publishers' Sites

The Internet has become a great source of information about numerous children's writers and illustrators. Typing in an author's name may result in a vast array of personal Web sites and Web sites maintained by publishers, fans, scholars, and readers. Fortunately, many of these sites are designed to promote enjoyable reading experiences and encourage growth in reading. Some of our favorite authors who have amazing Web sites are listed here.

- **David Adler**

  http://www.davidaadler.com/

- **Judy Blume**

  http://www.judyblume.com

- **Beverly Cleary**

  http://www.beverlycleary.com

- **Sharon Creech**

  http://www.sharoncreech.com

- **Roald Dahl**

  http://www.roalddahl.com/

- **Lois Lowry**

  http://www.loislowry.com/

- **Walter Dean Myers**

  http://www.walterdeanmyers.net/

- **Katherine Patterson**

  http://www.terabithia.com/

- **Gary Paulsen**

  http://www.randomhouse.com/features/garypaulsen/

- **Patricia Polacco**

  http://www.patriciapolacco.com

- **J. K. Rowling**

  http://www.jkrowling.com

- **Jon Scieszka**

  http://www.jsworldwide.com/

- **Lane Smith**

  http://www.lanesmithbooks.com/

- **Jerry Spinelli**

  http://www.jerryspinelli.com

- **Chris Van Allsburgh**

  http://www.chrisvanallsburg.com

- **Jane Yolen**

  http://www.janeyolen.com/

Publishers of children's literature often have fabulous Web sites designed to hook kids on reading and, of course, promote their publications in the process. So be sure to check out your favorite publisher when searching for new electronic reading sources.

- **HarperCollins**

  http://www.harpercollinschildrens.com

- **Scholastic Kids**

  http://www.scholastic.com/kids/kids.asp

- **Random House Kids**

  http://www.randomhouse.com/kids/

Online Books

In addition to Web pages of authors of children's and young adult books, the Web also provides literature. Thousands of opportunities to read online are available. Many of the collections contain rare or out-of-print books that might be difficult to locate otherwise.

To preserve their treasures and to make them more accessible to the public, many universities are developing extensive online collections. You may want to check out the following:

- **University of Calgary**

  http://www.ucalgary.ca/~dkbrown/storclas.html

  One of the best collections of children's classics online can be found at the University of Calgary site.

- **University of Virginia**

  http://etext.lib.virginia.edu/eng-on.html

  Here, hundreds of titles dating from 1500 A.D. to the present are available for both children and adults. Some, however, are restricted to University of Virginia users due to licensure agreements.

- **The Online Books Page**

  http://onlinebooks.library.upenn.edu/

  This site offers a comprehensive guide to literature online, sponsored by the University of Pennsylvania.

- **The International Children's Digital Library (ICDL)**

  http://www.icdlbooks.org/

  The ICDL is a five-year project funded by the National Science Foundation and the Institute for Museum and Library Services in order to create a digital library of international children's books. This wonderful new site is user-friendly and includes search engines, color pictures, and books in dozens of languages. Don't miss this one!

- **The Rosetta Project**

  http://www.childrensbooksonline.org/

  http://books.google.com/

  http://etext.library.adelaide.edu.au/

  The Rosetta Project's collections currently contain thousands of antique children's books that were published in the nineteenth and early twentieth century. However, because the Rosetta Project is still collecting books from around the world, it is expected that its online library will eventually grow to millions of html pages.

Take a Test Drive! Exciting Web Sites for Students to Try

Are you searching for new destinations on the Internet? Do you want your students to explore something fresh? In this section, you will find resources that will enable students to safely explore the Internet and test drive interesting Web sites that focus on literacy and learning.

Originally, the following "Test Drive Instruction Cards" were featured as part of an Interest Development Center during Phase Three time, which helped students consider how to be thoughtful consumers of information found on the Internet. Other aspects of the interest center included the following:

- Student evaluation forms that facilitated a critical review of a Web site and its contents

- Opportunities to develop questions and enter them into various kid-friendly search engines to find and compare answers

- Student recommendations to classmates of interesting Web sites

The White House for Kids

http://www.whitehouse.gov

Take a tour of 1600 Pennsylvania Avenue without ever leaving your classroom. At this site you can learn more about the families and pets who have called the White House home over the years. This is also a great place to visit if you want to learn more about U.S. history and how the government works.

How many Secretaries are serving in the President's Cabinet? Which position would you want to hold? Why?

Kid Pub

http://www.kidpub.org

Check out this cool Web site filled with stories and poems written for kids, by kids. The links include "Newest Stories," which offers a lengthy list of choices, "Book Reviews," which let you see what other kids recommend, and "The Stacks," which houses older stories.

Notice that you can contact the Web site's publishers with an e-mail address. Why do you think that is?

Starchild Project

http://starchild.gsfc.nasa.gov/docs/StarChild/StarChild.html

Blast off with NASA and explore the solar system, the universe, and cool space stuff. If you are stuck on a vocabulary term, there are links to glossary definitions with tons of interesting pictures. Each segment also has interactive activities to reinforce what you have learned.

What languages can you identify at this Web site?

Imagine the Universe

http://imagine.gsfc.nasa.gov/docs/homepage.html

If you are interested in science, check out this Web site filled with the latest discoveries from the crew at NASA. Investigate the "Ask an Astrophysicist" and "Featured Scientists" sections to tempt your curiosity. You can also explore Special Exhibits with video images. There is also a site-based search engine for astronomy information.

What do you think is the most interesting question answered by a scientist at this site?

Comics.com

http://comics.com

If you are drawn to the funny papers, this is the site for you! It includes a comic of the day, as well as links to Peanuts, Big Nate, and Marmaduke. You can also check out a variety of comic categories like sports, cats, or dogs.

Which comic character most resembles you?

History Channel

http://www.historychannel.com

Want to find out something about the past? This site is a great place to begin. One of the most interesting features is "This Day in History," which tells you what happened on a particular day of the year throughout history. Covered are events of the day in crime, automotive history, sports, the American Civil War, technology, and literature.

What great events occurred on the day that you were born?

How Stuff Works

http://www.howstuffworks.com

Have you ever wondered how quicksand really works or what makes the inside of a refrigerator cold? This Web site has the answers. You can look for answers to your specific questions or simply browse the colorful articles and video clips to learn something new.

What are the top ten questions asked at this Web site?

National Geographic for Kids

http://www.nationalgeographic.com/kids

National Geographic has a special spot just for kids. Even though the information is changing all the time, some of the favorite features stay the same. Check out the wild animal facts by clicking on *Creature Features*. Show off your sense of humor at the Cartoon link found in the activities section of the Web site.

Can you find the link to read some of the featured articles from *National Geographic Kids Magazine*? Which ones did you find most interesting?

Mystery Net: Kids Mysteries

http://mysterynet.com/kids

Looking for a clue about what to read? This site features mysteries for you to solve, mystery stories by kids, magic tricks, and even a link to a Nancy Drew mystery. You can also write your own mystery! If the judges at this Web site select your story, it will be published on the site and you may win a prize.

According to the publisher, all of the stories are changed regularly. Why would that be important to know?

Stone Soup

http://www.stonesoup.com

There are no recipes here, but you can taste a number of great stories written for kids, by kids. This site is the online version of the popular *Stone Soup Magazine.* Check out the illustrations.

Can you figure out how to listen to young authors read their tales for you? What is the currently featured story?

Between the Lions

http://pbskids.org/lions/index.html

Explore the Web page for the popular TV show, "Between the Lions." You can click on the *Stories* link to take you to a list filled with tales to read by yourself or with a friend. You can also download stories to take with you and test out the video clips with cool songs and pictures.

When you have finished reading the story, try some of the fun games to test how well you read *between the lions.*

The Mint

http://www.themint.org

Do you have the feeling that you never have enough money? Or do you want to know how to make your money grow? This Web site has been developed to help you gain a better understanding of economics and personal finance.

Can you find instructions for how to write a check? What is the memo line for?

Zoom!

http://pbskids.org/zoom/

Ready to zoom into action? If you click on the *Zoom* icon at this site, you will reach the Web page for the television series *Zoom.* The focus here is on volunteering. You can take a poll, learn more about the cast members, express your ideas, and be yourself. At *Zoom into Action!*, you can find project ideas, submit your own stories, and investigate great ways to volunteer.

Can you find stories that others have shared about their own volunteer efforts? What project might you want to try?

How Are Hollywood Films Made?

http://www.learner.org/exhibits/cinema/

Have you ever wanted to make your own movie? At this site, you can go through the steps of making a film, from screenwriting to directing, producing, acting, and, finally, editing. Hands-on activities include writing part of a comedy script and managing a budget as the producer.

Can you find a page on film jargon to help you learn the lingo? What new term did you learn?

Page by Page—Creating a Children's Book

http://www.nlc-bnc.ca/pagebypage/

Explore the development of the children's book *Zoom Upstream* from the creative process to the printing process and beyond. Sections discuss the idea, the writing, finding the illustrator, the pictures, printing, and selling the book.

What did you do to crack the code in the printing section?

Grimms' Fairy Tales

http://www.nationalgeographic.com/grimm/

Step into the world of the Brothers Grimm, but beware of the dangers that lurk in the woods! The tales the brothers collected in Germany were often frightening and cruel. This National Geographic feature brings you fourteen tales based on a 1914 translation. Click on the treasure box to find information about the Grimm brothers, a map, an activity for kids, as well as the list of stories.

Did any of the stories surprise you? What was so unexpected?

Harry Potter

http://www.scholastic.com/harrypotter/

Are you a Harry Potter fan? Then cruise to this site to use your knowledge of the Harry Potter books to try the activities listed. Or visit the discussion board to find out what other Harry Potter fans are discussing. Find out more about author J.K. Rowling by reading interview and chat transcripts. What is a Veela and in which book was it featured?

Redwall

http://www.redwall.org

Enter the gates of Brian Jacques's Redwall series. There are twenty books so far, full of mice, moles, badgers, and others with the good characteristics of humans, who face the evil side of humans in the forms of rats, weasels, and foxes. Find crossword puzzles for each book, a gallery of characters, and information about illustrators of the Redwall books. You'll also find transcripts of interviews, a biography, and answers to questions that readers have asked Brian Jacques.

At what age did Brian complete school and what did he do after school? Would you like to do that? Why or Why not?

A. Pintura: Art Detective

http://www.eduweb.com/pintura/

The clues are everywhere! At this Web site, you will learn about famous artists, composition, style, and perspective as you play A. Pintura, a 1940s detective who helps Miss Featherduster identify a mystery painting. As you collect clues, you can use the vocabulary list and study sheet to help you solve the mystery. Did you correctly solve the mystery before the end of the story? What clues were helpful to you in solving the mystery? If you did not solve the mystery correctly, what clues did you miss and why?

Ranger Rick's Go Wild!

http://www.nwf.org/kids/

Take a walk on the wild side at this site, which is sponsored by the National Wildlife Federation. If you love animals, nature, or weird facts about the world around you, then this is the spot for you.

Can you find the latest reading suggestions in the book nook? Which book would you choose to read? Why?

The Pencil Page

http://www.pencils.com/

Have you ever wondered how pencils are made? And just how do they get those little erasers on each one? Click through the Great Eraser Caper to see how. This site offers little known facts about pencils, such as why they are traditionally yellow. Additional resources are provided for those who wish to sharpen their pencil knowledge.

At the pencil factory, what is a Groover machine used for?

Leonardo's Workshop

http://www.alifetimeofcolor.com/play/leonardo/

Join Carmine Chameleon for an ArtEdventure into the mystery of a missing painting. You'll find information about the Renaissance and Leonardo da Vinci as you track down the stolen painting. Investigate clues in Leonardo's room that lead you to information about his inventions, paintings, and interesting tools he used, such as a perspectograph. The toolbar at the bottom of each page takes you out of the Leonardo section, but the art activities and ideas you'll find are well worth investigating.

What is Leonardo da Vinci's most famous and beloved work? In what year did he paint it?

Kids Planet: Defenders of Wildlife

http://www.kidsplanet.org/

Are you ready to make the world a better place for animals? Then check out this Web site. You'll discover fact sheets on many endangered and threatened animals. Check out the games and activities, too. List the status of endangered wolves in at least five countries. What do you think can be done to keep this animal from becoming extinct?

Molecular Expressions

http://micro.magnet.fsu.edu/

A whole new world is waiting for you, right before your eyes! The Molecular Expressions Web site goes where no microscope has gone before, by offering one of the Web's largest collections of color photographs taken through an optical microscope (commonly referred to as *photomicrographs*). Visit the Photo Gallery for an introductory selection of images covering just about everything from French fries and ice cream to circuits and superconductors.

What would you examine if you had the chance? Why?

The World of Beverly Cleary

http://www.beverlycleary.com/index.html

Explore the colorful world of Beverly Cleary. Not only is there a section in which you can find out all about the author, but there are also links to a neighborhood map of places in Beverly Cleary's books, descriptions of all of your favorite characters from Ramona the Pest to Ralph and the Motorcycle, and some fun and games, too. If you like the Web site, you should check out her books!

Where can you go to read a chapter from one of Beverly Cleary's books? Which book would you choose to read? Why?

Baby-sitting Safety Tips

http://www.ci.phoenix.az.us/POLICE/babysi1.html

You got a job baby-sitting!! It's a very big and important job, but there is so much to remember. Learn how you can be a safe baby-sitter by taking a tour of the Phoenix, Arizona, Police Department's page of baby-sitting safety tips. You'll get loads of common-sense tips that will make your baby-sitting job easier and more fun.

If you are worried about remembering all of the details, locate the checklist and print it out. Name at least five dos and five don'ts that would make you a successful baby-sitter.

SEM-Xplorations: Enrichment Projects

Our SEM-Explorations (SEM-X) were created to help students explore their interests and passions with varying levels of support. Students who have an interest in completing and are able to work without the need for constant direction may be interested in trying one of our small-group, independent study SEM-X projects. These can also be adapted or students can even create their own independent project, using the same structure and outline. Using these options, any student can start an interest-based learning project that will engage him in independent work and more advanced readings.

The SEM-X projects are designed to help students think in an organized way about the process of conducting a multi-step project. When doing a project, we suggest that students and their teacher decide together on a start date, an intended completion date, and dates for meeting to discuss the project. These dates can be changed as needed if the project is extended or the student needs more or less time, but we have found that students need a plan and also need help to identify the steps necessary to complete a project, which is what we have given them in the projects in this section of our resource guide. Each project will involve the use of resources related to the project and may also involve steps such as going to the library, using the Internet, and using creative thinking skills such as brainstorming.

Materials, books, and Web sites necessary for the project will have to be discussed with you, the teacher, as will the student's ultimate choice of an end product, which might be a story, an art project, a performance, or any other culminating creation. Students should be specific when they begin to plan their work and should generate new ideas about their intended end product as they gather more information.

In our work on the Enrichment Triad Model (Renzulli, 1977) and the Schoolwide Enrichment Model (Renzulli & Reis, 1997) and the SEM-R, we have found that an audience is an essential part of any project. Sharing their work with others helps students learn how to escalate the process of independent or small-group work but also how to brainstorm different venues for their work. Hundreds of contests, competitions, and literary magazines enable students to submit and display their work. Teachers should encourage students to seek out these types of opportunities as well as consider sharing within their school and home communities.

After they have completed their project, students should complete some type of product self-assessment to help them analyze how to change or improve their work and what they have learned about themselves by completing their project. The assessment can be a rubric that you design, or it can consist of questions like those in the following list:

Student Self-Assessment of SEM-X Projects

1. What did you enjoy about working on your project?
2. What did you learn as you were completing your project?
3. Were you satisfied with the final product? In what ways?
4. What could you have done to improve your final project?
5. How were you helped with your project? What resources helped you the most?
6. Do you think you might like to do another project in the future? Do you have any ideas about the content area of your next project?

SEM-X projects work like any other type of independent study, but they have more scaffolding to guide students step by step through the project process. Thus, while SEM-X projects allow students autonomy in performing the various steps of a project, they also offer plenty of structure for students unused to managing their own project or for younger students who may require more substantial support.

To familiarize you with SEM-X projects, we have included ten examples of our exciting projects in this book. We suggest that you review some of the SEM-X projects in this book. With these exciting interest-based SEM-X projects, independent learning is only a click away!

References

Renzulli, J. S. (1977). *The Enrichment Triad Model: A plan for developing defensible programs for the gifted and talented.* Mansfield Center, CT: Creative Learning Press.

Renzulli, J. S., & Reis, S. M. (1997). *The Schoolwide Enrichment Model: A how-to guide for educational excellence* (2nd ed.). Mansfield Center, CT: Creative Learning Press.

Build a Bridge

Build a Bridge

Have you ever thought of having a career as an engineer? No, not a train engineer, but a civil engineer! What's a civil engineer? A **civil engineer** is someone who identifies needs in society and finds creative solutions. Before you begin this project, spend some time learning about the specific jobs of civil engineers—for example, designing roller coasters, creating plans for traffic control, or managing water and sewage. Civil engineers also design tunnels, dams, and railroads. The following Web site provides information about civil engineering jobs and engineering design.

- Those Amazing Engineers

  http://www.asce.org/files/pdf/thoseamazing.pdf

  What sort of work done by engineers interests you? This site describes many different types of jobs for civil engineers. How are Slinky toys and engineers connected? Read to find out!

Charting Your Course

Another job of civil engineers is to design—you guessed it—bridges! The following Web sites provide information specifically about engineering bridges.

- How Bridges Work

  http://science.howstuffworks.com/bridge.htm

  Read about beam, arch, and suspension bridges, to learn where tension and compression affect each structure. This will help you when you are choosing the design of your bridge.

- Types of Bridges

  http://perth.uwlax.edu/globalengineer/draft/project/Types%20of.html

  This site is a great place to see real-life examples of the different bridge styles. You can review your knowledge of beam, arch, and suspension bridges while learning about girder, cable-stayed, and truss bridges.

  In addition to these excellent Web sites, there are several exciting books that you must see! Go to your local library and check them out today.

- *Bridges* by Nicole Baxter (Franklin Watts, 2000)
  ISBN: 0531154467
  Excellent photographs and drawings show a variety of bridges from all over the world.

- *Bridges* by Etta Kaner (Kids Can Press, 1995)
  ISBN: 1550741462
  Want to learn how to build some bridges right now? This book includes instructions for building models of beam, arch, suspension, and movable bridges.

- *Art of Construction: Projects and Principles for Beginning Engineers and Architects* by Mario G. G. Salvadori, Christopher Ragus, & Saralinda Hooker (3rd edition, Chicago Review Press, 1990)
  ISBN: 1556520808

This book explains how tents, houses, stadiums, and bridges are built and how to build models of these structures, using stuff you may have around the house.

- *Is There an Engineer Inside of You? A Comprehensive Guide to Career Decisions in Engineering* by Celeste Baine (2nd edition, Professional Publications, 2004) ISBN: 1591260205
  Would you like to become an engineer when you grow up? This book tells you how! Here you will find information about the different types of engineering, education for engineers, and more.

Now you have read about and observed some of the important responsibilities of being an engineer. Let's review what you've learned. There are four main types of bridges, and each bridge is used for a particular reason, as described in the following list:

- Beam/girder bridge: This type of bridge is simple and inexpensive. Made of concrete or steel, one strong beam is supported by two piers at each end, and compression occurs at the piers. This bridge usually spans less than 250 feet.
- Arch bridge: This type of bridge typically spans 200–1000 feet. Made of steel or concrete, every part of the bridge is under compression.
- Cable-stayed bridge: Only recently erected in America, this futuristic-looking type of bridge typically spans 500–2,800 feet. Cables are connected to one or two concrete towers; compression is carried by the towers.
- Suspension bridge: This type of bridge typically spans 2,000–7,000 feet and is suspended by large cables that lie on top of towers. The cables stretch from one side of the bridge to the other, and compression is carried by these cables.

Sometimes one type of bridge is combined with another type to suit the specific needs of the environment. Although this is a very challenging design task, it has resulted in creative and well-functioning bridge solutions to some of the problems that engineers have faced.

Engineers have designed a structure called a **truss** that enables bridges to span a great distance and carry more weight. Trusses are used most often in beam bridges. There are three types of truss bridges.

- Pratt: Thinner beams, more economical
- Howe: Uneconomical style, rarely used
- Warren: Most common type due to its simplicity

Exploration

Virtual Bridge Design: Learning to Design

You can now consider completing the first challenge of this project, which is creating your own virtual truss beam bridge. First, practice making several designs until you learn the necessary steps involved in the process. The following link is an excellent place for you to discover your best design.

(Continued)

- West Point Bridge Design

  http://bridgecontest.usma.edu/

  This contest is open to students ages thirteen through eighteen. You can experiment with creating truss bridges by using bridges from previous contests to practice decision making in bridge building. Don't forget to test your bridges for strength, to see if you pass the test!

  Have your teacher or a parent help you download the site and get you started. At the beginning of the program, follow the "Site Design Wizard" carefully, to teach yourself what to do. The program will allow you to create bridges by selecting your choice of metal and the strength of metal you want to use. You may also choose to create a one-span or two-span bridge and experiment with different styles of truss bridges (Pratt, Howe, and Warren). Keeping track of the cost of the bridge is important if you wish to win the competition, but since you are just beginning your exploration, take careful note of how much each piece of steel costs. Experiment with the different bridge structures and materials. Then test your examples to see if a truck can pass over your completed model. Once you have finished, keep practicing! You might consider making ten sample bridges to see which is most successful. This experience will help you to learn how to construct a model bridge by hand at the end of this project. Good luck.

Reviewing What You Know

Were you able to successfully construct a truss bridge? What steps did you learn? Which bridge design did you like best? At the end of this project, write a list of the important concepts that you have learned about bridge building. Keep your records so that you can review them at the end of the project.

One of the most important things to notice about bridges is that they are supported by triangles. Why do you think large structures like bridges, buildings, and airplanes rely on the strength of triangles? There is a relationship between the number of triangles used to support the bridge and the strength of the bridge. Take a few minutes to experiment with the program on the following Web site to see whether you can discover the relationship.

- Truss Bridges

  http://www.brantacan.co.uk/trussthree.htm

  This Web page provides the mathematical knowledge that goes into building a successful truss bridge.

Bridges remain intact despite the different stresses they endure. These stresses, or tensions, include gravity, vehicle weight, and forces of nature. Bridges must be designed to last for many years with minimum upkeep. These requirements are one reason why a great deal of planning and effort goes into the design and building of a bridge. For example, the famous Chesapeake Bay Bridge Tunnel (http://www.cbbt.com/) in Virginia, which spans seventeen miles of water, rests on four man-made islands, each of which was built especially for the bridge. It has the strength to support tractor trailers with 200,000-pound loads (equal to the weight of twenty-three elephants)! The Bay Bridge Tunnel is also designed to withstand high winds of up to 110 miles per hour, rain, and other extreme weather conditions. Try your hand at the mini-quizzes in the following Web sites, to test your bridge knowledge.

- Bridge Building
  http://www.bradford.ac.uk/acad/civeng/marketing/civeng/game2.htm#location1
  How do you know when to use a particular bridge? See whether you can choose the right type of bridge for a given environment.

- Super Bridge
  http://www.pbs.org/wgbh/nova/bridge/
  This site allows you to practice what you've learned and put the correct bridge in its correct environment. Click on "Build a Bridge" to get started!

- New Bay Bridge
  http://www.newbaybridge.com/classroom/
  Have you considered building a bridge to withstand an earthquake? This site is a blast!

Build a Bridge Challenge!

Now that you have learned about different types of bridges, different materials, bridge strength, and bridge construction, you should move on to the final challenge. Using what you learned while designing your virtual bridge, think carefully about your plan for building your own bridge. Use everything you have learned to construct a bridge that meets the following conditions:

- Your bridge must hold a weight of 10 pounds. (You can use two five-pound bags of sugar to test your bridge's strength.)
- Your bridge must withstand the forces of Mother Nature. (You can blow air from a low-speed fan on your bridge to simulate wind.)
- Your bridge must be labeled, to indicate the type of bridge you created.

You may use wooden toothpicks, wooden Popsicle sticks, glue, and your choice of one other material to construct your design. Your bridge should measure no more than thirty inches. Also, if desired, you can use a flat piece of cardboard, wood, or board as the support for your bridge. You may enlist the help of a brother, sister, or classmate so that you can teach him or her about bridges. But be sure to ask your teacher for permission!

Begin your planning by using paper and a pencil to sketch your plans. At the same time, you should start looking for the materials needed to complete your design. Ask your parent or teacher to help you collect the materials. Think about which materials

(*Continued*)

will work best for the conditions described. Once you have worked out a plan that works mathematically, you should begin your construction.

Remember that model construction takes precision and patience. There may be times when your plans fail and you have to go back to the designing or planning phase. Plan for setbacks so that you can be successful in spite of disappointments.

Launching Your Results

Once your design is complete, gather some members of your class, teacher, principal, friends, or family to watch you test your design. You'll need to have two five-pound bags of sugar and a fan at the testing site. Once the demonstration is over, take some time with your audience to describe what you learned through the process. Remember to ask whether anyone has questions about your design.

Congratulations on becoming an apprentice civil engineer!

Refining Your Skills

Now that you have finished your bridge construction, compare the bridge you created with some well-known bridges. Take a careful look at the engineers' design and construction. Think about possible changes to your design.

- Famous Bridges of the World
  http://www.civl.port.ac.uk/comp_prog/bridges1/
  Looking for a list of some of the biggest and best bridges in the world? Click here to see pictures and learn important facts.

- Brooklyn Bridge Web site
  http://www.endex.com/gf/buildings/bbridge/bbridge.html
  The Brooklyn Bridge is one of the most famous suspension bridges in the world. Take a peek at this marvel of New York.

If you are interested in learning more about different civil engineering jobs, keep reading! Become informed about other famous engineering wonders of the Americas, using the following Web sites!

- Panama Canal
  http://www.pancanal.com/eng/general/howitworks/index.html
  Visit Central America to view one of the greatest engineering marvels of all time, the Panama Canal. To view how the canal works, click on "Transit" and "Operation" to watch the animated video. Also try the link on the left of the home page entitled "Photo Gallery" in order to see actual panoramic and historical photographs!

- Hoover Dam
  http://www.sunsetcities.com/hoover-dam.html
  One of the largest dams in the world is located on the border of Nevada and Arizona in the United States. Consider reading the historical background and viewing the photos.

- New York Subways

  http://www.nycsubway.org/

  Many large cities have combated road traffic by developing alternative transportation. Take a look at one of the most complex subway systems in the world.

Treasure Chest of Tools

Still craving more information? Use the following Web sites for a comprehensive look at bridge-related facts, contests, and activities.

- Building Bridges

  http://www.newton.mec.edu/Brown/TE/GIRL/bridgelinks.html

  Find the best webquests, photos, contests, and more—all about bridges!

- Building Big: Bridge Basics

  http://www.pbs.org/wgbh/buildingbig/bridge/basics.html

  Engineers must consider many things—like the distance to be spanned and the types of materials available—before determining the size, shape, and overall look of a bridge. Read here to find out all about how they make these decisions.

- Climb the Sydney Harbour Bridge

  http://www.bridgeclimb.com/

  Did you know that you can actually climb an arch bridge in Sydney, Australia? Click here to take a virtual tour of a group climbing 440 feet above sea level!

As this project comes to a close, don't forget that there are other types of engineers. Someday, you might be interested in becoming a traffic engineer, a chemical engineer, an electrical engineer, or a mechanical engineer. Did you know that there are over twenty-seven engineering careers you could learn about? Or you might be interested in continuing to explore different jobs within civil engineering. Either way, these jobs will require you to earn good grades in math and science courses. Keep working hard!

2 Experiment with Sound

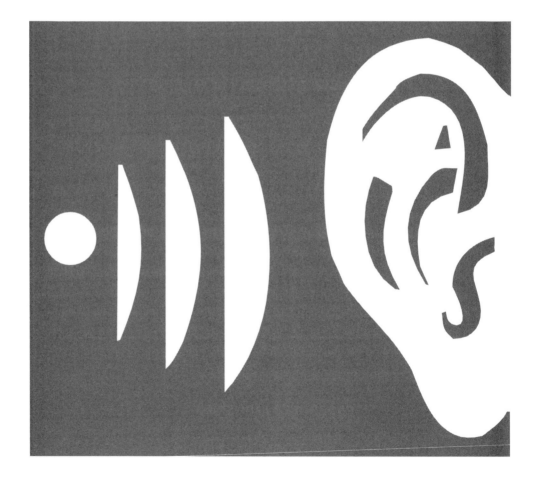

Experiment with Sound

Sound always has been and probably always will be a part of life. Sound provides valuable information about our surroundings—information that, at times, may be important for our survival. For example, prehistoric people may have depended on animal sounds, running water, thunder, and other natural noises to tell them what was happening in their environment. A rushing stream might attract thirsty travelers. An angry animal roar was probably a good signal to stay away!

What about today? Have you ever thought about the noise you encounter as you go about your daily business? We certainly live in a noisy world! Here are just a few examples of some noisemakers in our modern environment:

- Cars, trucks, and buses
- Planes and helicopters
- Home phones and cellular phones
- Stereos, personal CD players, and MP3 players
- Department store and mall soundtracks
- Police and ambulance sirens
- Crying babies
- Barking dogs
- Construction
- Conversation in school, at home, in the store, and on public transportation

Can you think of any others?

Do we, like our ancestors, use these noises to make decisions? Of course! For example, at the sound of an approaching truck, you might ride your bike a little closer to the side of the road. And when you hear a barking dog, you might change your course to avoid a confrontation.

So we know that noise serves a valuable purpose as a source of information, but have you ever wondered about other effects of noise? Have you ever felt energized and engaged by upbeat music? Have you ever been distracted from what you were doing by too much noise? Are you curious about the effect of noise on other people? If so, you can conduct an experiment to find out how sounds affect people's ability to perform a task. Then you can share the information with other interested people.

Charting Your Course

Creating a Hypothesis and Planning the Experiment

When scientists conduct research, they begin by making a prediction about what will happen during their experiment. This prediction is called a **hypothesis.** In this experiment, you will determine how well students can solve problems in a silent environment, while listening to classical music, or while listening to louder music such as rock, salsa, or rap. What hypothesis or hypotheses will you formulate for this experiment?

(*Continued*)

When do you think most students will be able to do their best work? Do you think they will excel when they're listening to loud, lively music? Or will they prefer the soothing sounds of classical music? Maybe you believe that silence is best for concentration. After you have given the matter some thought, take a minute to write down your predictions about the best and worst level of noise for doing work. You can create your own statements or just finish these sentences:

- Hypothesis # 1: I think students will do their best work while listening to . . .
- Hypothesis #2: I think students will be the least successful when listening to . . .

Now that you know your purpose and your hypotheses, you need a general plan for carrying out your experiment. For this project, you may want to have one or more groups of students work on math problems under each of the three noise conditions you have established: listening to energetic music, listening to classical music, and working in silence. Ask your teacher whether the students in your class may act as your research subjects by participating in your experiment. Your teacher can also help you arrange a time and place for your experiment. If you want to try the experiment with students in other classes, you will have to speak to their teachers, too.

Choosing Test Materials
Now that you have a hypothesis (or multiple hypotheses) and a plan for carrying out your experiment, you must choose materials for your test. For this experiment, you need to select two materials: math problems and music that you like.

Math Problems
Think about how many problems you will need and what kind they should be. A set of thirty to forty-five problems that ask students to multiply or divide long numbers might be appropriate. Here are some examples:

$$4685$$
$$\underline{\times\ 245} \qquad 2547/163 =$$

You can make up the problems yourself or find the problems and answers in a textbook. If you make them up yourself, be sure to solve them, too, so you have a correct answer key. You will probably want to check your answers with a calculator or have a teacher or another adult review your answers, not because you can't do the problems or because you are careless but because even adults sometimes make silly mistakes when doing math problems!

Once you have created your math problems, divide them into three sets: one for students to work in silence, one for students to work while listening to classical music, and one for students to work while listening to energetic music. Make sure that each set has the same number of problems, and try to make sure that the sets are equally difficult. This way, the results will depend on what students are listening to, not how easy or hard the test is.

Put each set of problems on a separate sheet of paper. Print "Rock Music," "Classical Music," or "Silence" at the top of each sheet so you can identify each set. You may need to ask your teacher for permission to make copies of the problem sheets. Also, you may need to make different sets of problems if you try the experiment with students in different grades. Teachers of classes in those grades will be able to suggest appropriate material.

Music

Next, you need to choose the music you will play during your experiment. You need about fifteen minutes of rock, salsa, or rap music and fifteen minutes of classical music. The music can be on CDs, tapes, or records, depending on what equipment you will be able to use. You can use your own CDs or tapes or borrow them from someone else. If you don't have the music you need at home, ask your local librarian or someone in your school music department whether they can loan you music for your experiments. They may even have some good suggestions about which music to select. Be sure to thank them for their help and offer to share your results.

Arranging the Experiment

Your next task is to set up at least three testing sections with different groups of students. To do this, you will need the cooperation of your teacher and possibly other teachers as well. Clearly explain the purpose of your investigation. Make sure that the teacher or teachers understand that you will need about half an hour for each group you plan to test and that you will use energetic music, classical music, and silence in your testing.

Each of your testing groups should be made up of ten to fifteen students, all from the same grade. Try to get nearly equal numbers of students in each of your groups, and offer to report back to each group with the results of your investigation.

Make a schedule of the testing times, and double-check the schedule with any teacher whose students are involved. Be sure to get permission from your own teacher if you need to be out of class to conduct a test.

Exploration

Conducting the Experiment

When you have a group of students ready to take the test, give them a brief explanation of your experiment. Tell them *not* to put their name on their paper. When everyone is ready, pass out the problem sets labeled "Classical Music" and turn on the classical music. After fifteen minutes, when everyone is finished, collect the papers. Then follow the same procedure with the problem set for the rock, salsa, or rap music and for the problem set to be done in silence. At the end of the test section, thank everyone for cooperating and tell them that you will let them know the results. Try to make sure that you play the energetic music and the classical music at about the same volume for each group.

(*Continued*)

Analyzing Your Results

After you have collected and scored all the papers, you will be able to calculate an **average,** or mean, score for each group. You may even want to compute the median (the score that is exactly in the middle when all the scores are put in order from highest to lowest) and the mode (the score that occurs most frequently) for each group. Check a math book or ask your math teacher if you don't know how to figure out the mean, median, or mode.

When you have completed your calculations, make one or more graphs of your research findings. Graphs can help you understand and analyze your data, or information. The following example of a bar graph may give you one idea of how to show your results. Your graph may look different, depending on your results. You can draw a bar graph by hand on graph paper or regular paper, or you can ask your classroom or computer teacher about creating a graph with computer software. You may think of other ways to display your findings or look for ideas in math books.

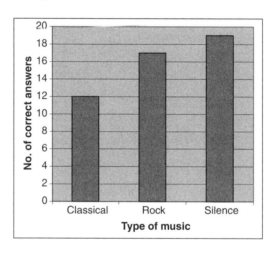

Comparing the scores of the three groups of students should allow you to draw some tentative conclusions about how students perform while listening to different types of music and while working in silence. What do your results show? Does the sound in a room make any difference in how well students work?

Launching Your Results

Once you have analyzed the data from your experiment and drawn some conclusions, you will want to share your experiment with other interested people. Here are some components of your research that you should report:

- Your hypotheses
- A description of your materials (your math problems and music)
- An explanation of your methods (who participated in your experiment and how you conducted it)
- Your findings (data)

- Graph or other visual aids
- Conclusions

With whom should you share your project? First, of course, you will want to share your results with the students who took part in the experiment and the teachers who helped you arrange it. Then consider others who might benefit from learning about the results of your study. For example, you might want to share your results with other students in your school and their parents.

How will you present your results? One option is to write an article for your school or local newspaper or for your parent teacher association (PTA) newsletter. You could also make a display of your results. Professional researchers and scientists often share their findings in poster sessions. The following Web site provides some information on how to create a scientific display board.

- The Ultimate Science Fair Resource: Display Boards
  http://www.scifair.org/articles/reports/display.shtml
  You can find information here about the content and structure of scientific posters.

Once your poster is completed, ask your teacher to display it in your classroom. Your principal may even be interested in placing it somewhere where the whole school can benefit from your work!

Another option is to submit your poster or project to a school or state science fair or to another type of contest. The following link provides information about how to prepare for a science fair.

- Science Fair Help
  http://homeschooling.gomilpitas.com/explore/sciencefair.htm
  This Web site offers pointers on how to pick a project, present information, and plan your time for science fair entries.

Here are some links to science contests that might interest you:

- Christopher Columbus Awards
  http://www.christophercolumbusawards.com/guides/student/start.htm
  This Web site has a contest that allows students to conduct experiments and research of interest to their communities.

- Discovery Channel Young Scientist Challenge
  http://school.discovery.com/sciencefaircentral/dysc/
  This cool science contest is designed for kids in grades 5–8.

- The National American Indian Science and Engineering Fair (NAISEF)
  http://www.aises.org/events/naisef/
  This is a special science fair for Native American students in grades 5–12.

(*Continued*)

- The World Wide Web Virtual Library: Science Fairs
  http://physics.usc.edu/~gould/ScienceFairs/
  This Web site has tons of links to science fairs all over the world, including international, national, state, and regional science fairs. Many of these have special requirements for entering, so be sure to read all the guidelines before planning a project.

Treasure Chest of Tools

Congratulations! You have completed a useful and interesting science project! Would you like to learn more about the effects of noise on living things? If so, you can do more research. For example, you can plan an experiment to find out whether plants grow better in silence or when music is played. Does the kind of music played around plants affect them differently? If so, how? How would you go about finding answers to these questions?

You may find suggestions for other experiments with noise in science books in your school library or public library. Or you may want to research a topic unrelated to noise. Here are some links to Web sites that provide experiments for kids:

- Energy Quest Science Projects
  http://www.energyquest.ca.gov/projects/
  This site offers links to energy-related science projects.

- Science Made Simple
  http://www.sciencemadesimple.com/
  You can find a variety of science projects and answers to your science questions on this Web site.

Here are some books that can give you ideas for science experiments:

- *Science Experiments You Can Eat* by Vicki Cobb & David Cain, Illustrator (revised edition, Harper Trophy, 1984)
  ISBN: 0064460029
  This book offers fun and tasty science experiments for kids.

- *The Everything Kids' Science Experiments Book: Boil Ice, Float Water, Measure Gravity—Challenge the World Around You!* by Tom Robinson (Everything Kids Series, Adams Media Corporation, 2001)
  ISBN: 1580625576
  This book contains dozens of kid-tested experiments using household items.

- *700 Science Experiments for Everyone* by United Nations Educational, Scientific and Cultural Organization (revised and enlarged edition, Doubleday Books for Young Readers, 1964)
  ISBN: 0385052758
  This book provides straightforward science projects about the world around us, using commonly available materials.

- *Physics Projects for Young Scientists* by Richard Adams & Pete Goodwin (revised edition, Franklin Watts, 2000)
  ISBN: 0531164616
  This book offers physics experiments with simple lists of materials and explanations of the scientific properties at work.

Remember, the first step on the road to a successful science project is picking a topic that interests you. What do you wonder about? What would you like to know? There are so many questions waiting to be asked! Don't you want to start right away?

3 Investigate Local History

Investigate Local History

As we go about our daily business, we often take for granted the hustle and bustle of our communities or neighborhoods. We hardly notice conveniences such as paved roads, halogen streetlamps, or drive-up ATMs, and we accept as natural the dress and behavior of our friends, family members, and neighbors. It may seem that your community has always been just this way.

But is that true? Has your community remained the same over time? Of course not! Many generations of people have lived and worked in your community. In your community, important local and national events have happened, some of which may still be remembered, others of which may now be shrouded in mystery. What stories would the streets and buildings of your community tell if they could speak? What kinds of people, past and present, have lived in your community? What were their lives like? Do you know? Could you be surprised by the answers? To find out, you could do some research on questions such as the following:

- What was this area like before it became a town or city?
- Who were the earliest settlers in this area? Were there native communities in the area before white settlers came? Are there written accounts about how early settlers and native communities interacted?
- Have natural disasters affected your community? If so, when or how?
- Which church was first established in the area? Who built it, and when was it built? What role did it play in the lives of the town's inhabitants?
- What folklore, if any, is associated with the area?
- How did certain historical events such as the Civil War, Prohibition, the Depression, the Civil Rights Movement, or the Vietnam War affect the people of the area?
- Did any famous person come from the area? If so, is there a written biography of that person? What effect did this person's accomplishments have on the town or city?
- Who was the town's first elected official? What factors contributed to his or her election? Does he or she have any living descendents in the area?
- What industries supported your community? For example, was your town built on sailing, fishing, or whaling? Or maybe on factories and textiles? Perhaps agriculture? What was life like for the everyday people who went to sea, worked in the factories, or tended the fields?
- What were clothing styles like when your town was founded? How have styles changed over the years? What political changes, if any, were reflected in changing clothing styles?
- What is the history of the oldest building in the area? Who lived or worked there? Has it ever been restored?
- Who was the first person to ever publish a newspaper in your community? Did the publication have a particular political viewpoint? What effect did the newspaper have on the history of the town?

(Continued)

- Did historically significant events occur in your area? What were the events? Where did they occur?
- What would life in your community have been like for a person your age in the sixteenth, seventeenth, eighteenth, or nineteenth century?
- When did your town first begin to keep written documents or records, and what were they? Who authored them?
- Is there a written history of your town, region, county, or state? Where might you find such a book?

Charting Your Course: Using Primary and Secondary Sources

In your research, you will encounter two types of resources: primary sources, and secondary sources. **Primary sources** are actual documents or images preserved from the period of time you want to investigate. Primary sources may include letters, diaries, journal entries, photographs, paintings, and legal documents such as census records or birth certificates. The following list provides information about potentially useful primary sources.

- Autobiographies: Autobiographies provide personal information that you may not find anywhere else. If you can find an autobiography written by someone who lived in your community in the past, you have a wonderful resource!
- City directories and telephone directories from the period you are researching: These sources are a good way to find information about ordinary people. City directories contain lists of all the town's adult inhabitants, their addresses, and their occupations. Telephone directories list names and addresses too, but they also contain advertisements that include useful information about town businesses of the past. By looking at the ads over a period of years, you can detect changes in the economy and in the social life of the town.
- Federal and local census reports: These documents can reveal changes such as shifts in population or family size.
- State "bluebooks": Bluebooks are reference books that are published each year and contain biographical information about important people who have served in state government. They are called *bluebooks* because they had blue covers when they first began to be published. Now they come in other colors, too.
- Old newspapers: Newspapers can provide important details about people and events in the history of your community. These may be found in libraries or in a newspaper office's "morgue," which is a collection of the past editions of the paper. In addition, an incredible digital collection of early American newspapers (1690–1876) provides thousands of pages from a variety of publications. It is searchable by date range, publication, and topic at http://tinyurl.com/5vaqag.
- Deeds, property maps, and building permits: If your question is about buildings or landmarks in your area, these types of documents may be particularly useful. You can probably find them in your city hall.

- Old catalogues and magazines: If you are studying the way people dressed in 1900 or the common tools that were used then, you may want to locate a mail-order catalogue from that period.

As you explore primary sources, you may find things that no one else has discovered. You may also discover two or three different versions of the same event or different views on an important local issue. When you come across conflicting stories, you must decide which record is correct or which person's account is most likely to be true. If there is no clear answer, you will probably want to include both versions of the event. Presenting all the sides of a story that you know about is called *unbiased documentation*. Primary sources are exciting because you never know what you will find! A Web site called Using Primary Sources on the Web at **http://www.lib.washington.edu/subject/History/RUSA/** provides information on how to find, evaluate, and cite online primary historical sources. If you find a primary source that isn't available through your library, a local university or college, or the Internet, you might ask a librarian whether you can get it through interlibrary loan.

- In an ideal world, you could always rely on primary sources to answer your research questions; in reality, however, you may have to check secondary sources. **Secondary sources** are materials written by other researchers who have examined the primary sources and drawn their own conclusions. Encyclopedias and other reference books are secondary sources. Biographies are also good secondary sources and may even contain reproductions of primary sources such as letters or journal entries. *Biography and Genealogy Master Index* is a reference that lists biographies. This database may be available online, but chances are you will have to contact your local library, historical society, or college history department to find out how to get access. You may also find useful information on the following biography Web sites:

- Biography.com
  www.biography.com
  Created by the makers of the popular TV show *Biography*, this site allows users to search a database of hundreds of biographies.

- Biographies for Kids: Famous Leaders for Young Readers
  http://www.gardenofpraise.com/leaders.htm
  You'll find easy-to-read biographies of famous leaders on this site.

- Lives
  http://amillionlives.com
  This site provides links to thousands of biographies, autobiographies, memoirs, diaries, letters, narratives, oral histories, and more.

- National Women's History Project
  http://www.nwhp.org
  This Web site offers opportunities for thorough research on topics in women's history.

(*Continued*)

- The Faces of Science: African Americans in the Sciences
  http://www.princeton.edu/~mcbrown/display/faces.html
  This site provides profiles of African American men and women who have contributed to the advancement of science and engineering.

Where to Find Primary and Secondary Sources

Now that you know about primary and secondary sources, you need to figure out where to get them. You might start by visiting your local library and checking the reference section. There you will find encyclopedias and other general reference books that can provide basic information about your topic. Your librarian can help you get started. Your local library may also have old newspapers or photos related to your topic.

In addition to your local library, you may find useful information through research libraries. You can visit research libraries in person or look for information online. Links to U.S. university history departments can be found at **http://www.ghgcorp.com/shetler/univ/america.html.** The list isn't inclusive, however, so be sure to check a search engine like Google or Ask Jeeves Kids if you don't find a link for a school near you.

Local historical societies are also a great source of information. Here's a list of U.S. historical societies compiled by Yahoo: **http://tinyurl.com/5f2lda**. This site provides only a sample of the historical societies in the country, so if you don't find a society for your town or community here, try another search engine, such as Google at **www.google.com**, or Ask Jeeves Kids at **www.ajkids.com**. The phone directory provided by the Internet Public Library at **http://www.ipl.org/div/subject/browse/ref80.00.00/** might also help you locate historical societies.

Historical societies specialize in the history of your state or region and often employ professional historians. Do you know what a historian does? Historians are like detectives. They usually focus on a specific time and place in history and try to figure out what life was like in that era by finding and interpreting documents and artifacts from that time. Historians often work for universities and colleges, and though they may teach some classes about what they have learned through their research, their primary job is to look for new information. Historians may also work as professional consultants, helping museums create accurate historical exhibits or maintaining and organizing collections of historical documents that are important to a region, state, or even a nation. These are just some of the jobs that historians do. If you are interested in learning more about what it means to be a historian, you might enjoy an activity called You Be the Historian (**http://americanhistory.si.edu/hohr/springer/**). See if you can figure out who the Springer family was and how they lived by examining the things they left behind.

Treasure Chest of Tools

Another very useful source of information is the Internet. Hundreds of historical Web sites provide links to both primary and secondary sources. Historians have never had so much access to information—and it's all at your fingertips! The following list provides information about digital collections of historical resources.

- Library of Congress, America's Story
  http://www.americasstory.com
  This Web site, created by the U.S. Library of Congress, the largest library in the
  world, is designed to make historical research easy and fun for young people.

- American Memory: Historical Collections of the National Digital Library, Library of
  Congress
  http://memory.loc.gov/ammem/
  This site provides access to sound recordings, photos, moving images, prints, maps,
  and sheet music from American history.

- National Archives and Records Administration, Digital Classroom
  http://www.archives.gov/digital_classroom/
  Use this site to find links to useful historical resources such as the Web site for
  National History Day, the Smithsonian Oral History Interviewing Guide, and more
  than one hundred American historical documents.

- American Journeys, Eyewitness Accounts of Early American Exploration and
  Settlement
  http://www.americanjourneys.org/
  This Web site, a project of the Wisconsin Historical Society, provides more than
  18,000 pages of first-person descriptions of North American exploration, from the
  Vikings in Canada in 1000 A.D. to the diaries of mountain men in the Rockies hundreds of years later.

- Oregon History Project (Oregon Historical Society)
  http://www.ohs.org/education/oregonhistory/
  The Oregon History Project offers an online archive of historical records from the
  Oregon Historical Society collections, focusing on the diversity of the people and
  events of Oregon's history.

- California Historical Society
  http://www.californiahistoricalsociety.org/main.html
  This site offers access to more than four hundred images from the society's fine
  arts library and photography collections, as well as articles about California history. The site also provides an extensive database of links to information about
  California's cultural history.

- UCLA Department of Special Collections
  http://www.library.ucla.edu/libraries/special/scweb/
  The library of the University of California, Los Angeles, provides online access to its
  collection of rare books and manuscripts, including more than 30 million documents, 5 million photographs and negatives, maps, art, architectural drawings
  and models, and other graphic arts material.

(Continued)

- FirstGov for Kids
  http://www.kids.gov/k_history.htm
  Visit this site to find links to more than forty Web sites on historical research.

- History Matters
  http://historymatters.gmu.edu/
  This challenging resource provides links to primary sources, guides to using primary
  sources, and articles that link history to the present.

- Making of America
  http://cdl.library.cornell.edu/moa/
  Making of America, a project of the University of Michigan and Cornell University, is
  a digital library of primary sources of American social history.

- Documenting the American South
  http://docsouth.unc.edu/
  This Web site provides primary sources for the study of American southern culture
  and history.

- American Colonist's Library
  http://personal.pitnet.net/primarysources/
  At this site, you will find a huge collection of literature and documents about colo-
  nists' lives in America.

- Connecticut's Heritage Gateway
  http://www.ctheritage.org/
  This Web site provides online exhibits, primary sources, and secondary sources such
  as encyclopedias of historical events pertaining to Connecticut history.

- Virtual Jamestown
  http://www.virtualjamestown.org/
  This digital archive explores the history of the Jamestown settlement and "the
  Virginia experiment."

Exploration: Interviewing

Once you have done some background research, you may find that you can get unique
information from an interview. Interviews are incredible primary sources, and oral history is an exciting way to learn more about your topic. The following case study illustrates how oral history can work.

Case Study: Oral History in Collinsville, Connecticut

Four Connecticut students with a strong interest in history decided to investigate
the role of the Collins Company in the evolution of their hometown—Collinsville,
Connecticut. All they knew when they began was that the company had strongly
influenced the development of the town.

The students talked about the primary sources they could use, including interviews with former employees. They agreed that information from people who had firsthand knowledge of the company would provide them with a better understanding of their topic. The students knew a ninety-six-year-old man who had been an executive of the company during its period of greatest strength and production. They decided that he would be an excellent source of information, and, after explaining who they were and what they were researching, respectfully asked if he would be willing to speak with them. They were very pleased when he agreed!

To prepare for the interview, the students reviewed the information they had gathered from print sources, looking for holes in the data, questions raised but not answered by their information. Then they brainstormed an extensive list of questions they might ask about the history of the factory and chose the best ones for the interview. They made sure to develop open-ended questions that required a complete answer rather than yes-or-no questions that would provide less information.

On the day of the interview, they dressed nicely, checked their equipment and supplies, and arrived at the interviewee's house on time. They then asked if they could tape the interview. In case the man preferred not to be recorded, they were prepared to take extensive notes. Even with the tape recorder running, they took notes on important points in case they had an equipment failure.

They spent about an hour asking the interviewee the questions they had prepared as well as additional questions that occurred to them during the interview. If an answer was too short to be helpful, they asked for more information.

The interview was a great success, for the students were able to gather detailed information from a personal perspective—a type of information that was not captured by company documents or other literature about the company. The students were also able to use taped portions of the interview to narrate a slide presentation about the company's history. The oral history approach proved very useful to their research!

Here are some tips we can draw from the students' successful interview:

1. Decide who will provide the best information for your purpose. Ask that person for an interview, and arrange the place, time, and date. If you plan to use a video recorder or tape recorder, make sure it's all right with the person you are interviewing.
2. Complete enough research to be able to ask intelligent questions and understand the answers.
3. Brainstorm all the questions you could ask. Choose the best ones, and practice asking them in an organized way. Remember that a response in an oral history interview may lead you in an unexpected direction, so be prepared to vary the order of your questions.
4. If you plan to use a video recorder or tape recorder, practice using the equipment until you are comfortable inserting the tapes, adjusting the volume, arranging the microphone (if there is one), and playing back the tape.

(*Continued*)

5. If you wish, practice an oral history interview with an older relative or an older resident of your community. For example, interview one of your grandparents about his or her childhood, memories, and family history. You will gain valuable practice for your local history interview and also have a wonderful record of your grandparent's family memories.

6. Check your notes and questions before your interview, and prepare a brief introduction of yourself and your project.

7. Arrange to have an adult drive you and come with you to your interview.

8. During the interview, listen carefully, maintain eye contact, and be polite. Make sure to ask follow-up questions if you don't understand something.

9. After the interview, thank your interviewee for his or her time and ask him or her if you can call or e-mail if you have any additional questions or need clarification on any of the responses.

10. Once you get home, look over your notes and play the tape of the interview, if you made one. This is the time to decide whether you need further clarification. If you do need a little more information from your interviewee (and don't feel bad if you do; professional journalists and writers often contact a source with follow-up questions), be sure to create short, to-the-point questions that will avoid wasting the time of your interviewee. Then thank him or her profusely for the extra time!

Launching Your Results

Now that you have done all this work, you need to find some way to share your interview and research experience! You may want to write an article for your school or local newspaper. Many states also publish historical magazines that accept the work of young people. You may even want to prepare a booklet for your own school library.

Another option is to write a historical fiction story about your research and your interviewee. If you are interested in reading a book that was written by using oral history techniques, look for the Foxfire books, edited by Eliot Wigginton. These books contain oral histories collected by students.

- If you videotaped your interview, you could also create a documentary that would feature the interview as an important segment. You could act as the narrator and provide background information, using the data you found through your research. The following book might help you to get some ideas on how to get started on a documentary.

- *Creating History Documentaries* by Deborah Escobar (Prufrock Press, 2001)
  ISBN: 1882664760
  This book provides information about researching, scripting, and editing a historical documentary.

A final option is to use your research to create a project for the National History Day contest.

- National History Day

  http://nationalhistoryday.org/

  National History Day is one of the oldest and best regarded academic contests in the country for students in grades 6–12. The Web site will provide you with more information about National History Day and how to get started on a project for the event.

  Whatever type of project you do, you should be proud of all you have accomplished! You have done valuable research about your community and shared it with others. Maybe someday your research will become a secondary source for a student with a question similar to your own!

Create an Artifact Box

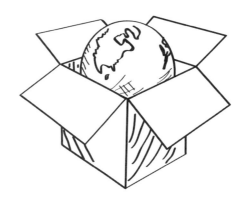

Create an Artifact Box

In the Indiana Jones movies, Indiana's search for ancient *artifacts*—human-made objects—from long ago, result in dangerous adventures. Archaeologists like Indiana Jones are scientists who use artifacts and *ecofacts*—natural objects such as seeds or animal bones—to study human life and activities of the past. Looking at the objects that people used in their daily lives, archaeologists can learn about the culture in which they were used or created. Take a look around the room you are in right now. What do you think archaeologists could learn about your life from the objects in the room? Because most archaeologists study artifacts from long ago, many people think that artifacts can only be historical items. However, an artifact is an object that people use or create to serve a purpose in their daily life. You use and create artifacts every day! Trees are not artifacts; they are ecofacts because nature makes them. However, tree houses are artifacts because humans make them! Perhaps if Indiana Jones had realized that artifacts were all around him, his life would have been much less dangerous!

Do you think that the artifacts that surround people in New York City are the same kinds of artifacts that surround people in San Francisco? Yes and no. People in New York City and San Francisco may share some common artifacts, such as silverware, soda cans, or baseball caps. But because each city has its own culture, some of the artifacts in each city are unique. For example, while people who live in New York City and San Francisco may both wear baseball caps, people in New York City are probably much more likely to wear New York Yankees or New York Mets baseball caps than are people in San Francisco. While New York City residents and San Francisco residents are both surrounded by buildings, only people in San Francisco can claim Alcatraz as an artifact. Can you think of any artifacts that are unique to your town or state?

A collection of current artifacts and ecofacts from a particular town or region of the country can also inform people who are unfamiliar with that area. For example, if you live in Connecticut, you may not have any idea what Louisiana is like. But if someone from Louisiana made a box for you filled with Mardi Gras beads, a CD of Cajun music, some Spanish moss, and a toy crawfish, it would help you learn about Louisiana's culture and landscape. Artifacts and ecofacts can help people learn about the social, economic, and environmental aspects of a particular area. By studying the products produced in a town or country, people can learn about the economic well-being of the area and about the importance of industry and agriculture. Information about an area's weather and recreational opportunities can tell people something about the lives of the residents. People can also learn about the area's environment by finding out about the local wildlife and vegetation.

Charting Your Course: What Is an Artifact Box?

For several years, teachers and students from across North America have been constructing sets of twenty to twenty-five artifacts and ecofacts about their hometown and

(Continued)

region. Each collection is then assembled and packaged as an Artifact Box. The box is exchanged for one from a mystery classroom in a distant area. Only the teacher in the classroom receiving the box knows the area from which it came.

Without revealing where the box is from, the receiving teacher shows the contents to students in the class. The students then use available reference books, Internet sites, and nonprint resources to figure out the country, state or province, and town from which the artifacts came.

If you would like to create an Artifact Box about your town, city, or community, you may want to join the Artifact Box Exchange Network. The network will send you the Artifact Box manual and connect you or your class with a partner for the fall or spring Artifact Box exchange. There is a fee for this service. If you explain the project to your teacher or principal, your school may provide the money. You may write to join the network, using the registration form at **www.artifactbox.com**. Once you've printed the form and filled it out, you're ready to mail it. You may also join by phone. Before you call, make sure to check with your parent, guardian, or teacher; calling this number may be long distance for you.

If you prefer not to join the network, you have another option. Ask your teacher if he or she might help you find a partner from another town or state with whom you can exchange Artifact Boxes. Your teacher may be able to find an artifact exchange partner by using the Epals.com Classroom Exchange. You can find out more about this program at **www.epals.com**. If your teacher finds an exchange partner for you, remind him or her not to reveal the location of your artifact box partner! You want to figure out that piece of information for yourself!

Exploration: Make an Artifact Box

There are five steps to follow in collecting artifacts and ecofacts that are typical of your area:

Step 1: Brainstorming
Step 2: Choosing items for your box
Step 3: Making clue cards
Step 4: Categorizing the items in your box
Step 5: Developing an answer sheet

Step 1: Brainstorming

To make an Artifact Box, start by brainstorming ideas of objects, or artifacts, that are representative of your community. At this time, don't worry about the sizes or shapes of your artifacts or whether something will spoil. When you brainstorm, there are no bad or silly ideas. Just think of anything that is typical—and especially of anything that is unique—to your area. Be specific. Jot down your ideas on a sheet of paper, and try to come up with at least twenty-five to thirty-five items.

You may want to ask one or more friends to brainstorm with you. The more ideas you come up with, the better! Here are a few suggestions, to help you get the ideas flowing for your Artifact Box.

- A local road map
- A soil sample
- A food item that is produced in your area
- A tree leaf or flower that is native to your area
- A product that is manufactured in your area
- A picture of a famous person who was born in your area
- Equipment for a sport that is popular in your area
- A local advertisement
- A population figure

Remember, you are an expert on your area; after all, you do live there! What ideas can you come up with that will help other students identify where you live and what it's like to live there? Going to your town hall for some brochures and information about your area may help you come up with even more ideas. Searching the Internet may help, as well. Use a search engine such as Ask Jeeves Kids (www.ajkids.com). As you brainstorm items for your Artifact Box, remember to find clues about your general region, your state or province, your region of the state, and your town or city.

Step 2: Choosing Items for Your Box

Now it is time to think about how to package your items. For instance, you couldn't include a whole tree in your box, but you could add some dried leaves from a tree that is unique to your area. You couldn't include the newest version of a computer made in your area, but you could include an advertisement for it! If refrigerators are made in your area, you could include a small toy refrigerator. A photograph could represent a famous person from your state or town. Try to include as many three-dimensional objects as possible in order to make your Artifact Box more interesting.

If you are going to send your box to another student or class, remember that it should be a kind of puzzle. The students whom you send your box to will use research skills to figure out where your box is from. You shouldn't make the puzzle too easy. For example, if you include a map, be sure that it doesn't show the name of your town or state. On the other hand, don't make the puzzle too hard. Make sure that there is a way for other students to solve the mystery of each clue. You want your Artifact Box to be a rewarding challenge.

Step 3: Making Clue Cards

Package each artifact in a separate bag or envelope, and use string to attach a clue card to each item. Clue cards are three-by-five-inch index cards with clues written on them.

(*Continued*)

Make a clue for each item, listing a reference book, a Web site, or another resource that could be used to identify the artifact and where or when it is from. For example, if you enclose an evergreen cone in your box, one clue might ask the reader to use a field guide to identify the tree that produced the cone, as well as the region in which it grows.

Make sure that the students studying your Artifact Box will be able to obtain enough information from the clue and the artifact together to identify the item and figure out where or when it came from. When you are finished gathering your items, you should have at least twenty to twenty-five artifacts with clues in individual bags.

Step 4: Categorizing the Items in Your Box

Now, separate your artifacts and ecofacts into four piles, according to these four categories:

1. Clues that identify the general region of the country
2. Clues that identify the state or province
3. Clues that identify a region of the state or province
4. Clues that identify your city or town

Step 5: Developing an Answer Sheet

Now you are ready to develop an answer sheet for your Artifact Box. Begin by numbering your clue cards. The first clues will be the most general ones—those that identify the general region. Save the most specific clues—those that identify your city or town—for last.

List the number on the answer sheet. Next to each number, give the name of the artifact or ecofact and tell why it is useful in identifying your community. For example, if you included a toy tractor and sunflower seeds in your Artifact Box, your answer sheet might read like this:

1. Toy tractor: This clue shows that our region is mainly agricultural.
2. Sunflower seeds: This clue represents our state flower, the sunflower, which identifies our state as Kansas.

Do you see how these clues become increasingly specific?

Once you are finished with your answer sheet, enclose it in an envelope marked as follows: "Answer Sheet: DO NOT OPEN until you have attempted to solve all the clues!"

Launching Your Results: Sharing Your Artifact Box

Pack your artifacts carefully in a box, with the envelope containing the answer sheet on top. If you are exchanging Artifact Boxes, ask your teacher to send it to the other school.

Making an Artifact Box is a great way to learn more about history, government, economics, and everyday life in your area. In fact, your Artifact Box should make you a real resident expert on your community!

Good luck figuring out your Artifact Box partner's location!

Treasure Chest of Tools

Look at these books on archaeology if you'd like to find out more about how to learn from artifacts and ecofacts.

- *Archaeology for Young Explorers: Uncovering History at Colonial Williamsburg* by Patricia Samford & David L. Ribblett (Colonial Williamsburg Foundation, 1995)
  ISBN: 087935089X
  Explore colonial Williamsburg like an archeologist! Learn how artifacts end up in the ground, how archeologists choose dig sites, what types of artifacts have been found, and how archeologists make sense of their findings.

- *The Young Oxford Book of Archaeology* by Norah Moloney (Oxford University Press, 2000)
  ISBN: 0199101000
  Discover the study of archaeology, including the world of underwater archaeology. This book may be a challenge to read, but it will introduce you to many interesting archaeological facts!

- *Archaeology for Kids: Uncovering the Mysteries of Our Past* by Richard Panchyk (Chicago Review Press, 2001)
  ISBN: 1556523955
  Projects in this book will teach you some of the techniques archaeologists use. Build a sifting screen to use at archaeological sites!

- *The Usborne Young Scientist: Archaeology* by Barbara Cork (E.D.C. Publishing, 1985)
  ISBN: 0860208656
  Read this fascinating book and discover how archaeologists do their job.

If you liked the books in the preceding list, you might also want to explore these Web sites on archaeology:

- Artifacts Gallery
  www.kidsdigreed.com/artifacts.htm
  Explore artifacts from the Reed Farmstead Archaeological Site in West Virginia.

- Dig Magazine Online
  www.digonsite.com
  This archaeology magazine is just for kids, and you can read it online! Read stories about archaeologists' discoveries, and search their Fantastic Factoids section.

- Colonial Williamsburg Archaeology: Dirt Detectives
  http://www.history.org/kids/games/dirtDetective.cfm
  Take this challenge and test your archaeological skills!

- Geocaching
  www.geocaching.com
  Geocaching is an activity in which you use a GPS unit to hunt for hidden caches. It's a little like searching for buried treasure! Visit the Web site to learn more.

(Continued)

Draw a Comic Strip

Draw a Comic Strip

Do you like to read the comics in the newspaper on Sunday mornings? Do you enjoy comic books as much as the books you read in school? Would you be interested in drawing a comic strip? Well, you can do just that—even if you have never drawn comics before or heard about how comic artists work. All you need is your imagination and a few supplies! Here is a list of materials you will need for this project:

- A notebook for ideas and rough sketches
- A drawing pad with unlined paper (You can buy these at a grocery store, pharmacy, or art store. Your school's art teacher may also be able to give you some drawing paper. You can staple the pages together to make a homemade sketchbook.)
- Sharp pencils
- Some pens with black ink
- Colored pencils, crayons, or other drawing supplies with which to color your comic
- Some great ideas!

Charting Your Course

What do you think of when you think of a comic strip? Do you think of silly characters and jokes? Or superheroes? These are popular types of comics, but there are other types of comics that might interest you as well.

Graphic Novels

Did you know that in 1992, a long comic book won the most famous literature prize in the country? This book was called *Maus.* It was a serious story about World War II. Book-length comics—called *graphic novels*—may be serious or funny, but they always tell interesting stories. They are becoming increasingly popular as people realize that they are informative, beautiful, and fun to read. Some students are even reading them for school. If graphic novels sound interesting to you, you may want to read some, such as those listed here. You can ask your school or local librarian where to find these and other graphic novels.

- *Out from Boneville (Bone, Book 1)* by Jeff Smith (Cartoon Books, 1996)
  ISBN: 0963660993
  After being kicked out of their hometown, three cousins—Fone Bone, Phoney Bone, and Smiley Bone—wander into a magical valley. There they find wondrous beings, a human girl named Thorn, and terrible rat creatures. This is the first book in the very popular Bone series.

- *Amy Unbounded: Belondweg Blossoming* by Rachel Hartman (Pug House Press, 2002)
  ISBN: 0971790000
  Amy is like many nine-year-old girls: she's excited about her tenth birthday, doesn't always feel like doing her chores, and has a crush on a neighborhood boy. But

(Continued)

Amy lives in a medieval town called Goredd, where sometimes dragons disguise themselves as humans and statues talk to surprised strangers. This is a fun graphic novel about a kid whose life is different—or maybe not so different—from yours!

- *Clan Apis* by Jay Hoseler (Active Synapse, 2000)
  ISBN: 096772550X

  Do you like bees? You might, after reading this graphic novel! Nyuki, a worker bee, has lots of adventures with her family and friends as she grows up in her hive. This book is funny, interesting, and very cool!

Political Cartoons

Political cartoons are another important type of comic. Political cartoons use humor to share ideas about government and important events. Many people read political cartoons because they are funny—even if they usually find politics boring or hard to understand. For this reason, political cartoons are a very powerful way for cartoonists to express opinions about what is happening in the world. For example, a political cartoonist may think that a government official (also called a *politician*) has made a bad decision. The cartoonist might create a cartoon that shows the politician doing or saying something very foolish. The cartoonist may also exaggerate the politician's features, so that he or she has a huge nose, giant ears, or buckteeth. This type of drawing—an exaggeration of a famous person—is called a **caricature.** Political cartoonists have been drawing caricatures for hundreds of years. You can still find caricatures and political cartoons in any newspaper today.

Funnies

Of course, some comics tell stories just for fun. The following comics are good examples of some fun comic strips. Reading them may give you some ideas of your own!

- Snoopy.com; http://comics.com/peanuts/index.html

  This Web site provides information and sample comic strips from the famous cartoons of Peanuts. You can read about Snoopy, Charlie Brown, and all their friends in the comic strip of the day.

- Amazing Kids Comics

  http://www.amazing-kids.org/akcomics.htm#akcindex

  This Web site displays a number of comic strips drawn by kids. Check out Amazing Kids Comics Adventures by seventeen-year-old Laura Tisdale and Kid Works by twelve-year-old Betsy Brown. You can link to other kid comics through this page as well.

Exploration

Short, fun comic strips like Peanuts or Amazing Kids Comics Adventures may be good models for a new comic artist like you. But how do you begin your comic strip? There's no one right way, but the following steps may be a good guide for this project.

Steps for Creating a Great Comic Strip

1. Develop a story that you would like to show in your strip.
2. Choose a character or characters for your strip.
3. Choose main ideas for the squares of your strip.
4. Create a storyboard.
5. Draw your strip.
6. Ink or color your strip.

Step 1: Developing Your Story

Most comic strips show characters acting out very simple stories or jokes. You can get ideas for a story from your own life. Funny things make good comic strips, but you can also make a comic strip about surprising, scary, or exciting events. Any story that can be told with a few pictures and words and that also has an interesting point at the end, can make a good comic strip.

For example, maybe you recently had your first roller-coaster ride. You could write a comic strip about what happened before, during, or after the ride. You might write about how you felt while you were waiting, how you behaved during the ride, or how others acted around you.

Or maybe you have had a bad day recently, and that's what you want your comic strip to be about. That's fine, too. In that case, you might take out your comic strip notebook and write down all the things that made the day bad for you. Your list might look like this:

A Bad Day!
- I overslept.
- I forgot my lunch at home.
- I tripped and fell in class, and everyone laughed.
- I lost my favorite pencil.
- My teacher snapped at me for having a messy desk.

Choose an idea and make your own list of events that could support that idea. Which of the ideas on your list would you most like to show in your comic? Choose one event from your list that you think would make a good story. Then write a brief description of what happened, making sure that you have a clear beginning, middle, and end. Try to make your description interesting or funny. Let's say you decided to write about over-sleeping. Your paragraph might look like this:

The Bad Morning

The alarm rang, and I reached over and turned it off so I could sleep for a few more minutes. Then I heard my dad yelling that I was going to miss the bus if I didn't wake up! I jumped out of bed and started getting dressed. I was in such a hurry that I got tangled up in my clothes and fell over. My dad had made me some oatmeal, but I didn't have time to eat it before running to the bus stop. On the bus, I was squished between two

(Continued)

of the biggest kids in the school. When I finally sat down at my desk, my teacher smiled at the class and said, "Good morning! I hope everyone is having a great day so far!"

Choose a few different events from your list and write a paragraph for each. Read the paragraphs, and decide which is the most interesting. Go back to that paragraph and make any changes or improvements you think are necessary. Are there sentences that don't add to the story that you can cross out? Or do you need to add a sentence or two to show an important event that you had forgotten? Just remember to keep your story short and simple. Four or five sentences should be plenty for a good comic strip.

Step 2: Choosing a Character

Now that you have a story, it's time to think of a character for your comic strip. Think about what you have written. What type of character would react in an interesting way to the situation you have described?

For example, if you had decided to create a comic strip about oversleeping, what type of character would be likely to oversleep? How would he or she react to oversleeping? Or you may want to ask yourself what type of character might be very *unlikely* to oversleep. How would *that* character react to oversleeping?

Remember, you don't have to limit yourself to realistic characters. If you like superheroes, you could create a comic strip about a superhero who oversleeps. Animals, toys, household appliances, and plants may also make good characters for your comic strip.

Take out your comic strip notebook, and brainstorm some characters that might fit well into the scene you have written. Write down all of the interesting ideas you can think of.

Step 3: Choosing Main Ideas for Your Squares

Think about the comic strips you see in the newspaper. They're made of individual squares that show what's happening to the characters and what the characters are saying. For your comic strip, you may want to create six squares. This will give you just enough room to tell your short story.

But what will happen in each square? Now is the time to make a plan. Let's look back at the scene about oversleeping. Can we break it into six pieces—one for each square? Of course we can! Here's how it might work for this comic:

The Bad Morning

Square one: The alarm rang, and I reached over and turned it off so I could sleep for a few more minutes.

Square two: I heard my dad yelling that I was going to miss the bus if I didn't wake up!

Square three: I jumped out of bed and started getting dressed. I was in such a hurry that I got tangled up in my clothes and fell over.

Square four: My dad had made me some oatmeal, but I didn't have time to eat it before running to the bus stop.

Square five: On the bus, I was squished between two of the biggest kids in the school.

Square six: When I finally sat down at my desk, my teacher smiled at the class and said, "Good morning! I hope everyone is having a great day so far!"

Take out your comic strip notebook and try breaking the scene you wrote into six easy pieces. Remember, you are going to have to show the action in each square with a simple drawing and maybe a few words. This means that you must have only one idea for each square. If you have two ideas, you may want to use only the more important idea. For example, look back at square three:

Square three: I jumped out of bed and started getting dressed. I was in such a hurry that I got tangled up in my clothes and fell over.

Here we have three ideas or actions in the same square: "jumped out of bed," "started getting dressed," and "got tangled up in my clothes and fell over." It might be difficult to show these three actions in one square. But what's the most interesting and funny part of this square? The part where the character falls over, right? You can cross off the other parts. Your readers will understand that if your character is falling over while getting dressed, he or she has already gotten out of bed. Look over your plan for your squares, and make sure that each square shows only one action.

Step 4: Creating a Storyboard

Now that you have a main idea for each square, you will need to create a storyboard for your comic strip. A storyboard is like a rough draft of your comic strip. Your goal is to figure out the pictures and words that will best represent the main idea you have chosen for each square. Your storyboard doesn't have to be fancy; you can use stick figures and very basic sketches. Next to each square, you can write any conversation that will be in the final draft.

Before you get started, you may want to think a little about the conversations your characters will have. It's important to remember that we read comic books from left to right, just as we read regular books. If you have more than one character speaking in the same square, make sure the character who speaks first is on the left side of the square as you look at the page. This will make it easier for you to arrange the conversation in the square in a logical way.

You may also want to practice arranging figures, objects, and words in a square before you create your storyboard. If so, you can practice online at the site Comic Creator (**http://www.readwritethink.org/materials/comic/index.html**). This Web site allows you to choose people, animals, conversation bubbles, props, and captions to create an online comic strip. The Garfield Comic Creator site (**http://www.nhlbi.nih.gov/health/public/sleep/starslp/missionz/comic.htm**) is also useful for practicing. This site allows you to arrange and create your own Garfield comic strips. When you have finished creating your online comic, you can print it out or clear it and start over. Here's an

(*Continued*)

example of how you might create a storyboard for the comic strip on oversleeping. Let's imagine that you chose a superhero for the main character. The storyboard might look like this:

1. **Square one:** A girl lies in bed. Next to her is a table with an alarm clock. The clock reads "8:00," and the words "beep, beep, beep" show that it is going off. The girl's hand is hitting the top of the alarm clock. Hanging off her bedpost is an eye mask and a cape with a superhero emblem.

2. **Square two:** A superhero man is standing at the bottom of the stairs in a house. He is wearing a superhero outfit. He has a briefcase in his hand and is looking at his watch. He is yelling up the stairs with his other hand next to his mouth. Next to the square are the words "Wake up! You're going to miss the bus!"

3. **Square three:** Back in the superhero girl's bedroom, she is trying to tie her cape around her neck but is stepping on the hem and falling over at the same time. Behind her, the clock reads "8:35."

4. **Square four:** The superhero man is standing next to the stove in his superhero outfit with an apron around his waist. He is holding out a bowl to the girl superhero, who is literally flying out the door. Next to the square are the words, "Bye, Dad!"

5. **Square five:** The girl superhero is squished between two big, tall boys on the bus. Her wings are all crunched between them.

6. **Square six:** The girl superhero is sitting at her desk. Her cape is crooked. Her wings are still crushed. Her hair is sticking out. Her mouth is turned down. She is surrounded by other children at their desks. At the front of the room, the teacher is speaking. Next to the square are the words "Good morning, class! I hope everyone is having a great day so far!"

Create sketches for all six squares of your strip. Write **dialogue,** or conversation, for the squares that will have words. Try different pictures for the squares to see which best tell the story you have imagined.

For example, look back at square two. Here the square shows the father yelling, "You're going to miss the bus!" But couldn't we instead show the girl in bed hearing her father's voice? Of course! There are many different ways to tell (or in this case, show!) a story. You just need to find the way that works best for you! And remember, for your storyboard, you can keep your pictures simple. You will want to save your best talent for when you really actually draw your comic strip!

Step 5: Draw Your Strip

How is drawing your comic strip different from creating a storyboard? First, you will want to use your sketchpad or drawing paper instead of your comic strip notebook. Each square will show more detail than the squares of your storyboard, so you will want to make the squares as large as they can be while still fitting all of the boxes on one page. Depending on the shape of your pad, you may want to turn your paper sideways so that you will have plenty of room. The squares should all be about the same size and an equal width apart. Once you have a little more practice in creating comics, you may want to try different arrangements of squares or different sizes of squares in the same comic strip.

Using your storyboard as a guide, begin to draw pictures in your squares. If you have never drawn comics before, you may want to check out these Web sites for some drawing tips.

- Draw and Color with Uncle Fred
  http://www.unclefred.com/index.html
  This Web site will show you, step by step, how to draw some cool but very simple cartoon characters. You can do a lot with a few lines, circles, and squares!

- Cartooning with Blitz, Cartooning Tips
  http://www.bruceblitz.com
  This Web site shows easy ways to draw cartoon faces that express cartoonish feelings. Use the drop-down menu to see tips from past dates.

Books like the ones here may also be useful. You can ask your school librarian or public librarian where to find these and other books about drawing comic strips.

- *Cartooning for Kids* by Mike Artell (Sterling, 2002)
  ISBN: 140270111X
  This book says you don't have to be a great artist to be a good cartoonist; you just have to learn how to think and draw funny things. The book provides instruction on how to draw a bunch of cartoon animals and people, as well as explanations about why each cartoon is funny.

- *Cartooning for the Beginner* by Christopher Hart (Watson-Guptill Publications, 2000)
  ISBN: 0823005860
  This book is good for beginning comic strip artists of all ages. It provides information about drawing cartoon heads, facial expressions, and bodies, as well as instructions on drawing cartoon animals and other objects. It also points out ten common mistakes that new comic strip artists often make and offers advice on how to avoid them.

As you create your strip, work in pencil and draw lightly. Don't worry if it looks messy; you will erase all the pencil lines later anyway. Add detail and facial expressions. Let your imagination guide you as you create this new world! Remember, if you have conversation in a strip, you will need to leave room around (usually above) your characters for the words.

Once you have drawn the pictures for each square, figure out where you want the words to go. Then take a ruler and lightly draw lines on which to write your dialogue. This will keep your letters straight. Write the words neatly with a sharp pencil, remembering that the first thing that is said must be on the left. It should also be higher in the square (or at the same height) as what the second character says. Once you have

(*Continued*)

written out all the words, you can draw a conversation bubble around the lettering. Never draw the bubble first; you may not leave enough room for all your words!

Step 6: Ink or Color Your Strip

The final step in creating your comic strip is to go over your pencil lines with ink and, if you want, to add color. You may decide that you like your comic strip better in black and white, and that's okay, too.

To ink your strip, take one of your black pens—gel pens work well—and go over the final pencil lines of your strip. Ink all the dialogue in your comic, too. Once the ink is dry, use a soft eraser to remove the pencil lines beneath.

To add color, use your judgment and your imagination! You may want to work with colored pencils, watercolor paints, pastels, or other supplies. Experiment in order to figure out which drawing materials are most comfortable for you. Books about drawing comics, such as those listed earlier, may provide information about inking and coloring as well.

Launching Your Results

Congratulations! If you have completed this project, you have learned a little about comic strips and created one of your own. Now you just need to share your results with others. One option is to enter a comic strip contest such as the one listed here.

- The Amazing Kids! Comic Strip Drawing Contest!
  http://www.amazing-kids.org/comicscontest.html#top1
  This annual contest has divisions for several age levels, including one for kids aged eight to eleven. The grand prize is a $1,000 scholarship from the popular cartoon Web site **Toonville.com** and a chance to learn from a professional cartoonist. Plus, if you win, your comic strip will be featured on the Amazing Kids! Web site. Click this link for contest contact information: http://www.amazing-kids.org/contactus.html.

Another option is to create a **small-press comic,** a comic book that you put together yourself. If you have a photocopy machine at school, you may be able to draw your comic book and then make copies for your school library and your classmates. Many well-known cartoonists have gotten started by creating small-press comics— including Jeff Smith, who wrote *Out from Boneville* and its sequels.

You may also want to check with your school newspaper to see whether you can publish your comics there. Maybe they need a cartoonist to create an ongoing comic strip! A regular comic strip would give you an opportunity to develop your cartooning skills while sharing with others.

Local papers may also offer opportunities to publish your comic strip. Click on your state in the directory of U.S. newspapers at http://dir.yahoo.com/news_and_media/ newspapers/by_region/u_s__states/, and then select the "Complete List" link to view a list of all the major newspapers in your state. Just remember, like all artistic adventures, publishing your comics may take persistence. Don't give up! In the meantime, if you enjoyed this project, keep drawing comics. You may be amazed at what you can create with a little time and lots of practice!

Would you like to take a comic strip field trip? Here are some museums entirely dedicated to comics and cartooning:

- Charles M. Schulz Museum

  http://www.charlesmschulzmuseum.org/home.html

  This museum in Santa Rosa, California, is all about the famous creator of the Peanuts comic strip. Here you can see Snoopy and his friends as they changed over time. For more active learning, you can also walk through an outdoor Snoopy-shaped labyrinth and visit an education room with drawing materials, activity sheets, and books about drawing cartoons.

- Museum of Comic and Cartoon Art

  http://www.moccany.org

  Did you know that comic books were first created in the United States? This New York museum focuses on the history of comic art and its importance in our nation's history. You can see exhibits of comic book heroes, such as the X-Men, and also more serious comics about world events.

- Cartoon Art Museum

  http://www.cartoonart.org/

  This museum in San Francisco has exhibits about current comic artists as well as famous artists of the past. Here you might find a special exhibit on one talented artist, a focus on small-press publishing, or information about graphic novels that are seen as literature.

Treasure Chest of Tools

- How to Draw Cartoons

  http://www.how-to-draw-cartoons-online.com/

- Learn How to Draw Cartoons

  http://www.teachmecartoons.com/

- Cartooning for Kids

  http://www.cdli.ca/CITE/cartooning.htm

6

Design a City of
the Future

Design a City of the Future

Can you imagine how people lived one hundred years ago? Would you be surprised to learn that people did not have the luxuries of cars, televisions, computers, or fast-food restaurants? People who lived in the past experienced a different life than people of today. Knowing that the world changes with each passing year, stop for a moment and think about how our world will change in the future. What will change, and will those changes improve or make problems for our world? No one can be quite sure, but if people are trained on how to solve problems, our future can be improved.

- Future City Painting

  http://davidszondy.com/future/city/futurecity.htm

  Take a look at Frank R. Paul's painting of his vision of the future, and scan the contents of the Web site as it illustrates views of the future from different time periods.

  Have you ever traveled to a city? Think about what you see and hear in a city. Do you hear traffic? How about sirens and wind?

Cities are different than towns because more people live in cities. Very big buildings, known as **skyscrapers,** were created to provide more space for city dwellers. Space was found when architects discovered that the best way to have large numbers of people live and work in limited areas was to build up into the air. Do you know any cities that have skyscrapers? The most densely populated cities in America are New York, Los Angeles, and Chicago. The first skyscraper was built in 1885 in Chicago and was named the Home Insurance Building. Often, people see large skyscrapers and busy streets and this becomes the definition of a city, but there are many other important features of a city.

This project is about how you can plan a city of the future, and it requires imaginative and productive thinking. Persons who plan cities are called **city planners,** and they know that there are no wrong answers, just careful planning.

Charting Your Course

Do you know what it takes to plan and build a new city? This section will explain some unique features of cities that are important to consider when designing a city. Cities have a large concentration of persons from different cultures in one place. A person's **culture** refers to their traditions, holidays, country of origin, and other beliefs and customs. Persons from many cultures live in cities because housing is affordable and jobs are more plentiful in cities. This mix of cultures results in a culturally diverse city. If you were to travel to a big city, you might notice a variety of houses of worship as well as culturally diverse restaurants and grocery stores that are different from those you find in rural or suburban areas. In addition, cities are places where the arts can grow! In cities, you may see art museums, city libraries, symphony halls, and opera halls in addition to sports arenas, parks, numerous fire stations, cemeteries, courts, hotels, and hospitals. All of these services are close to each other and help to provide a variety of services

(*Continued*)

to the people who live in a city. Opportunities for work and this mix of services are the reasons that masses of people live in cities. These factors are also what makes cities crowded and what makes each city unique.

Cities require special laws so people can live in peace. For example, Salt Lake City in Utah adopted a liquor policy that reduces the number of places where alcoholic beverages can be purchased. Many cities have adopted laws making it illegal to use a cell phone while driving. These types of laws were enforced to protect the people who live in a city. Some laws are not as clear. For example, in Hartford, Connecticut, a law says that people may not educate dogs. In Anniston, Alabama, it is a law that people may not wear blue jeans on Noble Street. Isn't that amazing? Finally, in Cape Coral, Florida, it is unlawful to hang clothes on a clothesline outside. Considering some of these laws, what laws do you want for your city? You might want to jot a few ideas down to get yourself started in thinking about it.

Transportation needs are very important in a city, as well. Many people do not use cars in large cities because parking is difficult and expensive and because too many cars cause slow traffic. People have worked to create easier ways to get around cities, such as *subways*—trains that run underground. It helps to have trains underground so that they take up less space in the city. Thirteen major cities in America have subway systems that are both cheap and convenient to ride, and most cities have public bus systems. Railroads were also developed to help people travel greater distances than they can on subways. Finally, airports were built in the largest cities in the world. Airports help to transport people, packages, and goods quickly and efficiently. All of these forms of transportation are important in helping the city function well. What types of public transportation have you used? What kind would you like to try?

Exploration

Planning your city will be easier with the help of a few good Web sites:

- Building the Windy City
  http://library.thinkquest.org/J002846/
  Take a virtual field trip to see unique buildings and learn about people who make Chicago a great place to live and to visit.

- What Is a City Planner?
  http://www.planning.org/kidsandcommunity/whatisplanning/Default.htm
  Read about two people's experiences that helped them become city planners and what each person's job requires.

- City Creator
  http://www.citycreator.com/
  Try your hand at designing a city of dreams. Pick a city theme, buildings, streets, and even people to make a city you can call your own! This is a great place to spend some time understanding the elements of city design. City Creator allows you to suggest your own city theme for future consideration.

Launching Your Results

Are you ready to begin designing your own city? Remember that many cities have problems with transportation, and new cities have to be planned carefully to avoid these transportation problems. Consider the forms of transportation to use for this project and the types of people you hope will live in your city. If you want to have a diverse culture, a variety of exciting restaurants and other gathering places should be included in your city. Finally, once your city is designed, you may want to create some laws that are unique to your city. Remember that laws are meant to help people live their lives better and more safely.

Consider three possibilities for designing your city: ask your teacher whether you can (1) use a bulletin board to create a mural of your city, (2) use clay or other materials to create a city by hand, or (3) use a computer animation program—for example, something like City Creator—to create a city. When you are finished designing, check to be sure that your city will attract a variety of people and that there will be a wide choice of transportation.

Someday, you may have the opportunity to design a real city. It is a difficult job, but I know you can do it!

Treasure Chest of Tools

- *City: A Story of Roman Planning and Construction* by David Macaulay (Sandpiper, 1983)
  ISBN: 0395349222
  City describes the planning and building of an imaginary Roman city.

- *The Supernaturalist* by Eoin Colfer (Hyperion 2004])
  ISBN: 0786851481
  A futuristic adventure about an orphan.

- *The Girl Who Owned a City* by O.T. Nelson (Laurel Leaf, 1977)
  ISBN: 0440928931
  When a plague kills all of the adults, the children must rebuild a new way of life.

- *Crispin: The Cross of Lead* by Avi (Hyperion, 2004)
  ISBN: 0786816589
  A historical fiction tale of a boy's journey across England.

Create an Illustrated Book

Create an Illustrated Book

Think back to when you were a very small child. Did you have a parent, teacher, brother, or sister who occasionally read out loud to you? Did you enjoy the experience? What do you remember about it? The stories? The soothing sound of the reader's voice? Certain pictures from your favorite books?

If you said that you still remember some of your favorite illustrations, you wouldn't be alone. Human beings are programmed to notice and store visual stimuli—and for good reason. Think about it: if we weren't capable of remembering the appearance of poisonous plants, dangerous animals, and edible fruits and vegetables, we wouldn't have survived as a species.

Illustrations aren't a matter of life or death, or course, but their bright colors and often emotional or energetic content make them stand out in our memory. If you're like many people, you may be able to remember certain illustrations from childhood in great detail, even if you haven't seen them in many years.

Would you be interested in revisiting some of your special childhood images? Would you like to create some illustrations of your own? If so, you can track down some favorite picture books from childhood. You can examine them to see if they're still appealing to you today. You can learn about famous children's book illustrators and become acquainted with their broad range of styles and techniques. Finally, you can create and illustrate a book yourself, using your own style, talent, and imagination to express a favorite or original story. Does this sound appealing? If so, read on!

Charting Your Course

Take a Trip Down Memory Lane

Are you ready to have some fun? Grab a notebook and a pen, find a comfortable chair, and then close your eyes and think about books and reading. Was there a special picture book that you read again and again as a child? Was there a series of illustrated books (with or without words) that you particularly enjoyed? Did you inherit any favorite illustrated books from parents, grandparents, or neighbors?

Are you having trouble remembering? Try picturing the environments in which you encountered books as a child. Did you go to a story hour at a local library or bookstore? Which books were read to you there? Did your parents or guardians read to you before bed? What stories saw you off to sleep?

Once you start remembering books, write down as many as you can recall in your notebook. Try to capture not just the well-known books—such as *Where the Wild Things Are* by Maurice Sendak or *Goodnight Moon,* written by Margaret Wise Brown and illustrated by Clement Hurd—but also the obscure or little-known books that may have seemed like your own special secrets.

How do you feel when you think about these books and their illustrations? Did some pictures scare you? Did some comfort you? Did some images seem dreamlike and

(Continued)

fantastic? Take notes in your notebook about any specific memories, emotions, and associations. You may want to try to evoke, or call up, similar emotions when you illustrate your own book. If so, you can refer to your list for books that may demonstrate the emotion in question.

Now that you have a list, it's time to do a little detective work. Take your notebook to your school or local library. How many of your books can you find? Bring the ones you locate to a quiet corner of the library, or better yet, check them out so you can examine them at your leisure. Then read! (Or look, if your books don't have words.)

Are these books still vibrant and entertaining? Do the illustrations still amuse or captivate you? Take particular note of those that do. You may want to put a star or some other reminder next to these titles in your notebook. This way, you can return to them if you need guidance in illustrating your book. You may also find it useful to record specific observations about the illustrations or the interaction of the illustrations and the words.

If you don't find many of the books on your list at the library, try a local bookstore. Most bookstores offer comfortable spaces where customers can spend some time reading or examining books before they buy them. Bring your notebook, and record your observations right in the store. You may also want to look online at Amazon.com (**www.amazon .com**) or another online bookstore. Some of these stores enable publishers to upload portions of books, which means that you can read several pages or view an illustration or two from a remembered favorite.

Learn About Famous Illustrators

In addition to reading your favorite authors again, you may want to do some research about illustrators who have been recognized for their craft. The following list provides examples of well-known illustrators who, although very different, have all been successful. Try to look at one or two of the books listed for each author, and take notes as you go. Record details of style, subject matter, color, and composition that particularly stand out for you. What do you like or dislike? How do the words and pictures work together? How do illustrations provide information that is not explicitly offered in the texts? How do different illustrators convey emotions and ideas? These are some of the questions you may want to keep in mind as you explore.

Quentin Blake

- *The BFG,* written by Roald Dahl, illustrated by Quentin Blake (Puffin Books, 1998) ISBN: 0141301058
  Quentin Blake attributes his unique style to his lack of artistic education. This famous illustrator never even went to art school! He says he particularly enjoyed illustrating *The BFG* (big friendly giant) because communicating the relationship between the BFG and his small human friend, Sophie, was challenging for him. How do you illustrate a relationship? Which illustrations do you think show the relationship between Sophie and the BFG? Which features of the illustrations show how they feel about each other?

- *Clown* by Quentin Blake (Henry Holt & Company, 1998)
  ISBN: 0805059334

  How do you tell a story without words? Look to this fun book to find out. Do the illustrations give enough information to make the story feel whole and complete? Do you feel you know Clown by the end of the book? How did Quentin Blake provide information about Clown's personality solely through illustration?

- *Dirty Beasts,* written by Roald Dahl, illustrated by Quentin Blake (paperback, Puffin Books, 2002)
  ISBN: 0142302279

  How do Quentin Blake's illustrations convey the humor in these silly verses? Does he convey the characters of the different animals? How so, or why not?

R. Gregory Christie

- *Only Passing Through: The Story of Sojourner Truth,* written by Anne Rockwell, illustrated by R. Gregory Christie (Knopf Books for Young Readers, 2000)
  ISBN: 0679891862

  In this gorgeous book, R. Gregory Christie uses color and unique perspectives to create illustrations that are as powerful as their subject matter. How does his style affect your feelings about the story? Do you think he had a reason for exaggerating Sojourner Truth's head, hands, and facial features? If so, what might his reason have been? Could you use a similar technique in your book?

- *The Palm of My Heart: Poetry by African American Children,* edited by Davida Adedjouma, illustrated by Gregory Christie (Lee & Low Books, 1996)
  ISBN: 1880000415

  Gregory Christie won the Coretta Scott King honor award for the illustrations in this book of poetry. What similarities do you see between the pictures in *The Palm of My Heart* and *Only Passing Through?* Did Christie's style change in the time between the publishing of the two books? What do you like or dislike about his style? Do you feel that it conveys emotion? If so, what about the illustrations works this way?

- *Yesterday I Had the Blues,* written by Jeron Ashford Frame, illustrated by Gregory Christie (Tricycle Press, 2003)
  ISBN: 1582460841

  This book is entirely about moods. How do Gregory Christie's illustrations convey the different feelings? How does he use color to reinforce each mood? Are his illustrations effective? Do they make you feel the feelings discussed in the book? How can you use color to convey emotion in your illustrations?

Raúl Colón

- *Roberto Clemente: Pride of the Pittsburgh Pirates,* written by Jonah Winter, illustrated by Raúl Colón (hardcover, Atheneum, 2005)
  ISBN: 0689856431

(*Continued*)

This book beautifully illustrates the life of famous baseball player Roberto Clemente, one of the first young Latino players to dominate the game. Raúl Colón worked with watercolors, colored pencils, and litho pencil to portray Clemente in his native Puerto Rico, as well as in his other natural habitat—on the baseball field.

- *What Is Goodbye?* written by Nikki Grimes, illustrated by Raúl Colón (Hyperion, 2004)
  ISBN: 0786807784
  In this poetic book, Raúl Colon illustrates the feelings of Jesse and Jerilyn, whose older brother has died. Do the pictures add to the deep emotion of the book? How so, or why not? What specific features of the illustrations are effective or ineffective?

- *Pandora,* written by Robert Burleigh, illustrated by Raúl Colón (Silver Whistle, 2002)
  ISBN: 0152021787
  This retelling of the famous myth of Pandora showcases Raúl Colón's strong technique and artistic style. Note Colón's skill with texture and surfaces. How does he depict Pandora's flowing robes, the cracked veneer of an ancient vase, reflections in a marble floor? How do you feel about this style? Are you more or less formal? Do you prefer a greater or lesser degree of realism? What do you like or dislike about these illustrations?

Maira Kalman

- *What Pete Ate from A–Z: Where We Explore the English Alphabet (In Its Entirety) in Which a Certain Dog Devours a Myriad of Items Which He Should Not* by Maira Kalman (Putnam Publishing Group, 2001)
  ISBN: 0399233628
  This book is illustrated in a medium called gouache (pronounced gwash), which is kind of like watercolor, only less transparent. What do you think of gouache? What do you think of Maira Kalman's illustrations?

- *Fireboat: The Heroic Adventures of the John J. Harvey* by Maira Kalman (G. P. Putnam's Sons, 2002)
  ISBN: 0399239537
  How do you illustrate a children's book about frightening real-world problems? This book tells the true story of an old-fashioned fireboat that was used to fight the flames from the terrorist attacks of September 11, 2001. How do you feel about Kalman's illustrations of this difficult topic?

- *Next Stop Grand Central* by Maira Kalman (Putnam Publishing Group, 1999)
  ISBN: 0399229264
  Have you ever been to Grand Central Station in New York City? How about another large train station or even an airport? Have you ever noticed all the people running around trying to catch their trains or planes? Did Maira Kalman capture that hustle and bustle in this colorful book?

Graeme Base

- *Animalia* by Graeme Base (Harry N. Abrams, 1987)
  ISBN: 0810918684

  This beautiful book will walk you through the alphabet animal by animal. See "eight enormous elephants expertly eating Easter eggs," "two tigers taking the 10:20 train to Timbuktu," and more. Every page is packed with illustrations that have one thing in common. No doubt you can figure out what that is!

- *The Worst Band in the Universe* by Graeme Base (Puffin Books, 2001)
  ISBN: 0140565876

  Graeme Base struggled with the illustrations in this book because his original concept—to bring a musical space alien to earth—limited his imagination. After years of work, he cut the portions of the book that dealt with earth so he could focus with freedom on imagining other planets. What does this say about the craft of illustration? How do you like the end result?

- *Discovery of Dragons* by Graeme Base (Harry N. Abrams, 1996)
  ISBN: 0810932377

  In this book, Graeme Base complements elaborate, exotic drawings of dragons with humorous captions. How do the rich illustrations work with the text? Do they mirror or contrast with the tone of the writing?

Exploration

Are you interested in doing some exploring on your own? The American Library Association's Caldecott Medal is a prestigious annual award for children's book illustrators. Visit (http://www.ala.org/ala/alsc/awardsscholarships/literaryawds/caldecottmedal/caldecottmedal.htm) to find information about Caldecott Award–winning illustrators and books from 1938 to the present. You may want to find some of the books and illustrators as the first step in your independent exploration. It may be interesting to give special attention to the works that *don't* appeal to you. You can read the descriptions of the books provided on the Web site and maybe even find some reviews of these works by using a search engine such as Google (www.google.com) or Yahoo! (www.yahoo.com). Reading others' opinions may provide information about the criteria that critics and artists use to judge children's book illustrations. Once you have read more about these books, do you think about these or your favorites differently?

The following Web sites provide another option for independent exploration. Each offers examples of work by well-known illustrators of the past and present. Click through some of the different links just for fun. If you don't like the style of a particular illustrator, move on to another artist. Who knows what wonderful things you may find? Just keep in mind that the purpose of some of these sites is to sell illustrators' work. For this project, remember that you're just window shopping. Many of these illustrations are quite expensive!

(*Continued*)

- Storyopolis

  http://www.storyopolis.com/artistlist.asp

  Storyopolis is a Los Angeles gallery and bookstore dedicated to illustrations. Its Web site provides access to hundreds of full-color illustrations by respected artists. Find a few artists whose illustrations appeal to you and write down their names. Maybe you can take some of their books out of the library.

- Art Passions

  http://www.artpassions.net/

  This Web site focuses on antique fairy-tale illustrations. Click through different artists, taking note of similarities and differences in style. As a group, is their work different from that of more modern illustrators? If so, in what way?

Would you like to learn more about the illustrators themselves? The following sites provide information about the people behind the pictures.

- Hans Christian Andersen Award

  http://www.library.northwestern.edu/exhibits/hca/illustrator.html#berner

  The Hans Christian Andersen Award is awarded every other year to an illustrator whose work has been an important contribution to children's literature. Here you can read biographies of and see book covers by the 2004 nominees for the prize.

- Hans Christian Andersen Collection interviews

  http://www.library.northwestern.edu/exhibits/hca/interviews.html

  Listen to two master illustrators talk about their craft. Maurice Sendak and Quentin Blake discuss inspiration and illustration in two full-length interview clips.

- Houghton Mifflin Authors and Illustrators

  http://www.eduplace.com/kids/hmr/mtai/index.html

  This Web site provides biographies of authors and illustrators. Are any of your favorite illustrators here?

The following book may also be interesting to you. You can look for it at your school library or public library.

- *Ways of Telling: Fourteen Interviews with Masters of the Art of the Picture Book* by Leonard M. Marcus (Dutton Juvenile, 2002)

  ISBN: 0525464905

  Learn about the lives and work of famous illustrators in this interesting book. Each artist discusses his or her process for creating illustrations, as well as how he or she views the art of illustrating. Other topics include the effect of history and politics on art, childhood memories of the artists, and early artistic influences.

Exploring Your Own Talent

So now you know a little bit about illustrations and illustrators. Are you ready to do some work of your own? If so, the following Web sites may help you to get started.

- Page by Page

  http://www.collectionscanada.ca/pagebypage/

  This extremely interesting Web site walks you step by step through the making of two children's books. You may want to pay particular attention to *Zoom Upstream,* the more sophisticated of the two books; the creative processes of the author and the illustrator are described in depth. Spend some extra time on the section called "The Pictures." Here you will find lots of details about how one illustrator works.

- An Illustrator's Guide to Writing and Creating a Picture Book

  http://www.meghan-mccarthy.com/illustratorsguide.html

  There's lots of good technical information here on illustrating a children's book—for example, advice on sketching, page layout, and pacing. You will also find information that may be useful if you want to publish your book once it's finished.

The following books may also interest you. Ask your school librarian or public librarian where to find them or others like them.

- *Writing with Pictures: How to Write and Illustrate Children's Books* by Uri Shulevitz (Watson-Guptill Publications, 1997)

  ISBN: 0823059359

  This is a great book for a beginning illustrator. The author addresses features of children's stories but gives most of his attention to illustrating. Starting with basic ideas, he uses more than six hundred pictures to demonstrate key ideas of the illustrating process.

- *Illustrating Children's Books: Creating Pictures for Publication* by Martin Salisbury (paperback, Barron's Educational Series, 2004)

  ISBN: 0764127179

  Although this book doesn't provide direct drawing instruction, it may give you a useful overview of the illustration process. Tons of illustrations from a variety of picture books demonstrate different ideas and techniques.

Finding a Story

Did you notice on the Page by Page Web site that the making of a children's book starts with an idea and a story? This makes sense, doesn't it? It's hard to illustrate when you don't have any actions or characters to draw!

If you don't enjoy writing, you may want to ask a friend or family member to write a story for you to illustrate; real writers and authors often collaborate in this manner. If you do enjoy writing, go ahead and write your own story. The famous illustrator Maurice Sendak is an example of an artist who often writes his books.

Another option is to rewrite a classic folktale or fairy tale. If you decide to do this, try setting the story in a new environment, such as a different historical period, a distant planet, or an imaginary world. Or you may want to change the main character in some way or add a twist ending. Use your imagination and originality to make the story

(Continued)

your own. The following Web site provides links to some online versions of well-known fairy-tale books. You can choose a story from among the ones you find here or select something else entirely.

- Legends and Fairytales on the Net
  http://www.legends.dm.net/fairy/
  Here you will find hundreds of fairy tales and folktales. Explore some of the dark tales by the Brothers Grimm (http://www.freebookstoread.com/grimm10_1.htm); read about the Irish/Scottish seal-people known as Silkies (http://www.sealsitters.org/learning/silkie_lore.html]); check out classics by Hans Christian Andersen (http://hca.gilead.org.il); and more.

Planning and Dreaming

Once you have selected or written your story, you can start thinking about the illustrations. Not sure where to start? Try reading through your story and making notes where you would like to insert pictures. Once you have some ideas, contemplate your illustrations as you go about your daily business—on the bus, in the car, or walking home from school. Carry a pad or notebook with you so you can capture your ideas or images as they occur. You may want to make brief sketches, or you may find that writing a few key words will help you remember your ideas. You may also want to keep a pad and pencil next to your bed. Many artists and writers experience creative ideas in the final moments between waking and sleeping. Think about your illustrations as you prepare for bed. Then, if you become aware of a creative image forming as you drift off to sleep, wake yourself quickly and get it down on paper. Another idea is to take up walking, running, or some other physical activity. Many creative people find that if they stretch their bodies, their minds stretch, too. Repetitive exercises that require little conscious attention are typically best. With your body in "autopilot" mode, your imagination is free to roam. This can be a very fruitful time to do some creative planning.

As you plan, you may want to consult some of the resources you have already explored in this project to see if they can provide insight and inspiration for your illustrations. For example you may now be ready to implement:

- Information from the illustration books you explored
- Technical advice you may have found in illustrators' biographies
- Tips from the Page-by-Page Web site
- Ideas gleaned from books by favorite illustrators
- The notes you took while exploring the work of favorite illustrators

Sketching

You have some great ideas now, but what's the best way to present them on paper? Maybe you're new to drawing and sketching, or maybe you're a talented artist who just wants a little extra instruction. No problem! Now is the time to brush up on—or learn—some drawing basics. Look for these books at your school library or your public library. If they aren't available, a librarian can help you find some other volumes that will be equally useful.

- *Drawing for Dummies* by Brenda Hoddinott (John Wiley & Sons, 2003)
  ISBN: 076455476X

  This basic drawing book, written by a professional illustrator and art instructor, is a great place to start your drawing education. Written for beginners, it covers a broad range of techniques, including shading, adding texture, cartooning, and more. It also provides instruction on both figure drawing and landscape or scenery drawing, making it a good one-stop guide.

- *Drawing for the Artistically Undiscovered* by Quentin Blake, John Cassidy (Klutz, 1999)
  ISBN: 1570543208

  If you're not too sure about your drawing skills or you need a little encouragement or you just like to have fun, this fantastic drawing book is for you! Here you will find lots of friendly advice on drawing and plenty of positive support from famous illustrator Quentin Blake. One note: Blake warns that while the book will help you to draw "properly," its focus is more on capturing the "essence" of things. This is a great attitude for free spirits and even better for people who need to be a little more free-spirited.

- *How to Draw Animals* by Jack Hamm (Perigee Books, 1982)
  ISBN: 0399508023

  This is a nice straightforward book for beginning artists. Tons of illustrations, diagrams, and instructions cover the basics of drawing animals, including dogs, bears, giraffes, monkeys, and many more. There's even a section called "Odd and Unusual Animals."

- *Drawing the Head and Figure* by Jack Hamm (paperback, Perigee Books, 1983)
  ISBN: 0399507914

  This book is not a children's drawing book, but the language is direct and simple and the instructions are very clear. In this book, you will find information about drawing faces and bodies, differences in children's faces and adult faces, how to join arms and legs to the body in a natural manner, and much, much more. Hundreds of diagrams and illustrations provide extra guidance.

- *Cartooning the Head and Figure* by Jack Hamm (paperback, Perigee Books, 1982)
  ISBN: 0399508031

  Depending on your style, you may find this book more helpful than a basic book on figure drawing. Useful topics include drawing cartoon faces in four easy steps; drawing cartoons from life; and mastering proportions of cartoon people, which aren't usually true to life. Lots of sketches provide examples.

(*Continued*)

- *Perspective Made Easy* by Ernest Norling (paperback, Dover Publications, 1999)
  ISBN: 0486404730
  This book will teach you, in great detail, how to manage perspective in your art. Learn about figures in perspective, objects in relation to each other, rooftop perspective, and more. More than two-hundred illustrations complement the simple text.

Here are some books that examine drawing in a slightly different manner:

- *Picture This: How Pictures Work* by Molly Bang (Seastar Books, 2000)
  ISBN: 1587170302
  This sophisticated book examines the way images send messages we don't always notice on a conscious level. Using the tale of Little Red Riding Hood as an example, the author shows how illustrations work with a story to create emotions in readers: Why are some types of lines exciting and other types relaxing? Why do certain colors convey particular feelings? You will find a lot of interesting information in this unique book.

- *The New Drawing on the Right Side of the Brain* by Betty Edwards (Putnam Publishing Group, 1999)
  ISBN: 0874774241
  This fascinating book uses information about the brain to teach you to draw more accurately. Learn techniques for seeing the world like an artist, accessing your creativity, and thinking about the world in a different way. There's a workbook that goes along with the book to help you practice your new skills. It may be a useful complement to the text, but it's probably not necessary.

As you sketch rough drafts of your illustrations, you will want to keep some practical details in mind—for example,

- Do you want to faithfully reproduce scenes from the text, or would you like your illustrations to build on the text while adding some new ideas? (For more information about this concept, check the illustration books referenced earlier in the project or other books on the same topic.)
- What size margins do you need? How will you frame your illustrations so that all of the margins are the same?
- Where will the words of your story go? On pages opposite the illustrations? On the same page as your illustrations?
- If you plan to have words and illustrations on the same page, how will you arrange the content? Will the words be at the top of the page? At the bottom? To the side of the illustrations?
- Will any illustrations take up more than one page? If so, how will you create your illustrations to accommodate the binding of the book (which will run down the center)?
- How many illustrations do you want to do? What is a practical number? How many do you need to accomplish your goals for your book?

Creating Your Illustrations

Once you have sketches to work from, you may be ready to create your illustrations. For this part of the project, you will have to choose which medium you will work in. Do you want to use watercolors? Acrylic paint? Black pencil? Oils? Talk to your art teacher at school about the benefits and drawbacks of different mediums. Look back at the professional illustrations you like best. Are they in color? Black and white? Are they pale and dreamy, or are they bright and bold? Select your medium based on what is practical for a new illustrator, what is available to you at school or at home, and what appeals to you visually. You can also refer to the following books (or others like them) to get an idea about how particular mediums work and what effects they produce.

- *The Acrylics and Gouache Artist's Handbook* by Sally Harper (Barron's Educational Series, 2003)
  ISBN: 0764156217

  Acrylics are often used by beginners because they're inexpensive, easy to use, and versatile. Gouache is a traditional medium of illustrators. This book provides information about both mediums, including how to mix colors, fix mistakes, produce particular effects, and choose tools. More than four hundred illustrations provide examples and brighten the text.

- *The Beginner's Guide to Oil Painting: A Complete Step-by-Step Guide to Techniques and Materials* by Angela Gair (Sterling Publishing, 1998)
  ISBN: 1853686026

  Oil paint is often considered a difficult medium to master, but you may want to experiment if you have tried other mediums—or even if you haven't. What some find difficult others find comfortable and inspiring! This book may help you choose reasonably priced materials, develop technique, and explore different styles. It also provides lots of examples of oil paintings by beginners.

- *Watercolor Basics: Shape and Light Value* by Chinkok Tan (North Light Books, 2001)
  ISBN: 1581800436

  The author of this book states with "absolute certainty" that anyone can learn to paint. This is the perfect attitude! Learn what tools you'll need to start painting with watercolors, beginning techniques, and what to avoid when using watercolors. Beautiful illustrations complement the text.

- *All About Techniques in Pastel* by Parramon's Editorial Team (Barron's Educational Series, 1998)
  ISBN: 0764151053

  This big book provides tons of information about getting started with pastels. Learn about beginning techniques; how to represent particular subjects (for example, buildings, skies, water, or people); how to choose colors; and more.

(*Continued*)

- *Colored Pencil for the Serious Beginner* by Bet Borgeson (Watson-Guptill Publications, 1998)
  ISBN: 0823007618
  Colored pencils are inexpensive and relatively mess-free. In this book, find out how to use them to your best advantage. Topics include materials needed to work with colored pencils, beginning instruction on drawing forms, and how to draw from life and photographs.

- *You Can Sketch: A Step by Step Guide for Absolute Beginners* by Jackie Simmonds (Watson-Guptill Publications, 2002)
  ISBN: 0823059928
  Maybe you prefer black and white to color. That's fine! This book offers information about drawing with pencil and charcoal as well as colored pencils and pastels. Individual lessons show how to sketch people, animals, buildings, landscapes, and seascapes. You can also learn how to combine mediums to create a unique finished product.

In addition to traditional mediums, some professional illustrators now use software programs to create their art. If this sounds interesting to you, use a search engine and key words such as "illustrating software" or "software illustrators" to find more information about the topic. Once you have an idea of the types of programs that exist, you can ask your school computer teacher or information technology teacher if the school owns a suitable program. Make sure to explain your project when you ask so that he or she can decide how best to help you. And remember that enthusiasm is contagious! In this instance, sharing your excitement and commitment may encourage your teacher to explore unique solutions even if the school doesn't own the software you need.

Whichever medium you select, don't be afraid to experiment and make mistakes. Use the illustration and art books as guides to develop your process. Will you first draw on tracing paper and then transfer the image? Will you paint directly on your art paper without sketching at all? The following Web site provides information about one illustrator's drawing and painting process. This may or may not be a process that works with your medium and style, but it should give you some insight into the types of questions you may want to ask as you teach yourself the art of illustration. Besides, it's fun to see how one artist works!

- Drawing Step-by-Step
  http://www.geocities.com/~teddarnold/drawing.html
  See how illustrator Tedd Arnold transforms a simple sketch into a colorful finished illustration.

As questions emerge during this stage of your project, talk to your classroom teacher, an enrichment or resource teacher, an art teacher, or a helpful person at a craft store. Refer to the books and Web sites you have previously explored. You may need to create the same illustration several—or even many—times before you are satisfied with your results. This is fine. Professional illustrators often spend a year or more on one book! While you may not want to take that much time, you should work at a comfortable pace. If this means working slowly and painstakingly, no problem! If you prefer to work briskly and without too much rumination (thought), go ahead; some illustrators find that speed frees their minds. Remember, this is your project. Your work style should suit your skills and preferences.

Binding Your Book

So now you have a story and a stack of illustrations and you just need to put them together into a book. Good for you! You have a few options at this stage, depending on the resources available and your aesthetic sense (your idea of what is attractive and visually engaging). If possible, it would be a good idea to create your book from reproductions of your originals. What does this mean? Ideally, you can use a color copier to duplicate your illustrations or you can scan them into a computer to create digital images.

Duplicating has several advantages. First, if you use copies of your illustrations in your book, you can store your precious originals (which may be worth millions one day if you become a famous illustrator!) in such a way that they will be safe and protected. Using duplicates may also make it easier to join your text and your illustrations. If you can copy or scan the illustrations onto good quality typing paper or computer paper, you can use a typewriter or word-processing program to create the text on the same type of paper.

If you choose to put text and illustrations on the same page, you will have other considerations, but duplication may still be the easiest course of action. Scanning may allow you to insert text boxes into the digital images of your illustrations. If so, you could then type your text right onto the image. If you photocopy your illustrations, you could first type or write your text on sheets of clear tracing paper, cut around the text, and then attach the tracing paper to your illustration with clear glue (you may have to experiment to see what works best). When you copy the original with the tracing paper attached, your text should be printed on the image.

If you can't create your book from copies, don't worry! You can always bind your original illustrations. While this would make reproducing the book more difficult, it may also make it more special. This book will be totally unique! Plus, there is something inherently compelling about original pieces of art. Copies just can't convey all the tiny details that make original paintings and drawings so beautiful.

Whether you use copies or originals, you will have to decide how best to bind your work. You can choose a simple method such as hole-punching the pages and tying them with ribbon, twine, or yarn, or you can choose a more complicated binding process. If you choose a more complex technique, you may want to consult one of the following books or another volume about bookbinding.

- *Cover to Cover: Creative Techniques for Making Beautiful Books, Journals and Albums* by Shereen LaPlantz (Sterling Publishing, 1998) ISBN: 0937274879

(Continued)

This amazing book provides detailed instructions and almost two hundred photos to help you bind your book. Learn about bookbinding materials and traditional and more creative methods of bookbinding. This book is good for beginning bookbinders as well as those who have already experimented with this art form.

- *The Essential Guide to Making Handmade Books* by Gabrielle Fox (North Light Books, 2000)
  ISBN: 1581800193
  Here you will find detailed information about bookbinding tools, formats, and techniques. Eleven projects walk you step by step through different bookbinding processes. Gabrielle Fox, the author, holds a degree in fine bookbinding.

Launching Your Results: Sharing Your Book

Congratulations! If you have researched, planned, illustrated, and bound your book, you are to be commended! Now you just need to share your results. One option is to give a copy to your school librarian and another to your classroom teacher. If your book is geared toward younger children, you could give a copy to one or more classroom teachers in the lower grades of your school. This way, many children could enjoy your efforts over the coming years. You could even make many copies and distribute one to each of the schools in your district. Why not take one to your local public library as well?

You may also want to share your illustrating talent by entering a contest. Here are some contests that may interest you:

- The Society of Children's Book Writers and Illustrators
  http://www.scbwi.org/index.htm
  The Society of Children's Book Writers and Illustrators hosts contests periodically throughout the year. Visit http://www.scbwi.org/contest.htm to go to the contest page. Check it regularly to see if whether there's an upcoming contest that appeals to you. You may also want to visit the society's home page via (by way of) the link shown earlier. Here you will find featured illustrators, writing prompts, and a calendar of events of interest for writers and illustrators.

- The Scholastic Art and Writing Awards
  http://www.scholastic.com/artandwritingawards/enter.htm
  These awards are open to students in grades 7–12. Your book would qualify as a mixed media entry. Prizes include cash, scholarships, and publishing opportunities.

Online or print magazines may also accept some of your illustrations—although you will probably have to submit them individually (without the text), which may or may not be of interest to you. The following publications accept student art submissions.

- The ChildArt Magazine
  http://www.icaf.org/resources/magazine/Magazine.htm

This cool journal was created to inspire creativity in learners of all ages and from all countries. You can submit artwork or writing geared to kids ages eight to twelve via e-mail. Just make sure to check out the submission guidelines on the Web page.

- Kidsonlinemagazine.com
  http://www.kidsonlinemagazine.com/index.html
  This e-zine is a great place to start the process of submitting your work to different publications, because every artist who submits will have his or her work placed somewhere on the Web site. Go to http://www.kidsonlinemagazine.com/submitartwork.html to obtain submission guidelines and information about how to send your work electronically.

Treasure Chest of Tools

If you have enjoyed this project, you may want to take a field trip to learn more about illustration. The following museums may be of interest to you.

- The National Center for Children's Illustrated Literature
  http://www.nccil.org/visiting.html
  This museum in Abilene, Texas, has rotating illustration exhibits and regularly scheduled art activities for young people. Admission to the museum and most of its events are free. Visit http://www.nccil.org/meet_artists.html for information about past, present, and future exhibits.

- The Society of Illustrators Museum of American Illustration
  http://www.societyillustrators.org/index.cms
  Located in New York City, this gallery and museum is dedicated to illustration of all types. Contact information is listed at http://www.societyillustrators.org/info.html, while information about exhibits can be found at http://www.societyillustrators.org/exhibition_competition/schedule.html.

- The Eric Carle Museum of Picture Book Art
  http://www.picturebookart.org/
  This museum in Amherst, Massachusetts, was the first in the United States dedicated to international children's book illustrations. Here you will find three galleries of rotating exhibits, a hands-on studio, a library for reading and storytelling, and an auditorium for lectures and performances.

8 Invent Something New

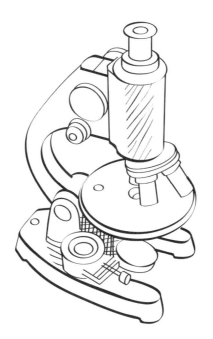

Invent Something New

Do you have what it takes to become a famous inventor? Some of the most creative thinkers in the modern world were inventors of gadgets and tools that improved peoples' daily lives. This type of person is not afraid to reach for the stars and try new ideas and new ways of thinking.

When you see a problem, do you sometimes think of your own means of solving it? That's what inventing is all about! An **invention** is something that no one ever thought of before. It is also something that solves a problem. It may be completely new, or it may be an improvement on something that has already been invented.

Almost everything you use on a daily basis is the result of an invention. Take a moment to think about different items you use each day—for example, pens, notebooks, backpacks, mirrors, white boards, computers, telephones! You might even be thinking of other things. Are there other items whose history you wonder about? When and where did these inventions take place? This project will give you an opportunity to find answers to these questions by conducting research on the Web and in nonfiction books. It will also give you a chance to reflect on the patterns of inventions over time. What current inventions are making news? What inventions have we not even dreamed about? Do you have what it takes to predict trends?

Inventions that stand the test of time are true marvels to study more closely. Do you know any inventions that were created before the twentieth century? Did you know that screwdrivers were invented in the fifteenth century? In 1564, pencils were invented! The first eyeglasses were invented around 1270. But before those great moments in time, marshmallows were invented! Over three thousand years ago, the Egyptians used a plant sugar found in marshes to create marshmallows. It sounds exciting to invent things like candy! What types of inventions would be exciting for you to create?

An inventor is a combination of scientist and dreamer. Be an inventor—dream, play with ideas, take gadgets apart, build some unusual contraptions, and have fun!

You might be interested in reading one of the following fiction books to whet your creative appetite. Take a look in your local library to see whether you can find them.

- *Ben and Me* by Robert Lawson (Little, Brown Young Readers, 1988)
  ISBN: 0316517305
  Benjamin Franklin's companion, Amos the mouse, recounts how he was responsible for Franklin's inventions and discoveries.

- *The Time Machine* by H. G. Wells (Tor, 1992)
  ISBN: 0812505042
  A scientist invents a time machine and uses it to travel to the year 802,701 A.D., where he discovers the childlike Eloi and the hideous underground Morlocks.

Charting Your Course

To become an inventor, you must learn to let your mind wander creatively and think about many possible solutions to each problem you meet. Sometimes the best ideas

(Continued)

come when you think of as many ideas as you can or when you think of unusual or strange ideas that seem impossible or even funny at first.

Inventors are problem solvers, so learn to look at problems in new ways. Try to see lots of possibilities for using any object. Try to visualize pictures in your mind, and look for ideas you can improve on. Try to combine objects or ideas in a new way or for a new purpose.

To create an invention, you will have to find a problem to solve. Start by making a list of all the problems you believe can be solved with an invention. Take a piece of paper, and get started with your list. Think of lots of ideas. Look for a variety of possibilities, and be unusual. Feel free to add details and encourage yourself to look for wild and different ideas. Give yourself plenty of time to think of and list your ideas.

When your list is finished, reread it and revisit each item. Have you thought of problems from many different contexts? Think about items you use at home, items you use at school, communication troubles, environmental problems, governmental problems, societal problems, and toy problems. Think hard, and keep writing different ideas on your list.

Add to your list by conducting a survey. In your survey, you can ask other people what bugs them or what doesn't work the way they think it should. After a few surveys, your list should be complete.

Exploration

From your list, identify a few problems that you would be interested in trying to solve. To help you figure out the best way to find a solution to the problem, you might try using a brainstorming tool that people use to help them think of a variety of solutions. One tool for brainstorming is called SCAMPER, which is an acronym. Do you know what an acronym is? It means that each letter in the word stands for the first letter of another word or part of a word. One famous acronym you might know is DNA. DNA stands for **d**eoxyribo**n**ucleic **a**cid, but DNA is much simpler to pronounce in its shortened form, and that is why the acronym DNA is used more frequently. Another popular acronym is TV, which, as you know, stands for **te**le**v**ision. SCAMPER stands for **s**ubstitute, **c**ombine, **a**dapt, **m**odify/magnify/minify, **p**ut to other uses, **e**liminate, **r**everse/rearrange. Take a look at the following Web site to learn how to use SCAMPER to help you create good ideas.

- SCAMPER Training
  http://www.brainstorming.co.uk/tutorials/scampertutorial.html
  Learn how to use this brainstorming technique to come up with a variety of unique ideas.
  Use the directions in the Web site to learn the important questions to ask yourself when brainstorming for each category. After you go through the SCAMPER process with each idea you are considering for an invention, begin narrowing down to just one or two ideas that you really like.

Ask yourself the following questions:

1. Will my invention idea solve a problem?
2. Is it something no one has ever thought of before?
3. Is this idea a new invention and not found in a store or a book?
4. Is it an improvement on something that has already been invented?
5. Is it something that someone will find useful?
6. Will I enjoy working on it?

You can probably think of some other questions to ask yourself. If you answered yes to the questions on the list, then you are ready to make your final pick and begin creating your invention! If you answered no, go back to your original list of ideas and try SCAMPER until you come up with a new and better idea for an invention.

Keeping a Log

It is very important to keep a record of your work. You can do that by keeping a log, which is a record that you keep as you work. In your log, you can record your ideas and inspirations. Your log can prove that you were the first person to have the idea, and it can help you plan your invention. It becomes an official record of the progress of your invention.

Describe all your ideas in your log, and tell how you went about exploring them. Make drawings of your ideas. Date your notes every time you work. When you have finished a page in your log, have a parent or friend date it and sign it in order to verify that the work and ideas are your own.

Your complete inventor's log becomes important evidence that shows when you first got your idea and that you worked hard on it. This evidence may help you if you decide someday to apply for a patent. A **patent** is the way the government protects inventors. It says that no one else is permitted to manufacture or sell a certain invention but the person who has the patent.

Remember the questions you asked yourself when you were choosing what to invent? Your reasons for choosing a particular idea should go into your log, along with the date. You can record information about your ideas in any way you choose, but you should include the following information: your name, grade, and school; the date of your entry, the time, and place; your idea, reasons you chose the idea, and a drawing of the idea; and a witness signature, along with the date, time, and place.

Now the work begins! Before you start, make a plan so your work will be easier. A written plan takes some time, but it will help you think through your idea before you begin and may save you trouble along the way.

Begin your plan on a new page in your log. There are four parts of your plan that you should record.

Part 1: General Information

Describe in one or two sentences what you intend to invent. Don't worry if you don't have a name for your invention yet. Also, make drawings of how your invention will look and work. Label your drawings clearly.

(Continued)

Part 2: Materials

List all the things you think you will need to build your invention. Make sure you include everything, even things like glue and staples. If you don't know the name of something, draw a picture of it.

Part 3: Steps to Follow

In sequential order, list all the steps you will need to do to complete your invention. Close your eyes, and picture how you will begin. Write that down. Then picture the second step, and write that down. Continue with this procedure until you have completed your invention in your mind and on paper. You can include drawings here, too. This step may take several pages in your log.

Part 4: Possible Problems

List some of the problems you think you might have with this project. All inventors run into problems. Trying to think of some of the problems ahead of time may keep them from happening when you begin to make your invention.

Creating Your Invention

Now the building begins! Make sure you have all the materials on your list before you begin. This preparation will save you time. Find a place to work where you are sure that you can leave your project and materials. It may be a good idea to create your invention at home, because it may take you a while to finish and you don't want to lose any important pieces.

Follow the steps you listed in Part 3 of your plan. If you add or change any steps, be sure to record the changes in your log. As you work, also write down any problems you meet and how you solve them.

While you are working, you may find it easier to tape-record your thoughts than write them down. If you do, you can play the tape back later and write your thoughts down in your log.

Naming Your Invention

What will you call your invention? It deserves a great name. There are many kinds of names:

- A name such as *hair dryer* can describe what an invention does.
- A name such as *skateboard* can tell what an invention is made of.
- An invention can tell who invented it; for example, the Ferris wheel is named for it inventor, G.W.G. Ferris.
- A name can be funny, as the names of many toys are. Can you think of some examples?

Make a list of your ideas for the name of your invention. Play with words and combinations of words. Ask other people for ideas. Have other people listen to your list, and watch their reactions. The right name is important because it will interest people in your invention and help them understand it.

Launching Your Results: Sharing Your Invention

Can you think of a certain person or people who would benefit from your invention? Try to find out who those people might be. For example, a local community group might really be interested in your invention because it helps solve a problem of the community. Reach out and share your great work!

If you are convinced that your invention is really good, you may want to enter it in a contest. Many schools, communities, and states have contests for young inventors. Take a look at the following Web sites to learn about invention contests.

- Young Inventors Contest

  http://www.nsta.org/programs/craftsman/

  The Young Inventors Awards Program challenges students to use creativity and imagination along with science, technology, and mechanical ability to invent or modify a tool. This competition began in 1996.

- Create Your Own Web Site

  http://www.thinkquest.org/competition

  Click on this link to find information on the competition in which teams of students create a Web site. You can team up with students and teachers across the country to make your Web site a success.

- ExploraVision Awards

  http://inventors.about.com/gi/dynamic/offsite.htm?zi=1/XJ&sdn=inventors&zu=http://www.toshiba.com/tai/exploravision/

  ExploraVision is a competition for all students in grades K–12 attending a school in the United States, Canada, a U.S. territory, or a Department of Defense school. It is designed to encourage students to combine their imagination with their knowledge of science and technology to explore visions of the future.

You might be interested in learning more about inventing and inventions as a result of this project. If that's the case, you might want to look into these summer workshops:

- Camp Invention

  http://inventors.about.com/gi/dynamic/offsite.htm?zi=1/XJ&sdn=inventors&zu=http://www.invent.org/camp_invention/

  Camp Invention is a summer day camp that offers a weeklong enrichment program at elementary schools across the country for children in the second through sixth grades. Search the Web site to find the site nearest you.

- Kids Invent Toys

  http://inventors.about.com/gi/dynamic/offsite.htm?zi=1/XJ&sdn=inventors&zu=http://www.kidsinvent.org/

  This program develops and distributes curriculum for one-week summer camps, after-school programs, and classroom learning that fosters creative thinking, inventing, and entrepreneurial enterprise among elementary and middle school children.

(*Continued*)

The following Web sites will inspire you with stories about many famous inventors and help fuel your creativity.

- Invention Dimension
  http://web.mit.edu/invent/invent-main.html
  Learning about inventions can be fun! Read about the inventor of the week, play games and do puzzles, and use the inventor's handbook to find answers to many questions you might have.

- Become an Inventor
  http://library.thinkquest.org/C006094/
  Become an Inventor is designed to educate visitors in concepts and methods related to finding and solving inventive problems, performing patent searches, and marketing ideas pertaining to inventions.

- Inventions and Their Inventors
  http://library.thinkquest.org/5847/?tqskip1=1
  This Web site is dedicated to the people who have shaped our lives through their inventions. You can read articles, play a game, search time lines for inventions, or even take a quiz. If you have an idea, click on "Share Inventions." Lots of fun!

- Exploring Leonardo da Vinci
  http://www.mos.org/sln/Leonardo/LeoHomePage.html
  This is a comprehensive Web site about Leonardo da Vinci's contributions to society. The four content sections provide information on Leonardo's futuristic inventions, Renaissance techniques for drawing perspective, a biography of the man, and his curious habit of writing in reverse.

- National Inventors Hall of Fame
  http://www.invent.org/hall_of_fame/1_4_0_channels.asp
  Find a topic that interests you, then search within the link for that topic to see the people who made human, economic, and social progress in that area possible.

- Renaissance Inventions
  http://www.twingroves.district96.k12.il.us/Renaissance/University/Inventions/Inventions.html
  Go back in time to learn about seven inventions from around the fifteenth century. Learn about the people and events that led up to the important inventions from long ago.

Treasure Chest of Tools

Take a trip to your local library to pick up a great book and learn more about people and their inventions. The books in the following list are both inspirational and informative.

- *Brainstorm! The Stories of Twenty American Kid Inventors* by Tom Tucker (Farrar, Straus, and Giroux, 1998)
  ISBN: 0374409285
  Tom Tucker reveals some of the amazing inventions of the past and present that have come from young Americans aged eight to nineteen. The achievements of some of the kid inventors gathered here were prominent once but have become obscure over time; others are relatively unknown.

- *Steven Caney's Invention Book* by Steven Caney (Workman Publishing Company, 1985)
  ISBN: 0894800760
  This project book for the would-be inventor offers activities, a list of contraptions in need of invention, and the stories behind thirty-six existing inventions.

- *How to Enter and Win an Invention Contest* by Ed Sobey Enslow Publishers, 1999)
  ISBN: 0766011739
  This book describes the history and process of invention; lists regional inventors' clubs and national invention contests for middle school and high school students, along with entrance rules; and provides ideas for projects.

- *Inventing Stuff* by Ed Sobey (Dale Seymour Publications, 1995)
  ISBN: 0866519378
  Students who use this book will sharpen their critical thinking and problem-solving skills as they learn to ask questions, look for patterns, and keep tinkering with their inventions. Sections include information on inventing backward and finding new uses for things as well as facts about inventors and inventions. Information about invention contests may help youngsters find outlets for their inventions.

- *A Nation of Inventors,* edited by JoAnne Weisman Deitch (History Compass, 2001)
  ISBN: 1579600778
  Shine the light on American inventors and inventions by reading primary documents such as journals, advertisements, newspaper articles, and much more. In addition to historical documents, definitions of unfamiliar terminology, discussion questions, and follow-up activities are included.

- *Nobel Prize Women in Science: Their Lives, Struggles and Momentous Discoveries* by Sharon Bertsch McGrayne (Joseph Henry Press, 2001)
  ISBN: 0309072700
  This book tells the stories of the lives and achievements of fifteen women scientists who either won a Nobel Prize or played a crucial role in a Nobel Prize–winning project. This book reveals the relentless discrimination these women faced both

(Continued)

as students and as researchers. They succeeded because they were passionately in love with science.

- *Extraordinary Women Scientists* by Darlene Stille (Extraordinary People series, Children's Press, 1995)
  ISBN: 0516405853
  Forty-nine women scientists from the past two centuries are profiled in this extensive survey. Each brief, readable biography is accompanied by a portrait and contains personal and historical information, an account of challenges faced, and a summary of the woman's scientific work.

The next two books are filled with great information but are geared toward adult readers.

- *Inventing, Inventions, and Inventors: A Teaching Resource Book* by Jerry D. Flack (Teacher Idea Press, 1989)
  ISBN: 0872877477
  This outstanding book is filled with information about past inventions, and it teaches critical thinking skills; discusses topics related to inventions, including patents; predicts the type of inventions needed for future years based on what's been done so far; and includes information on contests and programs.

- *Inventing Beauty: A History of the Innovations That Have Made Us Beautiful* by Teresa Riordan (Broadway, 2004)
  ISBN: 0767914511
  In this fascinating, meticulously researched romp through the annals of the beauty industry, *New York Times* columnist Teresa Riordan explores that strange intersection of science, fashion, and business where beauty is engineered. From the bustle boom to the war on wrinkles, from kiss-proof lipstick to surgical face-lifts, *Inventing Beauty* reveals how, for centuries, social trends and technological innovations have fueled a nonstop assembly line of gadgets, potions, and contraptions that women have enthusiastically deployed in the quest for feminine flawlessness.

Write a Short Story
(Grades K–4)

Write a Short Story

Do you ever find yourself telling family or friends about something funny, scary, or surprising that has happened to you? Do you enjoy sharing these events in an exciting way? Maybe you're a quieter sort of person who likes to keep a diary or journal. Do you write about the things you see or experience? If your answer to any of these questions is yes, you're a storyteller. Lucky you! People who share stories bring pleasure, wisdom, and a sense of common experience to the world.

One of the best ways to share a story is to write it out in an organized and interesting way. Writing allows you to plan exactly what you want to say and how you say it. You can use colorful words, exciting scenes, and interesting characters to illustrate a real or imagined event. If this sounds like fun, you can become a writer yourself!

But where do you start? Many authors carry writing notebooks with them to capture their ideas. Three-ring notebooks work well, or you can staple notebook paper together for a homemade pad that folds easily into a pocket. Another idea is to keep a few index cards handy at all times. When you get a good idea or see or hear something interesting, you can jot it down. Make sure you always carry a pen or pencil with you. But if you keep your paper and pens in your pockets, remember to take them out before they go into the laundry! This way you won't lose any spectacular ideas—or clothes.

Charting Your Course: Getting Ideas

A good rule for beginning writers is to write about what you know. This doesn't mean that you can't write about aliens on a distant planet or a group of girl detectives from the future; it just means that great ideas are all around you. Aren't there some things from your everyday life that can fit into your space alien story? Maybe the main alien likes to sing opera like your older sister or thinks the dish detergent your mother buys makes a delicious drink. You never know what you'll think of! Keep your eyes and ears open, and the ideas will flow right in.

Once you start getting ideas, you will want to write them down in your writing notebook. Make your list official by writing, at the top of the page,

IDEAS

Now for the fun part: write down as many experiences, events, and ideas as you can think of. Write down all of the good ones, all of the bad ones, and everything in between. This process is called **brainstorming.** When you brainstorm, it doesn't matter how good the ideas are; it just matters that there are lots of them!

Here are some questions to help get your brainstorming started:

- Has anything really special ever happened during a holiday or birthday in your family?
- Have you ever done anything that was super scary for you?
- What makes you happy?

- What makes you sad?

- Have you ever solved (or even come across) an intriguing mystery?

  These books might also be good sources of ideas:

- *Blazing Pencils* by Meredith Sue Willis (Teachers & Writers Collaborative; 2nd printing edition, 1991)
  ISBN: 0915924196
  This book provides over 150 writing ideas to help kids through every step of the writing process.

- *The Writer's Express: Grades 4–5* by School Specialty Publishing (Instructional Fair, 1999)
  ISBN: 1568228627
  The activities in this book are designed to foster creativity in young writers.

- *Quick Writes* by Pamela Marx (GoodYear Books, 1999)
  ISBN: 067358643X
  More than sixty short writing activities inspire kids to write tall tales, song lyrics, journal entries, and more.

Exploration

Developing a Good Idea

Look over your list of ideas. Is there a topic that you feel especially interested in? Will it interest other people? A good story idea usually includes some problem or dilemma that gets solved or resolved by the end of the story. Does the story you're considering include a dilemma? Weigh all the factors, and then write your chosen idea at the top of a new page in your notebook, like this:

A Daring Rescue

On the same page, write as many things as you can think of that will happen in the story you want to tell. If your story will be about a real event, remember as much as you can about it. Don't worry about the order yet. Just try to get lots of ideas and details down on paper. You can list things like the following:

- Heard a dog barking when walking home from school

- Walked around to side of building

- Saw smoke

- Ran to police officer on corner

- Officer called firefighter

- Firefighter went into the building

- Crowd of people gathered around

- Dog and puppies rescued!

(*Continued*)

Another way to get your ideas down is to make a web. Your web might look something like this:

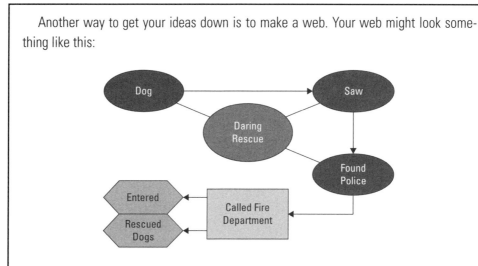

Developing Your Main Character

Every story needs a main character. You will tell your story through the eyes of your main character. Your readers will see events happening as they happen to that character. If you choose to illustrate a real event in your life, creating a main character will be easy, because the character will be you!

When authors write about characters, they often start by creating character sketches. A **character sketch** is a picture in words. Close your eyes, and imagine what your character is like. You can use words to create that picture in someone else's mind. The more clearly you describe what you see in your mind, the better the picture will be for your reader.

Turn to a fresh page in your writing notebook. At the top of the page, write
CHARACTER SKETCH

Now think about your main character. If you're writing about something that happened to you, the main character is yourself! Write as many things as you can think of to describe your main character. You can use words, phrases, or whole sentences—whatever you think is best.

Here are some questions you might want to ask yourself:

- What does this character look and act like?
- What is this character good at (or not so good at)?
- What does this character like to do?
- Where does this character like to go?
- What words or phrases describe this character—for example, *friendly, imaginative, energetic?*

What other things might you want to let your reader know about the character? Think of some other important questions, and answer them.

Developing Your Plot

Just as every story needs a main character, every story needs a beginning, middle, and end. In a short story, the main character usually runs into some sort of problem or conflict. When the problem comes up, more events happen. When the problem finally gets worked out, there is an interesting ending. The author's plan for the events that happen in a story is called the **plot**, or **story line**. At the top of the next new page in your writer's notebook, write

PLOT

Now make a rough outline of what will happen in your short story. Your outline might look something like this sample:

The Beginning (how your story starts)

I was walking along Third Street on my way home from school. . . .

1. Major details about your character and the problem she or he will have:
   Love dogs and was concerned when I heard dog barking as if in trouble
2. Other details
   Ran around to side of building
3. More details
   Saw smoke coming from building

Middle (what happens in your story)

I ran to the corner and told the police officer.

1. Details
   Officer called firefighters
2. Other details
   Fire engines came screaming
3. More details
   Crowd gathered

The solution and ending

Firefighter went into building.

1. Details
   Rescued dog and puppies
2. Other details
   Crowd cheered
3. Provide a strong clincher statement—that is, a last sentence that will make a good ending.
   This is the one time when my troublesome curiosity really paid off!

When you know how your story will unfold, find a friend who will listen to your ideas. Ask your friend for ideas to make your story better. What changes, if any, are you going to make?

(*Continued*)

Writing a Good Beginning

Look on the following Web site for great opening sentences of stories written by kids like you. What do you like about them? What don't you like? Do they intrigue you? Now find several of your favorite books and reread the first paragraph of each. Is there something about the beginning paragraph that makes you want to keep reading? What is it?

- Cricket: Favorite First Sentences
  http://www.cricketmag.com/activity_display.asp?id=189
  This Web site lists provides students an opportunity to list the favorite first sentences of books.

When you read the beginning of a good story, you want to keep reading to find out what happens next. The author grabs your attention right away. This is why the beginning of a story is important! Open your writing notebook again, and find another fresh page. At the top of the page, write

BEGINNINGS

On this page, write at least three different beginning paragraphs for your story. Make sure to use exciting nouns, verbs, and adjectives to describe the opening scene of your story. For a review on parts of speech such as nouns, verbs, and adjectives, go to **http://www. eduplace.com/tales/help.html**. If you need a little word practice or just a warm-up, you might try some wacky Web tales at **http://www.eduplace.com/tales/**. See how colorful words make these stories a lot more fun? The same goes for the paragraph you're writing!

When you have finished writing some sample paragraphs, choose the one you like best. You may want to take your favorite parts of each sample paragraph and put them together to make a new, better paragraph.

Do you think that your opening paragraph would make someone want to keep reading? Ask one or two friends to read what you have written. Ask them which beginning makes them want to keep reading.

Writing Your First Draft

Now you have a good idea of what your beginning will be. What part of the story will you tell next? As you write your story, remember to show your readers as much as possible about where your main character is and what is happening. For example, which of the following scenes can you visualize, or see in your mind, more clearly?

The children played on the playground.

A dozen ten-year-old boys and girls dressed in shorts and bright T-shirts played tag, rode on swings, and yelled and laughed together on the dusty playground.

As you write, think about what your main character is seeing, hearing, feeling, smelling, and tasting. Picture in your mind how your character is doing the things you are writing about. Then describe everything you see in words, clearly, so your readers can tell where and who the character is.

Now that you have gathered all of this information about your character, you are ready to get going on the **first draft,** or **rough draft,** of your story. When you write a first draft, the important thing is to get all your ideas down in your notebook (or on the computer, if you would rather type your story). You can correct spelling and punctuation and make other changes later.

Revising and Proofreading

When you have finished the rough draft of the story, it is time to read it out loud, to see whether you like the way it sounds. Use the following checklist to figure out whether you have all the elements of a great story.

Story Checklist

❏ Does my story have an interesting first sentence?
❏ Did I describe how my main character looks and acts?
❏ Does my story have a problem or dilemma for my main character to solve?
❏ Do I have a beginning, middle, and end to the story?
❏ Did I use plenty of descriptive words?

Writers know how important it is to revise their stories. If you need to add more detail to give your story a strong beginning, middle, and ending, take the time to make the changes. If some parts of your story don't sound right, fix them. If you're working on paper, you can use arrows to show how you want to move sentences or insert words. Cross out words that don't have the effect you want. Replace them with words that give a clearer picture of what is happening in the story. Write the new words above the ones you've crossed out.

If you're working on a computer, delete words or sentences you don't like and replace them with better choices. You can also use the cut and paste commands to move words and sentences from one place in the story to another.

Once you have finished revising, read your story out loud again, this time to a friend. Ask whether your friend has a good mental picture of what you are describing and whether the action is clear. After listening to your friend's comments, make any other changes that you think are necessary.

After making sure that you like the ideas, characters, and images in your story, proofread your rough draft to check for errors. The following checklist will help.

Proofreading Checklist

❏ Did I spell all words correctly (or run a spelling checker to catch mistakes)?
❏ Did I indent each paragraph?
❏ Did I write each sentence as a complete thought?
❏ Do I have any run-on sentences?
❏ Did I begin each sentence with a capital letter?
❏ Did I use capital letters correctly in other places?
❏ Did I end each sentence with the correct punctuation mark?
❏ Did I use commas, apostrophes, and other punctuation correctly?

(*Continued*)

Choosing a Title

Now turn to a new page in your writing notebook, and write down several titles for your story. Make sure you have more than two or three possible titles. Look at some titles of other stories or books. Which ones make you want to read them?

Choose a title for your short story that would make someone want to read it. You might want to think of the five best titles for your story and then ask some friends to pick the two that they find most interesting. This will give you an idea of what other people think. As the author, though, you have the final say. Write or type your title at the top of your story once you have decided.

Writing Your Final Draft

Now it's time to write your final draft. The final draft should include all of the edits from your previous drafts.

Launching Your Results

Perhaps you would like to work with other student writers to combine your stories into a magazine. If so, decide whether you want the magazine to be handwritten or whether all the stories should be written on a computer, word processor, or typewriter. You might want to meet with the other writers to decide on a name for your magazine and how it will be put together. You might also want to talk about making a cover for your magazine and whether to include illustrations.

Other questions to consider are whether you want to publish more than one issue of your magazine and how you want to distribute it to others. Do you want to hand out copies of the magazine to people, or would you like to put them in your school library for interested students and teachers to take? What other good ideas do the other writers have?

If you don't put together a magazine with other students, you may want to see whether a professionally published magazine will accept your story. Here some two Internet magazines that publish work by kids:

- Amazing Kids eZine
  http://www.amazing-kids.org/ezine_11/ez.html
  Amazing Kids eZine is an online magazine for kids. Follow this link for submission directions: Kidsonlinemagazine.com.
- http://www.kidsonlinemagazine.com/index.html
  Every kid who sends something to this Internet magazine for kids, by kids will have his or her work placed somewhere on the Web site. You can send your work by e-mail or regular mail. If you send it by regular mail, you must print out the parent permission form (http://www.kidsonlinemagazine.com/parentpermission.html) and send it with your work.

These well-known print magazines also publish writing by kids:

- *Cricket*
  http://www.cricketmag.com/ProductDetail.asp?pid=2
  Cricket magazine contains stories written by top-notch authors and illustrated by award-winning artists.

- *Stone Soup*
  http://www.stonesoup.com/main2/whatisstonesoup.html
  Stone Soup is a unique magazine made up entirely students' creative work.

Another option is to submit your story to a contest like one of these:

- Reading Rainbow Annual Young Writers and Illustrators Contest
  http://pbskids.org/readingrainbow/contest/
  In 2004, 45,000 kids like you entered this yearly contest.

- Tattered Cover Annual Scary Story Contest
  http://www.tatteredcover.com/NASApp/store/IndexJsp?s=localauthors&page=238301
  Young writers from kindergarten through sixth grade are invited to write an original mystery, suspenseful thriller, or humorous Halloween tale.

- Lemony Snicket's Cunning Count Olaf Composition Contest
  http://www.rif.org/readingplanet/content/count_olaf_contest.mspx
  This contest, based on Lemony Snicket's popular Series of Unfortunate Events books, asks you to figure out what the villainous Count Olaf is up to now.

- Candlelight Stories Kids' Mystery Contest
  http://www.candlelightstories.com/D001/Mystery.asp
  Finish the mystery that has been started for you on the Web page by filling in the form at the bottom of the page. Then hit send. When the contest ends, check back on the Web site to see whether you won!

If you're interested in reading some other mysteries by kids, check out the stories at Amazing Kids eZine (http://www.amazing-kids.org/ezine_11/ez.html) or the mysteries at Mystery Net's Kids Mysteries page (http://kids.mysterynet.com/) .

These books have ideas for publishing your work, too.

- *The Young Writer's Guide to Getting Published* by Kathy Henderson (6th edition, Writer's Digest Books, 2001)
  ISBN: 1582970572
  Many books teach kids how to write; this one teaches them how to get published.

(*Continued*)

- *In Print!* by Joe Rhatigan (Lark, 2004)
  ISBN: 1579906095
  Provides tips for traditional publishing, as well as forty publishing projects, such as stamping words on an umbrella, creating a curtain of poems, and more.

You can look online or in the library for other magazines that publish material by student writers. Then check those magazines to see whether they accept the kind of story you have written. The address will be in the front of the magazine. Most magazines ask you to include a stamped, self-addressed envelope with your story. Remember, magazines and Internet publications get far more stories than they can print, so don't get discouraged if they can't accept yours.

Treasure Chest of Tools

- Cyperkids
  http://www.cyberkids.com/he/html/submit.html

- Book Crossroads
  http://www.ebookcrossroads.com/childrens-writing.html

- Children's Writing Resources
  http://www.bethanyroberts.com/writerresources.htm#More%20sites%20of%20interest
  Regardless of how—or whether—you choose to publish your work, you should be proud of yourself! Writing a story is a great accomplishment! And you have a list of ideas for more stories in your writing notebook. Have you thought of others to add to your idea list? What will you write about next? One thing that any good writer will tell you is that you have to keep writing if you want to get better. So keep writing, and this could be the beginning of a whole new chapter in your life!

10 Write a Short Story (Grades 5–8)

Author, Author! Write a Short Story

Have you ever loved a book so much that you didn't want it to end? Have you ever stayed up reading when you were supposed to be asleep? Do you secretly wish that you could write a story that would captivate others the way your favorite books captivate you? Well, you can!

Writing intimidates many people because they don't know where to begin or how to build the story once they have written the first few lines. To a beginning writer, the task of writing may seem hopelessly mysterious. It may almost seem as if their favorite books were spun out of thin air.

Of course, that's not the case! Books are written by regular people—people a lot like you. The only difference between those who write and those who only dream of writing is that writers have a secret: they know that writing isn't magic. Writing is a skill that can be learned, with practice. Think about all the skills you have mastered already in your life. As a baby, you learned how to walk and talk. In school, you learned other skills, such as reading, adding, subtracting, and measuring. You may be able to ride a bike or catch a fly ball. Or maybe you can draw, paint, or dance. Like learning to write, learning those complex tasks required time, patience, and hard work—but certainly not magic!

So are you ready to start writing? A good project for a beginning writer is a short story. Chances are that you have already taken the first step toward writing a good story. If you have ever described something that happened on the way home from school or how you felt when you were anxious about something or how happy you felt during a special moment with friends, you are already a storyteller. Now you just need to learn how to write your stories down.

For this project, you will need a pen or a pencil and a special notebook that you use just for writing. You may prefer a three-ring binder and loose-leaf paper or a spiral notebook with plenty of space between the lines. Then again, maybe yellow legal pads will work best for you. Or you may want to do most of your writing on a computer or word processor. That's fine, too. Choose whatever materials you are most comfortable with. Writers are well known for being particular about their tools! If you choose to work on a computer, just remember to set up a special file folder for your writing and make sure to save all your work where you can easily find it. When you finish this project, your computer file folder or writing notebook will be filled with ideas for stories.

Here are five steps for writing a great short story:

1. Prewriting
2. Writing a first draft
3. Revising
4. Proofreading
5. Publishing

Let's get started!

Charting Your Course

Step 1: Prewriting

A good tip for beginning writers is to write about things you know. This doesn't mean that you have to limit yourself solely to the truth; certainly, if you think of a fictional character, scene, or detail that will improve your story, you should feel free to use that idea. But if you're not sure what to write about, it may be easier to create a story if you use familiar places, characters, or situations.

To turn your experiences into stories, open your notebook or turn on your computer and list as many topics as you can that you know something or a lot about. Your list might look something like this:

Topics

- People—my family, friends, and relatives
- My hometown and places I have visited
- Experiences—exciting, frightening, funny, and so on
- Things I'm good at
- Things that really interest me
- Special events in my life
- Feelings—good, bad, and so on

Once you have listed five to ten topics, write or type each topic on its own page. Now brainstorm as many facts about each topic as you can. Write down all of your ideas. Remember, when you brainstorm, you shouldn't judge your ideas. Right now, your goal is quantity, not quality! Here is a sample list of ideas:

People

- Brother: Justin
- Mom and Dad
- Aunt Alex
- Uncle Juan
- Twins: Abbey and Jordan
- Mr. J and his barking dog
- The recess aide with the blue hair

If you think of lots of ideas, the first part of your writing notebook or file should fill up quickly. Now your job is to ask yourself, "How can I use these ideas in a story?"

Create a Main Character

Most stories need a main character. You can start creating your main character by doing a **character sketch,** a picture in words. Close your eyes, and imagine what your character is like. See your character in your mind, and use words to describe how he or she looks. With words, you can create a picture in someone else's mind. The more detail you

(Continued)

envision and capture about your character, and the clearer your words are, the clearer the picture of your character will be.

- Write or type *Character Sketch* on a fresh page. Then think about your character. Write down words, phrases, and whole sentences to describe your character. Ask yourself questions like these:
  - What does this character look like?
  - How does this character act?
  - What does this character do well or not so well?
  - What does he or she like to do?
  - Where does the character like to go?
  - Is this character friendly, full of energy, self-reflective, kind, or brusque?

Think of other important questions about your character. What other things do you want your reader to know about the character? Now look back at your list of people. Are there things that any of those people do that your character does, too? Is your character like any particular person, or does the character combine parts of several people you know? For example, your character might have a nose like your Uncle Juan's and a temper like your brother. As you get to know your character, you might find that he or she has your mom's sense of humor and your Aunt Alex's common sense.

After you have decided what your character will be like, you may be ready to give him or her a name. Sometimes the right name will just come to you, as if your character has whispered in your ear. If this is the case, you're all set!

Other times, you may think of many names before you find one that seems right. If you can't find a name that seems to fit, don't worry. You may just need to spend a little more time writing and thinking about your character. Perhaps you don't know him or her well enough yet to "hear" the right name. After all, we don't just give our names to strangers, do we?

Once you know your character's name and have an idea about who she or he is, try this exercise: write a character sketch as if you're telling a friend all about your character. Give your creativity lots of freedom and write down whatever feels right at the time. You may be surprised at what you learn about your character as he or she develops through your words.

Plan Your Story

Once you have a grasp on your main character, you can begin to think about what will happen in your story. Here's a simple rule: Every story needs a beginning, a middle, and an end. In a short story, the main character typically runs into some problem or conflict. As the story progresses, the problem touches more characters and causes more things to happen. At some point, the conflict will peak—that is, it will reach a critical point where either the situation must be fixed or there will be serious consequences for your characters. At this point, the author usually resolves the problem in an interesting way that makes sense according to what has happened previously in the story.

This pattern of tension caused by the character's problem, followed by its resolution, is called the **plot,** or **storyline.** A problem or conflict is crucial to a good storyline. And just remember, when it comes time to resolve the conflict, you, as the writer, will have to make a judgment call: Is it most interesting and believable to let your characters triumph? Or will the conflict win? Many writers find that their stories develop in surprising ways. This sense of discovery is one of the most wonderful things about writing. Sometimes writers entertain even themselves with their creativity!

Are you ready to work on your plot? If so, write or type *Conflicts* on a fresh page in your writing notebook or file. Then write as many kinds of conflicts or problems you can think of. One good way to get started is to write down some conflicts you've experienced in your own life. You can then add conflicts or problems experienced by people you know. Add conflicts from your own imagination as you think of them. Here are some examples of conflicts and problems that might work well for a short story:

Conflicts

* I sometimes argue with my brother, and I feel like my parents always take his side.
* I sometimes accidentally leave my bike outside, which upsets my mother.
* I want a paper route so that I can buy things for myself, but my parents don't want me to work during the school year.
* Sometimes my friends talk about another friend behind her back, and it makes me feel uncomfortable.

Select a conflict that you think the main character you have created might have. Now that you have a conflict and a character, you are almost ready to begin your story.

Choose a Point of View

As soon as you sit down to start writing, you will have to make an important choice. We know who the story is about, but who will tell it? One option is to have your main character tell the story as it is happening to him or her. This is called **first-person** point of view. The first-person point of view can make the reader feel as if he or she is in the middle of the story's events, which can make the whole story more exciting. An example of a story that uses the first-person point of view is "The Ransom of Red Chief" by O. Henry (available at http://www.classicshorts.com/stories/redchief.html). This is a story about two kidnappers who find that their captive may be more trouble than he's worth. O. Henry is a famous writer who authored hundreds of stories. If you like this one, your school librarian or public librarian can help you find more stories by O. Henry.

A different way to write your story is to use **third-person** point of view. In this case, the story is told by an outside observer who describes the events happening to the characters. An interesting effect of the third-person point of view is that your narrator may provide the reader with information that the main character does not have, such as

(*Continued*)

the thoughts and ideas of other characters. Third-person narrative can be suspenseful because the reader may know before the main character how the story will unfold. You can see the third-person point of view in action in the following stories:

*   *To Build a Fire* by Jack London
    http://www.readbookonline.net/readOnLine/1443/
    This famous short story is about a man who must build a fire or freeze alone in the wilderness.

*   *The Lottery* by Shirley Jackson
    http://www.classicshorts.com/stories/lotry.html
    The Lottery is a story about a deadly small-town ritual.

    If you like these stories, you can find others by Jack London and Shirley Jackson in your school library or your public library.

Let's return to our discussion of point of view. There is a third way to write a story. Stories using **second-person** point of view are told as if the reader is the main character. Does this sound confusing? Often, it is—for both the writer and the reader. When used well, second-person point of view can pull the reader right into the heart of the story. But it's very difficult to master, so few writers ever attempt it. For an example of second-person point of view, check out this online "choose your own adventure" story (http://friend.ly.net/users/jorban/adventure/index.html). You can also find this type of interactive story in many school libraries or local libraries.

Write Some Beginnings

Now that you have created a main character, crafted a plot, and thought about point of view, you are ready to experiment with some beginnings for your story. To get some ideas, find several of your favorite books or short stories. Reread the beginning of each—especially the first paragraph. Is there something about the beginning that makes you want to keep reading? What is it?

On a clean page in your notebook or computer file, write or type the heading *Beginnings*. Then write at least three or four different beginning paragraphs for your story. You may want to write some paragraphs from the first-person point of view and others from the third-person point of view. Or you may not feel the need to experiment with point of view because you know you prefer one style over the other. This is fine as well. When you have written a few beginnings, you can choose one to use as your opening paragraph or you can combine parts of several to make a new paragraph.

Before making your final choice, you should ask yourself whether this beginning would make someone want to continue reading. Ask a friend to read your beginnings and help you select one that makes the reader want to find out more.

Make an Outline

As you have worked on your story, you probably have thought about your plot and how it will develop. If you haven't, take some time to do that now. Think about the conflict and about the role your main character will play in the time leading up to the conflict, during the conflict, and in the resolution of the conflict. What specific events happen to produce the conflict? Does your character think, do, or say anything that helps to bring the conflict about? Or is the conflict an event outside of his or her control? How will your character react when faced with the problem? Will she or he be calm and collected? Scared? Angry? Energized? Will he or she resolve the problem in a positive way, and if so, how? If the conflict is not resolved in a happy way, what will your main character learn from the experience? How will the story come to a close?

As you consider these issues, you may want to take notes in your writing notebook or on the computer. You may also want to get feedback on your ideas from a friend, parent, or sibling. If you receive feedback that says you should make some changes, consider the ideas carefully. Sometimes a reader can see holes or problems in your story that you can't see. Having the valuable perspective of another person is why professional writers have editors to suggest changes for their books. You, as the writer, have the option of rejecting others' ideas, but you should first think about whether making the suggested changes would make the story more interesting, believable, or unique. If you think so, you can add the new ideas into your story, just as professional writers make changes to their stories based on the comments of their editors.

Once you have worked out the details of your storyline, it's time to make a rough outline of your story. On a fresh page in your writing notebook or in your computer file, make an outline that shows how your story will progress. You might organize your outline according to the following plan:

Story Outline

I. The beginning
    A. (List major details about your main character.)
        1. Detail
        2. Detail
        3. Detail
    B. (Introduce the conflict.)
        1. Detail
        2. Detail

II. The middle
    A. (Write about what happens to your main character, including details of how he or she reacts to the problem.)
        1. Detail
        2. Detail
        3. Detail
    B. (Write about another event that happens to the character and how it relates to the problem.)
        1. Detail
        2. Detail

(*Continued*)

III. The solution and ending
  A. (Write about how the problem gets solved.)
    1. Detail
    2. Detail
    3. Detail
  B. (Write the ending of the story.)
    1. Detail
    2. Detail

You also have the option of showing the storyline in the form of a diagram:

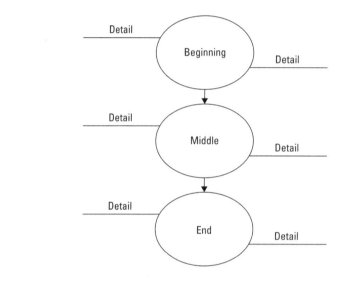

Whichever format you choose, you will find your outline to be a useful tool as you write your first draft.

Exploration

Step 2: Writing a First Draft

Congratulations! After all of your prewriting, you have finally reached the second step in your writing process. You're ready to actually write your story! And the best part is that you have done much of the hard work already. How so? Imagine that your story is a person. When you chose a main character and a point of view, you created a heart and a voice for your story. When you crafted your plot, you built the skeleton for your story. Now you just need to flesh it out and clothe it with your words, so that it can show its face to the world. Your story already has a structure, so all you have to do is write it out in its full form.

Are you ready to begin? If you are, sit down at your computer or open your notebook and let the story tell itself. While you write, think of how and what your main character is seeing, feeling, hearing, smelling, and tasting. A common saying among writers is "Show, don't tell." Picture your character doing and experiencing the events in your story, and describe what you see. Use words that communicate your mental pictures as clearly as possible, so that your reader will be able to tell what your character is like and where the story takes place. Write as fast and as freely as you wish. Later, you can correct any errors in spelling or punctuation and figure out how to say everything just right. For now, the most important thing is to get all those ideas down in story form. Have fun!

Step 3: Revising

When you have finished writing the rough draft of your story from beginning to end, it's time to read it out loud and see how it sounds. Do you need to make some changes in your wording? Do some parts of the story seem improbable now that the rest of the story is in place? Are the scenes in a logical order?

Make as many changes as you need to make your story just right. You can make changes right on your draft by crossing things out, using arrows to show how to move things, and adding words or sentences between the lines and in the margins. If you are someone who makes a lot of changes when you revise, you may decide in the future to write on just one side of the page. This way, you will have room to make changes and add notes on the back. If you are working on a computer, rewriting is easy. Just use your cut, paste, and delete functions to move sentences or even whole paragraphs, change wording, and add detail. You may want to save your changed story under a new name by adding "draft 2," or "final draft" to the original document title. This way, you will have a copy of the rough draft as well as your edited versions. You can save the document under a new name each time you make revisions. This may be important if you decide to change part of your story back to an earlier version.

Once you're satisfied with your story, read it to a friend, parent, or sibling. Ask whether your listener can see what you're saying in his or her mind. Did you show rather than tell? Does he or she have any last-minute suggestions for changes that might make the story better? If so, make the changes that seem right to you. Discard the suggestions that you don't like. Remember, this is your story and it has to please you.

Step 4: Proofreading

When your story is worded just the way you want it, you are ready to proofread it. The following checklist will help you correct any errors in your story.

Proofreading Checklist

❑ Did I spell all words correctly (or run a spelling checker to catch mistakes)?
❑ Did I indent each paragraph?
❑ Did I write each sentence as a complete thought?
❑ Do I have any run-on sentences?
❑ Did I begin each sentence with a capital letter?
❑ Did I use capital letters correctly in other places?
❑ Did I end each sentence with the correct punctuation mark?
❑ Did I use commas, apostrophes, and other punctuation correctly?

(*Continued*)

Finalizing Your Story

Now that you have written, revised, and proofed your story, you need to find the right title. In your writing notebook or on a new page in your computer file, write as many titles for your story as you can. Can you think of ten titles or more? Look at some of the titles of stories or books that you love. Which ones make you want to read them? What about them grabs your attention? Are some written as questions? Do they use interesting or colorful words? Are they mysterious? Try to pinpoint what you like and incorporate your observations into your titles.

Once you have chosen the title, you can write your final copy. Write it neatly on good paper, or if you used a computer, just add the title and print out the revised and proofed draft of the story. You may want to add a cover or a cover sheet to your story.

Launching Your Results

If you make your story into a book with a hard cover, you might want to ask your school librarian whether you can donate a copy to your school library. If the librarian says yes, don't forget to make a card for the card catalogue!

Step 5: Publishing

Another option for sharing your story is to submit it to an online magazine, or **e-zine,** that publishes works by young writers. The following list provides information about several e-zines that accept short stories from young writers.

- White Barn Press

  http://www.whitebarnpress.com/default.htm

  White Barn Press was formed to give young writers the opportunity to publish their work. This e-zine is serious about good writing, and in addition to publishing stories, essays, poems, and book chapters by young writers, it includes resources and activities to help authors improve their work. Use the link provided on the home page to get information about having your work published. Check out the Writing Ideas page (http://www. whitebarnpress.com/writingideas/writing_ideas.htm) for links to published works.

- Amazing Kids eZine

  http://www.amazing-kids.org/ezine_11/ez.html

  Amazing Kids eZine is an online magazine for kids.

- Kidsonlinemagazine.com

  http://www.kidsonlinemagazine.com/index.html

  This e-zine is a great place to start your submission process because every author who submits will have his or her work placed somewhere on the Web site.

  In addition to e-zines, there are print magazines that publish fiction by young writers. Several are listed here:

- *Stone Soup*

  http://www.stonesoup.com/main2/whatisstonesoup.html

Stone Soup is a magazine consisting of work by writers and artists aged eight to thirteen. *Stone Soup* has been published for more than thirty years and is one of the better-known children's literary magazines. Because the magazine receives about 250 submissions a week, don't feel bad if you don't get published the first time you submit. Just keep trying!

- *Potluck Children's Literary Magazine*
  http://www.potluckmagazine.org/
  This magazine publishes short stories, poetry, and other writing by authors aged eight to sixteen. Before you submit your work, make sure to read the writers' guidelines by clicking on the link on the magazine's home page.

- *The Claremont Review: The International Magazine of Young Adult Writers*
  http://www.theclaremontreview.ca/submit.htm
  This magazine publishes work by writers aged thirteen to nineteen, with a preference for fiction and poetry about the meaning or experience of life. The magazine doesn't publish science fiction, fantasy, or romance stories or most rhyming poetry. Spend some time reading the information on the magazine's Web site to get more information about the type of work that the magazine accepts.

Writing contests such as the ones in the following list are another good option for publishing your work.

- Tattered Cover Annual Scary Story Contest
  http://www.tatteredcover.com/NASApp/store/IndexJsp?s=localauthors&page=238301
  Young writers from kindergarten through sixth grade are invited to write an original mystery, suspenseful thriller, or humorous Halloween tale.

- The Claremont Review's annual fiction and poetry contest
  http://www.theclaremontreview.ca/annual_contest.htm#4
  This contest is open to writers aged thirteen to nineteen who are interested in writing about life and the human condition. There is an entry fee, but in addition to participation in the contest, you will receive a one-year subscription to the magazine. Winners will receive a cash prize. The contest is sponsored by the *Claremont Review: The International Magazine of Young Adult Writers*.

The following books have ideas for publishing your work, too.

- *So, You Wanna Be a Writer? How to Write, Get Published, and Maybe Even Make It Big!*
  edited by Vicki Hambleton & Cathleen Greenwood (Beyond Words Publishing, 2001)
  ISBN: 1582700435
  This book contains advice from other young authors and discusses where to find story ideas and how to approach publishers. It also provides profiles of ten young authors whose work has been published.

(Continued)

- *The Young Writer's Guide to Getting Published* by Kathy Henderson (6th edition, Writer's Digest Books, 2001)
  ISBN: 1582970572

  This book offers listings of magazines, contests, and online publications that publish the work of young writers. It also provides information about how to submit work to publishers and profiles young writers who have had their work published. There's even a profile of the famous author Stephen King and a story that he wrote when he was a teenager.

Treasure Chest of Tools

Congratulations! You have written a short story and learned a little about where you might be able to publish it. If you enjoyed this activity, you may want to learn more about writing short stories by reading some stories for kids and young adults. Here's a list of short-story collections (also called **anthologies**):

- *Shelf Life: Stories by the Book* by Gary Paulsen (Simon & Schuster Books for Young Readers, 2003)
  ISBN: 0689841809

  This anthology contains short stories with a common theme: each story mentions a book that is important to the author. The collection includes science fiction, historical fiction, fantasy, humor, and more.

- *Firebirds: An Anthology of Fantasy and Science Fiction* by Sharyn November (Firebird, 2003)
  ISBN: 0142501425

  This collection for readers aged twelve and up includes sixteen stories by well-known science fiction and fantasy writers.

- *The Color of Absence: 12 Stories About Loss and Hope* by James Howe (Simon Pulse, 2003)
  ISBN: 0689856679

  Twelve well-known authors explore teenagers' different experiences with loss. This book is for readers aged thirteen to eighteen.

You may also be interested in summer camps that offer creative writing classes:

- Idyllwild Arts and Summer Program
  http://www.idyllwildarts.org/

  This camp offers writing workshops for students aged nine to eighteen. Students have the opportunity to focus on fiction, playwriting, and poetry during two-week workshops.

- Passport to Summer
  http://www.mysummercamps.com/camps/Detailed/Passport_to_Summer_ L5729.html
  This Washington, D.C., camp offers academic programs to kids aged three to eighteen. Students who are interested in writing can take a creative writing course or a journalism course.

Frequently Asked Questions About Phase Three

Please elaborate on Phase Three; how should I start?

In Phase Three, students are encouraged to move from teacher-directed opportunities to self-selected activities. Activities can include the following:

- Opportunities to explore new technology (for example, using Renzulli Learning)
- Discussion groups
- Writing activities
- Creativity training in language arts
- Investigation centers
- Interest-based independent or small-group projects
- Continuation of self-selected individual reading
- Book chats

There are many examples of learning experiences you can offer students in Phase Three in *Joyful Reading*. The intent of these experiences is to provide time for students to develop and explore their interest in reading.

I know Phase Three happens for ten to fifteen minutes each day, but if our students can use their time wisely, can we extend their Phase Three time to forty or fifty minutes one day each week to give them extra time to do Phase Three activities? Extended Phase Three time might enable them to do independent projects.

Yes, this can be done. Ideally, remember that students should participate in Phase Two at least four days each week. This leaves one day a week for a longer Phase Three time, which will give students time for more advanced projects.

What have teachers using the SEM-R found to be the easiest way to start Phase Three?

We strongly recommend that you limit the number of choices that you provide for students as they start Phase Three. You may, for example, give students some of the following choices:

- Continue reading alone, if they like their book.

- Buddy read—that is, read a book with a friend (one student reads a page, then the other student reads a page).

- Work on a series of creativity activities for language arts (provided in this book). You may want to have your entire class do a couple of creativity training activities to get students ready for independent work.

- Write their response to a bookmark writing prompt (on the back page of their reading log for the week) at a writing center.

- Use Renzulli Learning. (This activity will be popular, so you may want to use a sign-up list; specify which students can use Renzulli Learning on Monday, Tuesday, and so on.)

- Listen to a book on tape or CD as they read.

- Do independent work of their choice, using Renzulli Learning or other resources for short-term projects (called Super Starter projects in Renzulli Learning).

Frequently Asked Questions About the SEM-R

In the five years that we have field-tested the SEM-R, we have found many different ways for teachers to implement this approach to reading. There is no single correct way to implement the three phases of the SEM-R, partly because individual teachers' creativity and interests are respected in the process and thus there is much room for variation. We hope you enjoy the freedom to use your own creativity to encourage students to read widely and to enjoy reading books that you introduce to them. Our research has demonstrated that when you use the SEM-R in your classroom, students' self-regulation in reading will continue to increase and that they will find pleasure in choosing reading and enrichment activities in their areas of interest.

How does a teacher integrate individual state standards and benchmarks into the phases of the SEM-R?

The SEM-R can be integrated with state and national reading standards and benchmarks in all three phases of instruction. Because the SEM-R is often used in conjunction with other reading programs, the combination of both approaches will determine how standards can be met. The goals of the SEM-R relate to increased reading comprehension and fluency, improved attitude toward reading, and differentiation of instruction. The instruction that occurs during Phase One and Phase Two can also help teachers to meet curriculum standards through the SEM-R. In Phase One, teachers have the opportunity to integrate reading skills and strategies into book hook activities, which constitute the only whole-group instruction in a SEM-R program. During Phase Two conferences with students, teachers can effectively present individualized reading skills and strategies to meet students' differing needs.

How do teachers grade students in the SEM-R?

In SEM-R programs, student grades have been earned based on the following: conferences, which result in a class participation grade; students' weekly brief written responses to questions about the books they are reading, resulting in a writing grade; the amount of time and quality of reading accomplished in Phase Two; or the level of differentiated reading strategies used by students. Of course, you can also combine these grades with grades that are earned during any traditional reading instruction or program that accompanies the use of the SEM-R.

How do we meet the needs of students with special needs who remain in the classroom during the SEM-R program—for example, students in programs such as Exceptional/Special Education (ESE) or English for Speakers of Other Languages (ESOL)?

Each Phase Two conference can be modified for students with special needs, and these conferences can address a student's Individualized Education Program (IEP) goals. We have been very successful in using the SEM-R with ESOL intensive students. Students who read in either English or Spanish made significantly higher gains than their ESOL peers who did not participate in the SEM-R.

When do we give the Reading Interest-a-Lyzers to students?

The Reading Interest-a-Lyzer has been developed to help you identify specific areas of student interest in reading and better understand when and what students are reading at home. You should plan to have your students complete the Reading Interest-a-Lyzer in the first week of your SEM-R program, to enable you to learn more about their interests. You can also have students complete the Reading Interest-a-Lyzer the week before your program begins.

How often are student logs completed?

Students should complete their reading log each day that they are involved in Phase Two of the SEM-R.

Can we use the assessment instruments included in Renzulli Learning to help us better understand our students' interests?

Renzulli Learning offers three general inventories: interest, learning styles, and product styles. When a student completes all three, plus a brief questionnaire about his perceptions of his abilities, a student profile is automatically generated. The student's interest, learning style, and product style preferences are then matched to hundreds of activity choices that he can pursue during Phase Three. Student profiles can be used to help you identify students' areas of interest and recommend books and enrichment activities for them.

Can you review the time we should spend for Phases One, Two, and Three during the SEM-R?

We hope that as students become more self-regulated readers, you can achieve a balance of spending ten minutes on Phase One, thirty to thirty-five minutes on

Phase Two, and ten to fifteen minutes on Phase Three. Some teachers spend ten minutes on Phase One and forty to fifty minutes on Phase Two for four days each week and then use the remaining week day for more in-depth time on Phase Three.

What about the student log? How did most teachers use it during implementation of the SEM-R?

Students should keep a log throughout the year. Student logs are a useful tool for helping students with the transition to the SEM-R instructional program. Each student can keep the book he or she is currently reading during Phase Two with the log. When students conclude Phase Two independent reading, they should enter the date and length of time they read their book in their log. Keep the logs in a secure place so that you can check students' progress with their current book selection. Students also use the logs to compose their brief writing response each week.

SEM-R Glossary

Bookmarks: Used in Phase One and Phase Two, the SEM-R bookmarks provide questions that help students and teachers think analytically about literature.

Enrichment Triad Model: The theoretical base of the SEM-R, Joseph Renzulli's model encourages enjoyment of learning and the opportunity to pursue creative work by exposing students to various topics, areas of interest, and fields of study and by training them further to apply advanced content, project management skills, and methodology training to self-selected areas of interest, using authentic methods of research and inquiry to do independent or small group projects.

Investigation center: An instructional component of Phase Three of the SEM-R, designed to create and develop interest and enthusiasm about a particular topic or theme. The goal is to engage students actively in reading, thinking, and researching.

Practicing professionals: Students working within a discipline who employ the methodological skills of a field in order to explore an authentic problem in a manner similar to a professional practitioner in that field.

Reading Interest-a-Lyzer: A student inventory consisting of questions designed to help students consider potential areas of interest in reading.

The Schoolwide Enrichment Model for Reading (SEM-R): An enrichment-based reading program with three distinct goals: to increase students' enjoyment of reading, to encourage students to pursue independent reading at appropriately challenging levels, and to improve reading fluency and comprehension. The SEM-R also has three phases, described following.

SEM-R Phase One: Experiences and activities within the SEM-R designed to promote listening comprehension and reading process skills. Teachers read aloud from high-quality, exciting literature and follow up with instruction in higher-order questioning and thinking skills.

SEM-R Phase Two: The component that emphasizes students' ability to engage in independent reading of self-selected high-interest books with content that is above their reading level. Reading material for these sessions should be one to one and a half grade levels above a student's current reading level. While students read independently, the teacher holds individual conferences with students.

SEM-R Phase Three: Experiences designed to provide training in project skills as well as opportunities for students to spend time engaging with activities in areas of interest to them. The ultimate goal of Phase Three is for students to progress from teacher-directed and teacher-provided opportunities to independent, self-selected activities over the course of the intervention.

Student reading log: A log in which students can record what they are reading and the amount of time spent reading silently in class each day. The log should be completed every day at the end of supported independent reading.

Supported independent reading (SIR): One of the main differences between a traditional Sustained Silent Reading program and SIR is that during SIR, teachers use the time when students are reading to meet individually with students. Individual student conferences focus on assessing the match between the student and her chosen book and on helping the student to select appropriately challenging reading material that is of personal interest.

Talented readers: As a group, talented readers are characterized by reading earlier than their peers, spending more time reading, and reading a greater variety of literature, even into adulthood. These students typically read at least two grade levels above their chronological grade placement, demonstrate advanced understanding of language, have an expansive vocabulary, perceive relationships between and among characters, and grasp complex ideas.

Type I enrichment: Experiences and activities that are purposefully designed to expose students to a wide variety of topics, issues, and activities not ordinarily covered in the regular curriculum.

Type II enrichment: The use of instructional methods and materials that are purposefully designed to promote the development of thinking skills and foster students' use of authentic investigative methods.

Type III enrichment: Investigative activities and artistic productions in which the learner assumes the role of a firsthand inquirer and practicing professional.

Weekly Teacher Log Lesson plan template: A form to assist teachers with organizing and recording the details of their individual implementation of the SEM-R framework.

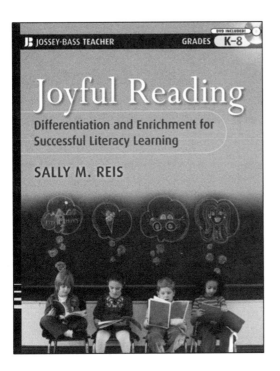

JOYFUL READING

Differentiation and Enrichment for
Successful Literacy Learning, Grades K–8
with DVD

Sally M. Reis

ISBN: 978-0-470-22881-4 | Paperback

COMPLETE YOUR RESOURCE LIBRARY WITH THIS COMPANION BOOK TO
THE JOYFUL READING RESOURCE KIT

*"This book is a must-read for all classroom teachers who are faced with meeting the
literacy needs of a diverse population; it provides powerful insights into the development
of thoughtful and self-regulated readers."*
—Nicole Gavin, director of literacy, City of Baltimore, Maryland

Joyful Reading offers teachers a differentiated instructional approach for motivating students at
varied levels to discover the rewards and delights of reading appropriately challenging books.
Authored by Sally M. Reis, an acclaimed scholar of gifted and talented education, the book
describes the Schoolwide Enrichment Model for Reading (SEM-R), an easy-to-implement
program that encourages students to read independently for a period of time during the school
day on books of their own choice while supporting them in learning comprehension strategies.

The program includes three phases: (1) a Book Hook component in which the teacher reads
aloud from a high-interest book while engaging the class in critical thinking responses; (2) a
Supported Independent Reading component in which students are encouraged to select and read
progressively challenging books while the teacher offers instruction through individualized
conferences; and (3) a Special Interest component in which students engage in reading-
enrichment activities.

The SEM-R program has been shown by research to improve students' fluency and
comprehension as well as their attitudes toward reading and is praised by teachers for getting
students excited about books. The book includes a DVD showing teachers using the program.